QUIET PROTEST

Effie Karageorgos is a Senior Lecturer in History at the University of Newcastle. She teaches and researches histories of protest, mental health, gender, war and violence. She was awarded the State Library of New South Wales David Scott Mitchell Fellowship in 2023. She is Deputy Co-Director of the UON Centre for Society, Health and Care Research and co-editor of *Health and History* journal.

'A new and original history of protests against the Vietnam War that also broadens our understanding of the meaning and forms of "protest" itself.'
Professor Sean Scalmer, University of Melbourne School of Historical and Philosophical Studies

'Effie Karageorgos dives deep in the archives, revealing the mechanics and diversities of a mass protest movement. There is nothing else like it.'
Rowan Cahill, historian and co-author of *Radical Sydney*

'An absorbing history, this book sizzles with thought-provoking insights into opposition to Australia's role in the Vietnam War. It is history that evokes a tumultuous past and speaks to our troubled present.'
Ann Curthoys, historian and protester

'Effie Karageorgos takes us under the bonnet of the anti-Vietnam War protests to provide a fresh perspective on Australia's democracy. Behind the familiar names and big protests, there were many thousands of Australians quietly debating and donating, writing to the papers and signing petitions, maintaining silent vigils and offering conscientious objectors their sympathy, understanding and moral support. This is a vivid account of a living democracy confronting one of the biggest controversies of the twentieth century.'
Frank Bongiorno, Donald Horne Professor of History and Public Ideas, University of Canberra

'More than a history book, *Quiet Protest* provides great insights into how protests deliver wins for progressive movements.'
Lee Rhiannon, former Australian Greens Senator

QUIET PROTEST

A NEW HISTORY OF ACTIVISM DURING THE VIETNAM WAR

EFFIE KARAGEORGOS

UNSW PRESS

UNSW Press acknowledges the Bidjigal people, the Traditional Owners of the unceded territory on which the Randwick and Kensington campuses of UNSW are situated, and recognises the continuing connection to Country and culture. We pay our respects to Elders past and present.

A UNSW Press book

Published by
NewSouth Publishing
University of New South Wales Press Ltd
University of New South Wales
Sydney NSW 2052
AUSTRALIA
https://unsw.press/

First published 2026

A catalogue record for this book is available from the National Library of Australia

ISBN 9781761170263 (paperback)
9781761179426 (ebook)
9781761178689 (ePDF)

Cover design Laura Thomas
Cover images Mitchell Library, State Library of New South Wales and Courtesy SEARCH Foundation, ON 161/Item 541
Internal design Josephine Pajor-Markus

CONTENTS

ABBREVIATIONS

AATTV	Australian Army Training Team Vietnam
ABC	Australian Broadcasting Commission
ACC	Abolish Conscription Campaign
ACCO	Advisory Committee for Conscientious Objectors
ACTU	Australian Council of Trade Unions
AICD	Association for International Cooperation and Disarmament
ALP	Australian Labor Party
ANU	Australian National University
APAN	Australian Palestine Advocacy Network
APC	Australian Peace Council
ASIO	Australian Security Intelligence Organisation
BWDC	Bill White Defence Committee
CFP	Catholics for Peace
CMF	Citizen Military Forces
CO	conscientious objector
COG	Conscientious Objectors' Group
CPA	Communist Party of Australia
CPV	Committee for Peace in Vietnam
CRCV	Committee of Responsibility for the Children of Vietnam
DCS	Draft Counselling Service
DLNS	Department of Labour and National Service
DRCC	Draft Resistance Counselling Centre
DRM	Draft Resistance Movement
DRU	Draft Resisters Union
ESAA	Ex-Services Association of Australia
ESHRAA	Ex-Services Human Rights Association of Australia
FPCA	Federal Pacifist Council of Australia
HOME	Hands Off Melbourne's Estates

ICCV	International Committee of Conscience on Vietnam
IPEC	Interstate Parcel Express Company
MCC	Moratorium Coordinating Committee
MLSLNSW	Mitchell Library, State Library of New South Wales
MULC	Monash University Labor Club
NCAC	National Campaign Against Conscription
NDVMG	Northern Districts Vietnam Moratorium Group/ Campaign
NGA	National Gallery of Australia
NLF	National Liberation Front
NSA	*National Service Act 1968*
PVC	Project Vietnam Committee
RAAF	Royal Australian Air Force
RHC	Rex Hewett Committee
RSA	Revolutionary Socialist Alliance
RSL	Returned Services League
RWA	Realist Writers' Association
SDS	Students for a Democratic Society
SLNSW	State Library of NSW
SMH	*Sydney Morning Herald*
SOS	Save Our Sons
SSITE	Secondary Students for International Tolerance and Equality
SUA	Seamen's Union of Australia
SULC	Sydney University Labor Club
UAW	Union of Australian Women
UNSW	University of New South Wales
VAC	Vietnam Action Committee/Campaign
VDDF	Vietnam Demonstration Defence Fund
VMC	Vietnam Moratorium Campaign
WAC	Workers' Art Club
WERG	War and Education Research Group
WIDF	Women's International Democratic Federation
WILPF	Women's International League of Peace and Freedom
WWF	Waterside Workers Federation
YCAC	Youth Campaign Against Conscription

INTRODUCTION

POSITIONING THE QUIET PROTESTER

On 3 July 1969, 72 Australians came together in Sydney Town Hall to sign a Statement of Defiance to the *National Service Act 1968* (NSA), which enabled the conscription of young men into the Vietnam War:

> Those young men whose principles will not permit them to register under the present National Service Act and who refuse to be coerced into any war which they believe to be immoral and unjust, have my wholehearted support, encouragement, and aid.
>
> If I were required to register under present conditions, I would refuse. Therefore, while young men may serve two years' gaol because they have the courage to defy conscription and oppose the Vietnam War, I am compelled to stand with them.[1]

The signatories were frank about their determination to breach the Commonwealth *Crimes Act 1960*, declaring: 'This is why we have come here today, and this is our clear intention'.[2] Specifically, they sought to breach section 7a, which declared that any person who 'incites to, urges, aids or encourages, the commission of offences against any law of the Commonwealth or of a Territory' could be charged with an offence meriting a $200 fine (equivalent to just under $3000 today), imprisonment for 12 months, or both.[3] The Committee in Defiance of the National Service Act was established at this meeting, one of many protest organisations formed in New South Wales (NSW) during

Australian involvement in the Vietnam War, which began with the dispatch of the Australian Army Training Scheme in 1962 and ended in 1972, and for which up to 19 000 young men were conscripted.

By the end of 1970, almost 8000 Australians would make a Statement of Defiance. The committee spent significant time and energy ensuring that as many members as possible would be prosecuted, hoping to cause a glut in the court system and resultant delays to the possible imprisonment of draft evaders. As the committee declared in a confidential letter of 1 September 1969 to signatories: 'We want the public to realise that what we are doing is executing a political act'.[4]

I first became aware of the full extent of the activities of the Committee in Defiance in the first months of 2023, as I worked through the many boxes of anti-Vietnam and anti-conscription materials held in the Mitchell wing of the State Library of New South Wales (SLNSW) in the early months of a David Scott Mitchell Fellowship. As I explored, I became more fascinated by these activists, few of whom align with the image of the young, loud protester considered within popular memory to be the typical Australian who opposed the Vietnam War. I realised that the diversity within the anti-war movement of the 1960s and 1970s closely parallels the groups of activists agitating about key issues today.

The Committee in Defiance was led and run by a range of well-known anti-conscriptionists, and according to the Australian Security Intelligence Organisation (ASIO) – which considered this group a public security threat – was influenced by the Communist Party of Australia (CPA), although its broad membership suggests that it was formed more organically.[5] Ken Thomas, founder of KW Thomas Transport (later known as Thomas Nationwide Transport, or TNT), was the committee's president, and its secretary was Ken McLeod of the Association for International Cooperation and Disarmament (AICD). Barrister Murray Sime, journalist and draft evader Simon Townsend, and founding member of the Ex-Services Human Rights Association of Australia (ESHRAA) Les Waddington were vice-chairmen. The signatories and fellow committee members came from many sectors of society and included Building Workers' Industrial Union President Frank O'Sullivan, botanist Thistle Stead, poet Robert D Fitzgerald,

Ken Thomas leading a Committee in Defiance of the National Service Act demonstration in Sydney, 1969

Noel Hazard/*Tribune* collection/Mitchell Library, State Library New South Wales [MLSLNSW]/courtesy SEARCH Foundation

Methodist clergyman Reverend Alan Jackson, Macquarie University academic Dr Ivor Newman, and Ella Outhred, who was listed on committee documentation as an Epping housewife, but was well known within the movement as a staunch organiser and member of the women's organisation Save our Sons (SOS).[6]

This was a revelatory year, during which I learned of courageous and transformative actions by Vietnam War-era activists that have largely been forgotten in collective public memory. Many days I left the library with dusty fingers from handling letters, pamphlets and stacks of cut-off slips. I walked from the library to Martin Place and through the city, passing public squares, streets and buildings that were slowly revealed to me as spaces where people had volunteered their time to stand, rally, sit, write, endlessly turn the handles of Roneo machines, and speak about how to bring an end to the Vietnam War and to conscription. Beverley Symons and Rowan Cahill, who experienced many of these actions first-hand, believe that the process of forgetting this work was

Committee in Defiance of the National Service Act demonstration in Sydney, 1969

Noel Hazard/*Tribune* collection/MLSLNSW/courtesy SEARCH Foundation

'deliberate', facilitated by conservative forces that 'rallied to destroy the hope and social justice legacies of the sixties and early seventies, promoting notions of democracy as theatre and entertainment rather than hands-on involvement and participation by informed, concerned, critical citizens'.[7]

As my research continued, I saw quiet protest all around me. I paid more attention to the signs of the organisational efforts behind petitions, open letters, calls for volunteers, and donations. I noticed the names of the printing presses that produced protest posters. As the year progressed, the unfolding genocide in Palestine caused a profound increase in quiet protest not only among people who would describe themselves as activists, but also the crucial non-activist, whose politicisation filled my social media feed.[8] Activists held conferences; writers, poets and other artists performed; businesses of all kinds raised funds through raffles, not only for Gaza but also for climate change, trans rights, Aboriginal rights and anti-colonialism. Whatever one's political stance, it is difficult to ignore that, across the country, ordinary Australians are increasingly integrating activism into their own daily lives. This mirrors the far-reaching and escalating campaign against Australian involvement in the Vietnam War in the 1960s and 1970s.

As I dove deeper into the protest archive, in this charged atmosphere, I reflected on my own early activism and recognised that a detailed account of the far-reaching and escalating campaign against the Vietnam War would be useful for other activists – and non-activists – organising today. My suspicion was supported when I held a teach-in of my own at the University of Newcastle's Palestine encampment in 2024 about historical quiet protest methods. As students diligently took notes and asked questions about spreading the word to local communities, I saw that newer generations of activists had much to learn from Vietnam-era protesters, particularly given the rising suppression of public protest across Australia.

In April 2022, the NSW Government outlawed 'illegal protesting', through the *Roads and Crimes Legislation Amendment Act 2022 No 7.* This law has introduced categories of 'offences for certain behaviour that causes damage or disruption to major roads or major public facilities;

and for other purposes', with a possible punishment of $22 000, or two-years imprisonment.[9] In 2024, this was extended to include railway lines. Further restrictions have more recently been placed on all forms of public protest in NSW following the anti-semitic attack in the Sydney suburb of Bondi on 14 December 2025 that killed 15 people.

Similar anti-protest laws have been passed in Tasmania, Victoria, Queensland and South Australia, specifically targeting environmental activists, which include anti-logging or anti-mining protesters.[10] On 22 June 2023, two anti-coal activists allied with Blockade Australia, one of whom was a 64-year-old woman, were charged for occupying a train in Singleton, NSW, aiming to disrupt coal production and draw attention to the environmental harm caused by mining.[11] Public acts of protest occur alongside quieter acts that demand climate action. The respectable presence of the Knitting Nannas at large numbers of climate protests and their unwavering work in 'saving the land, air and water for our kiddies' begs comparison to the intentionally quiet power of SOS vigils and demonstrations during the Vietnam War.[12]

These are only some of the many echoes of the Vietnam War period in contemporary Australian society. On 11 November 2023, Trade Unionists for Palestine and the Palestinian Justice Movement organised a large-scale public blockade of ships at Port Botany in Sydney, which echoes similar actions by the Seamen's Union of Australia (SUA) as they refused to take part in the transportation of military goods to Vietnam in the mid-1960s.[13] A silent auction of donated artworks held on 29 October 2023 at Capers coffee shop and bar in Thornbury, Melbourne, raised funds for the Palestine Children's Relief Fund, echoing the donation of artworks to raise money for the anti-war cause by well-known Australian artists including Russell Drysdale, Arthur Boyd and Ian Fairweather during Arts Vietnam Week in 1968.[14]

All such acts have a specific purpose that ultimately contributes to a broader social movement. During the Vietnam War, the Committee in Defiance aimed to 'ultimately force the complete repeal of the National Service Act' by obliging the state to spend valuable time and energy on minor crimes, diverting the attention of the authorities away from young men evading conscription.[15] The Statement of Defiance was to be publicised across the country as 'a deliberate political act designed to embarrass the coalition government on the eve of a General Election', which would fall on 25 October 1969.[16]

The NSA had been renewed on 24 November 1964, requiring all men aged 20 to register with the Department of Labour and National Service. This was two years after the Australian Army Training Team Vietnam (AATTV) was first sent to serve alongside the United States, in an advisory capacity. Following the communist Việt Minh victory over the French in the First Indochina War (1946–1954), Vietnam was split into two – the communist north and supposedly democratic south – and the US aided the south militarily to prevent communist occupation.

The conflict in Indochina represents one of the warmest phases of the Cold War between liberal democratic and communist world powers. In 1950, Australian Liberal Prime Minister Robert Menzies had attempted to ban the Communist Party. Although Australians ultimately voted against a ban, the general atmosphere of suspicion towards the CPA, added to international alliances ratified through the Australia, New Zealand and United States (ANZUS) Treaty and the Southeast Asia Treaty Organization (SEATO), made involvement in Vietnam an imperative for the Liberal–Country Party government.

Peace activists and others had objected to Australia's entry into the Vietnam War, but the reintroduction of the NSA spurred larger numbers to join the anti-war movement. Conscripts were chosen randomly by 'birthday ballot', which was was held in secret and then televised from 1970, and were required to serve for two years in the Regular Army unless they were members of religious orders, university students or could prove they were valid conscientious objectors (COs) in a court of law – the last of these was usually only possible if the conscript could demonstrate active religious pacifist belief. Anti-conscription activity intensified after the announcement on 29 April 1965 that Australia would send combat troops to Vietnam, and again after March 1966, when Menzies declared conscripts could also be sent overseas to fight. Activists agitated against this law until 5 December 1972, when it was repealed by newly elected Prime Minister Gough Whitlam.

The Committee in Defiance recognised that administering thousands of activist-criminals was no simple task. It had to both organise public signing events and coordinate informants, who regularly approached authorities to report on new signatories. Other Committee members managed publicity, through constant communication with politicians and the press, to ensure that the group's actions were not sidelined or ignored.

Australian authorities did not know exactly how to manage mass non-traditional protest events that intentionally broke the law. On 25 July, three weeks after its first meeting at Sydney Town Hall, the Committee sent Commonwealth Attorney-General Nigel Bowen a list of 2000 people who had by then signed the Statement of Defiance. It was ignored. The Committee was undeterred, writing again to Bowen that he had only two 'honourable' courses of action in response to the Statement of Defiance. The first was to prosecute the 2000 individuals under the *Crimes Act*, which the Committee hoped would be viewed by authorities as a waste of valuable state resources. The other, wrote the Committee, was to amend the NSA and abolish conscription, allow conscientious objection under reasonable grounds or include provision for alternative non-military service for conscripts.[17]

Over the following months, original signatories received summonses on the charge that they 'encouraged the commission of the offence of failing to register for the purpose of National Service'.[18] On 18 November, the Committee goaded the new Attorney-General Tom Hughes by writing to him to demand action. Hoping for publicity, it forwarded the letter to the press with a note stating that 50 more signatories would be charged in the following days and 30 past signatories would appear in court for sentencing on 20 November. Ken McLeod had told members in August that 'we now face a situation in which any activity undertaken by the Committee is either ignored by the press or receives only minimal coverage, and no metropolitan daily is prepared to sell space to the Committee for a paid advertisement', but the *Australian* agreed to publish the letter to Hughes.[19]

By the end of November, 38 of the original 72 had been convicted under the *Crimes Act* and sentenced to a $50 fine or 25 days jail. With the intention of making themselves liable for imprisonment, all bar one refrained from paying the fine – a bold act that authorities also chose to ignore. On 10 December, 48 additional signatories appeared in Sydney's Special Federal Court, where Ken Buckley, a University of Sydney economic historian and founder of the NSW Council for Civil Liberties, 'attempted to make a statement to the Court explaining why he had committed the offence and why he was pleading "guilty"'. Despite interruptions by the presiding judge, Buckley declared that the Commonwealth was inviting 'public contempt of the Court and the *Crimes Act*' by failing to engage all signatories in court. Following this appearance, most signatories marched to Hughes' Sydney office to deliver a document, signed by all 119 convicted, alleging the Attorney-General had failed to 'administer the law with impartiality'.[20]

The committee's aim of flooding the legal system to disrupt the prosecution of draft evaders achieved some success. In 1970, two ALP politicians made Statements of Defiance: the first at the Victorian ALP State Conference on 14 June, and the second in the Draft Resisters Union journal *Resist* on 7 October. Hughes responded by announcing that no action would be taken, spelling an end to this avenue of anti-conscription activism.[21]

The Committee in Defiance of the National Service Act represents just one of many creative and clever responses to military conscription by NSW activists during the Vietnam War. The Committee's surviving administrative records show us how much time and energy were expended in just one year to establish, administer and publicise this single protest organisation. Its activities quickly extended beyond the original Statement of Defiance: on 22 December 1969 it decided to discourage young men from registering for national service with a 'Don't Register' campaign, and placed advertisements in youth, trade union and other suitable publications. The Committee used sound trucks to broadcast 'Don't Register' messages in the city and at beaches. It also established a Draft Counselling Service for young men and organised an Anti-Conscription Pop Concert.[22] To promote and fund such activities, as well as to cover the legal costs of supporting prosecuted signatories, it asked members to donate money and attend the committee's regular meetings.

Although we are able to trace the activities of the Committee in Defiance and other groups in historical records, the fragmentary nature of the protest archive makes it difficult to see the full range of diverse actions carried out to oppose the Vietnam War in NSW. Even more difficult is the task of hearing the quieter voices within the movement. These voices emerge within brief or otherwise transitory documents that rarely survive. Those that have been preserved allow us into the lives of protesters whose activism was not publicly visible, but whose words and actions show us that they were fervently committed to the movement.

One such protester was Mabel Wilson, who sent a $5 donation, representing one-third of the weekly old age pension, to the Committee in Defiance in 1969, with this note:

> Dear people, I admire your courage and am completely in sympathy with your ideals. Alas! I am very old – six years an octogenarian and two years an old age pensioner. As you can see I can be of practically no use to you – or anyone ... My time is running out and it would take longer than I may have, positively, to save fifty dollars out of my pension. I am sorry to be so unworthwhile but wish you success. My heart is with you all the way.[23]

The Committee replied warmly only a few days later, reflecting the value they placed on Wilson's quieter contribution to the movement.

This relatively minor exchange suggests that the movement was larger than we have imagined. By 1969, polls showed that over 50 per cent of Australia's population of 12 million opposed military involvement in the Vietnam War – far more than the approximately 200 000 who marched across the country at the first Moratorium to End the War in Vietnam of 8 May 1970. There were certainly others who, like Mabel Wilson, were restricted in their ability to actively protest due to limitations such as disability, work schedules, caring responsibilities, or even fear.

How do we find these quieter activists? Many can be located within the administrative records of NSW protest organisations during the

Vietnam War. These records can help us move towards understanding the anti-war and anti-conscription movements as not just a homogenous group with similar lives and capabilities, but as a diverse mass of people with a variety of circumstances and motivations. Some activists preferred to act behind the scenes or protest in less traditional and less public ways, whereas others were unable to protest publicly for a range of reasons, including restrictions by family, employers or school authorities, or simply because they lacked the capacity to do so.

Quiet or private protest actions do not necessarily produce quieter results. As the following chapters will show, even the quietest of protest actions produced loud and dramatic responses from politicians, media publications and other pro-war advocates that reverberated through parliament, schools, universities and other institutions. Fully comprehending these requires us to shift our understanding of a protest event from simply one that occurs publicly among groups of young people, to activities that encompass many different sectors of Australian society. After all, as sociologists Richard White and Patricia Wood write: 'There is no singular activist response or form of organising. There is no ideal scale, no ideal mode of working, nor ideal activist. We see a diversity of forms and degrees of organisation, and sometimes basically none, just spontaneous outrage'.[24]

This was certainly the case in NSW during the Vietnam War. When NSW Premier Robert Askin labelled anti-war protesters 'long haired and short brained' in March 1966, the NSW branch of the Women's International League of Peace and Freedom (WILPF) said that he must be 'sadly misinformed as to the wide cross-section of the community which is now protesting ... people who take part are only a small fraction of those who support them'.[25] Although the dynamism of youth certainly drew attention to the cause by increasing the scale of public disruption during the war, such actions should be viewed as just one major part of a much broader campaign.

We must also place the protest movement in the 1960s and 1970s within a much longer tradition of activism that contributed knowledge to the fight against the Vietnam War, following the warning by Vietnam-era activists Beverley Symons and Rowan Cahill to avoid 'segmentation of the past into manageable units' that mean we ignore 'connections and relationships with what has gone before'.[26] Anti-conscriptionists during Vietnam sought the knowledge of veterans of the 'no' campaign against conscription during the First World War. Members of existing organisations such as the CPA, WILPF, AICD and other peace groups were key to the formation and ongoing administration of anti-Vietnam or anti-conscription groups, contributing their knowledge to the fight against the war.

It is also impossible to consider activism in this country without addressing the powerful legacy of Aboriginal anti-colonial protest, which has been vital to the survival of hundreds of Indigenous nations and cultures on these lands since European invasion. Actions by Aboriginal activists from the 1960s, such as the Redfern Black Power Movement based on Gadigal Country, built on the wide-ranging methods of Aboriginal protest developed since the eighteenth century and undoubtedly influenced the anti-Vietnam War and anti-conscription movements. Many non-Indigenous anti-Vietnam War protesters expressed support for Aboriginal rights, including through such actions as the 1965 Freedom Ride, led by Arrernte and Kalkadoon man Charles Perkins, president of the University of Sydney's Student Action for Aborigines.[27] The 1967 referendum to include Aboriginal and Torres Strait Islander people in the Australian Constitution took place during the Vietnam War but, as activist and Gumbainggir historian Professor Gary Foley writes, 'historians have trivialised, marginalised and dismissed the achievements and historical influence of the so-called Australian Black Power Movement'.[28] Foley explains that non-Indigenous people did not notice the strength of Aboriginal resistance movements until Wiradjuri activist Paul Coe addressed the May 1970 Sydney Vietnam Moratorium, labelling the anti-war movement 'hypocrites' for fighting more fervently for Vietnamese than Aboriginal lives.[29] Indigenous activism continues to lead the charge in this country, with groups such as Warriors of the Aboriginal Resistance organising Invasion Day rallies that fill Australian cities annually on 26 January.[30]

DEFINING QUIET PROTEST

Social movement theorists have long addressed the motivations for individual protest participation, and in doing so they have carved a space for quiet protest without directly identifying the quiet protester as an influential figure within activist circles. This means that the primacy of public protest persists. In 1976 the Marxist historian George Rudé defined protest as a 'social act (generally a collective act) that seeks to rectify an injustice, to ventilate a grievance of public concern, or to offer a more fundamental challenge to society or its established norm'.[31] This attention to the 'social act' suggests that protest only exists when in public view.

Alberto Melucci argues that twentieth century peace activism could only be truly comprehended by tracing 'submerged' or hidden networks that 'become visible whenever collective actors confront or come into conflict with a public policy'. Melucci does make room for what he calls 'latency' in activism, insisting that 'the potential for resistance or opposition is sewn into the very fabric of daily life'.[32] The 'archive of activist wisdom' Australian researchers Sarah Maddison and Sean Scalmer have sourced from interviews with prominent activists similarly shows that 'the challenge in a movement does not lie only in its ability to mobilise publicly', as 'much movement activity happens away from the public eye'.[33]

Some earlier theories on social movements attributed protest participation to personal psychology, including alienation or low self-esteem, but more recent thinking has turned to the importance of the structures or organisations surrounding individuals that draw them to protest.[34] As sociologist Paul Almeida writes: 'Only through the conscious volition of ordinary people deciding to join in a demonstration or other collective event can actions concatenate into a social movement'.[35] Today, scholars interpret social movements, or the factors that drive people from a position of sympathy to actual protest engagement, as multidimensional and consider many different factors in a person's life, including their personal availability, political stances, social networks, organisational memberships, collective identities and whether they have earlier participated in protest.[36] Increased attention to the lives and experiences of individual activists has led us more directly to reasons for quiet or alternative protest forms.

People participate in protest if they are able to fit it into their lives. As Anthony Orum wrote in 1974, 'without people who have time on their hands, great revolutions would probably never get off the ground'.[37] Clark McPhail and David Miller, writing three years earlier, describe the 'assembling process' that brings people together to work towards a certain objective.[38] McPhail considers activism to be a 'variety of individual and joined performances' that can only be truly understood through systematic knowledge of their immediate interactional environments that reveals what 'produces, maintains and alters them'.[39] Such knowledge has been vital to how we understand recent changes in political participation, and has meant that quieter methods, such as the use of political consumerism to express dissent through boycotts, and even 'clicktivism' or 'slacktivism', which usually occurs when individuals are alone and using an electronic device, are increasingly defended.[40]

This book draws attention to 'varied performances' within the anti-Vietnam War and anti-conscription movements in NSW in the 1960s and early 1970s. These performances encompass a range of protest acts, including donations of time, money, equipment or services, by many different groups including the elderly, migrants, teachers, public servants, railway workers, artists, veterans of past wars, lawyers and many others, as well as the 'assembling processes' that brought these people together in opposition to the war. Details about the infrastructure of the protest movement can be found in internal organisation documents, such as meeting minutes, membership slips, correspondence to and from protest organisations, religious leaders, politicians, newspapers and the general public, raffle tickets, competition entries, donation receipts and financial statements.

Fortunately, activists have recognised the value in these types of documents. Records have been deposited in SLNSW collections, as well as other Australian libraries. Along with posters, newsletters, leaflets and newspaper articles or advertisements, these archives allow us to draw closer to quieter protesters during the Vietnam War.

It is important to emphasise the role women activists played in creating these administrative archives, as they were so often allocated clerical duties within protest organisations. As University of Sydney graduate and Socialist Review Group member Sylvia Hale declared in her feminist critique of the anti-war movement at the 1971 National Anti-War Conference, 'women tend to type articles, not to write them'.[41] Historian and activist Ann Curthoys' work on feminists in anti-Vietnam War circles confirms that women were subjugated within the movement by these practices, which were justified by male activists who claimed they were striving for mass support, but reinforces that women were instrumental in the day-to-day running of the movement.[42] The value of the activist women's archive has been recognised since the Vietnam War. According to historian Patricia Grimshaw, feminist writers of the 1970s 'were convinced that mainstream historians had ignored women's life experiences because the men in fact denigrated the contribution women made to society', insisting that 'the sources which would write women back into history were out there waiting to be utilised'.[43]

The careful preservation by women activists of detailed records that document the everyday workings of the anti-Vietnam War movement echoes the 'archival activism' by 1920s and 1930s feminists through which they aimed to address their exclusion from political and public life, and ultimately enhance the value of the archive.[44] As Caswell and Cifor insist, forming and maintaining an archive, using a feminist approach centred in 'radical empathy' towards all who appear within the archive, can ultimately bring the public closer to the realities of their own communities.[45] Only through the 'radical empathy' of women activists is this study of quiet protest possible.

The pages of this book present some of the voluminous archives of anti-Vietnam War protest in NSW, alongside social and historical perspectives, that move us closer to activists who did not protest in public or traditional ways but who likely considered themselves just as opposed to the war as those who marched through the streets. Although there is very little research about why people who support a movement *do not* publicly protest, everyday documents within the archive tell us why many were not able to become involved in a more public way. The NSW protest archive alone is so vast it could fill multiple volumes. Accordingly, I have limited this study to one Australian state, although the archives show NSW activists avidly communicated with their contemporaries in other states and were linked to a broad national history.

Protest organisations constantly formed, transformed and re-formed, many changing names and identities throughout the war. For example, AICD took a central role in organising and hosting protest groups throughout the war, meaning that some established localised groups across NSW chose to re-identify as AICD offshoots. After the Moratorium campaign began in early 1970, many regional, suburban and occupation-based groups allied themselves with this phase of the movement by changing both name and structure, forming new collectives such as the Public Servants Moratorium Group, Railway Workers Moratorium Group, Journalists Moratorium Group and Teachers Moratorium Group. The radical anti-war organisation Vietnam Action Campaign, based during much of the war from Bob Gould's Third World Bookshop and run by Gould along with Hall Greenland and Steve Johnston, was also at one point called Vietnam Action Committee. It is not my aim to chart all these shifts, despite their importance – such a task would be better carried out by a Sydney activist who participated in the movement. Instead, this book explores the wide range of ways that people in NSW protested during the Vietnam War, focusing on non-traditional and quieter activism.

Many individuals spent hours, days, weeks, months or years quietly fighting against Australian involvement in Vietnam and conscription, but the enduring focus on loud and visible protest has meant that their names and identities have remained hidden within the archive. I have made every attempt to bring us as close as possible to these activists. I have included their addresses to show how seamlessly activism blended into Australian life. I have often quoted their words directly, to emphasise that their opposition to the war was just as fervent as those who protested more publicly. There are undoubtedly many activists I have unknowingly neglected or been unable to fit within these chapters. Nevertheless, I hope that this book has added to the vital work by previous scholars as well as the activists themselves, many of whom are cited throughout, in demonstrating just how many of our mothers, fathers, aunts, uncles, brothers, sisters and friends dedicated time and effort to the anti-Vietnam War movement.

Chapter One tells the story of the expansion of the movement during the Vietnam War, and how organisations formed, recruited and retained members. Protest organisations used a range of strategies to reach broader numbers of the population, including migrants, inspired by CPA ideas about a 'coalition of the masses' but adapted to local circumstances. Many joined the movement to express their opposition to compulsory military duty, so Chapter Two discusses the various ways, from public to quiet, that Australians, including lawyers, religious leaders and teachers, showed their opposition to conscription. Chapter Three positions the Moratoriums of 1970 to 1971 as the pinnacle of organisation against Vietnam, which brought together most protest groups to form a powerful coalition that built on tactics used before or during the war. An overview of this impressive multifaceted action against the war contextualises the aspects of quiet protest discussed in remaining chapters.

Chapter Four outlines the many creative ways protest organisations financed various forms of public protest, newspaper advertisements and medical support for Vietnamese victims of war, including direct appeals for donations and tax resistance, among other methods. Fundraising was one of the most effective ways to capture some of the quietest protesters. Chapter Five explores the ways artists, including dancers, filmmakers, gamers, writers, musicians, actors and poets, used their creativity, and their bodies, in non-traditional protest. Chapter Six focuses on voluntarism during the war, and how people donated their labour to the anti-war movement or provided equipment to aid the protest effort. Chapter Seven discusses the ways activists gave voice to their opposition to the war, including gatherings such as discussion groups, draft counselling schools, sit-ins, teach-ins, forums, public lectures, as well as private discussions among friends and family. Chapter Eight turns to the letter writing campaign to end the war, as well as other lines of communication such as advertising and legal support. Such avenues were particularly valuable to those who could not publicly protest due to age, disability, illness or bans by employers, teachers, parents or other authorities. Chapter Nine outlines how the 'quietest' activists chose to protest despite various constraints.

This book concludes with a reflection on the recent increase in quiet activism across Australia amidst increasing legal challenges to democratic protest. Quiet protest is essential to social movements, as mass movements can only be formed by working with the abilities and limitations of communities – or, in other words, meeting people where they are.

Laws that criminalise public protest only increase the opportunity for activists to create a public or louder disruption. To avoid alienating the new activist or non-activist within the current climate and ensure broader participation, activist groups must integrate a shift in tactics and a simultaneous focus on quieter protest. In Iran, citizens of all genders have engaged in anti-government protest in increasing numbers, which saw over 500 activists killed in the second half of 2022. The danger of protest, combined with the increase in activism, has seen the rise of 'micro-protest', involving small numbers of people acting over a short period of time.[46] Limited, or even quieter, forms of protest not only allow activists who wish to evade police action or other dangers to become involved, but also increase the ability of social movements to reach people of different ages and abilities.

Investigating quiet protest, then, can allow us to broaden popular definitions of the protester, and move past more ableist and ageist visions of social movements. Examining quiet protest during the Vietnam War, a significant conflict that socially and politically transformed Australia, will allow us to chart a more realistic estimate of the activist presence in this country. It will also ensure we do not ignore or neglect the frequently larger mass of quieter protesters who are just as staunchly determined to agitate for change as those marching on the streets.

CHAPTER ONE

REACHING THE QUIET PROTESTER

In July 1968, Rex Hewett appealed a Magistrates Court decision ruling that his request to be exempted from the *National Service Act* (NSA) as a conscientious objector could not be granted because he had failed to demonstrate 'absolute pacifism'. Hewett had been drafted in the first intake after the reintroduction of the NSA in 1964 and the introduction of conscription for overseas service in 1965, and had been battling since then for recognition of his objection to military service on moral principles. His mother Noreen May Hewett was an experienced activist, being national secretary of the Union of Australian Women (UAW) and a member of the CPA. In 1965, she and co-founder Joyce Golgerth had established Save Our Sons (SOS).[1] In the face of Hewett's inability to demonstrate his conscientious objection through the court system, supporters formed the Rex Hewett Committee (RHC) which mobilised around the family and reached out to recruit like-minded people to the movement.

On 19 July 1968, the Abolish Conscription Campaign (ACC) resolved to join with the RHC to sponsor a Caravan Against Conscription tour of the NSW countryside to 'make fraternal contacts – e.g. church members, young people, women, teachers etc.', and 'to distribute literature, hold public meetings, concerts, meet interested groups in homes, secure publicity'.[2] By sponsoring the Caravan, the ACC aimed to 'live up to the expectations of enthusiastic supporters in many country towns' resulting from 'deep responsibility to those valiant people in these towns who often feel isolated from the type of activity conducted in the cities'. The Caravan was to be 'big enough to make an impact' and 'colourful', with folk singers and entertainers to 'particularly attract young people', including an appearance by journalist and conscientious objector Simon Townsend.[3]

The ACC had decidedly democratic beginnings as 'an ad hoc committee set up from a meeting to which organisations opposed to conscription were invited', including members of the Quakers, Catholics for Peace, Conscientious Objectors' Discussion Group, SOS, Federal Pacifist Council of Australia (FPCA), AICD, Resistance, Secondary Students for International Tolerance and Equality and the Young Socialist League, among others.[4] It was intended to be a broad group representing the coalition approach I discuss later in this chapter. It would include ministers of religion, church members, businessmen, ex-servicemen, trade unionists, students, young people and women, with a stated aim to 'appeal to the local communities'.[5] The inclusion of 'respectable' members of the community alongside members of the radical left, CPA and the Australian Labor Party (ALP), was a deliberate strategy aimed at increasing broad support among non-activists.

The Caravan's organisers realised that many members of the public were reluctant to engage in demonstrations or rallies, so reassured rural residents that 'the object is not to hold protest demonstrations, but rather to exchange views and provide information about the NSA (including advice to young people about their legal rights under the Act)'.[6] The Caravan's itinerary – listing vans, caravan park berths, meeting rooms and rural contacts – reveals a vast amount of organisational work for a journey that can be viewed as 'mobile' quiet protest.[7] The Caravan was to travel to Goulburn, Wagga Wagga, Albury, Griffith, Forbes, Parkes, Orange and Bathurst from 27 August until 7 September, and briefly visit Cootamundra and Leeton. Fundraising before the Caravan set off was essential, and included a party organised by the RHC that featured folk singers, dancing and supper, for a donation of $1.[8]

On 8 August 1968, a group of AICD members in the town of Orange, including a meat inspector, housewife, businessperson, postal worker, production worker, retired health inspector, contractor and electrician, met to discuss their support for the Caravan, and decided to form a more

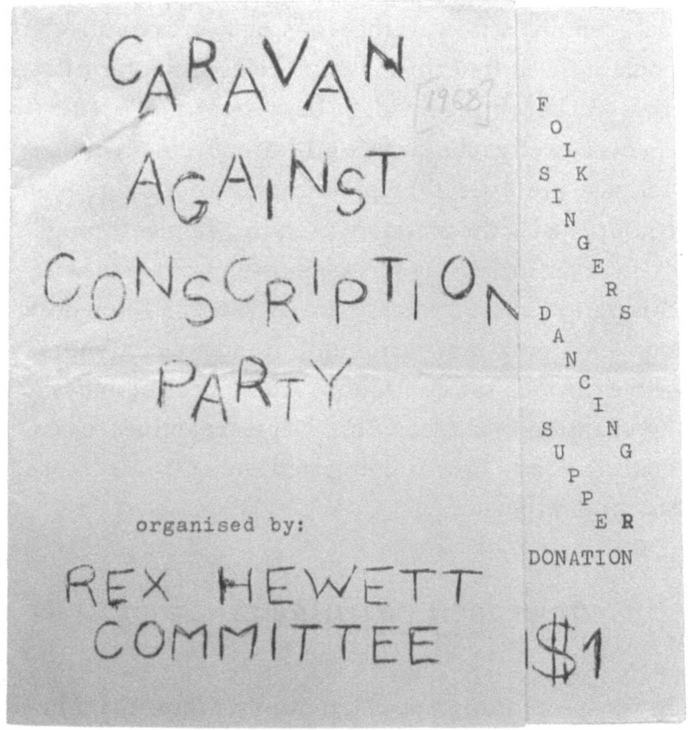

Caravan Against Conscription party invitation, 1968

People for Nuclear Disarmament/MLSLNSW

permanent group to 'pursue peace activities in the area'. Les Bromfield wrote to AICD the next day, suggesting the formation of an Orange AICD branch to engage in quieter activities such as 'publicising the parent body, the sale of publications, a drive for membership, inviting speakers from AICD, the showing of films, organising discussion events and sending delegates to AICD activities in Sydney'.[9] This fulfilled some of the Caravan's hopes for rural outreach, which represents one of many attempts made to reach the non-activist during the Vietnam War.

When the AATTV had been sent to Vietnam in 1962, existing activist groups from across the country began promoting the anti-war message. They diverted their attention from issues such as gender equality, Aboriginal land rights and the broader peace movement, to express open disapproval with the war, on anti-colonial, pacifist or ideological grounds. Anti-war, anti-conscription and anti-Vietnam War groups constantly shifted throughout the conflict, forming alliances, cooperating and becoming divided. They were influenced by both local developments as well as the larger anti-war movement in the US, where 'myriad forms of protest, self-help, community building and insurgency grew and flourished at the grassroots, sending ripples through the entire culture'.[10] The ever-increasing spread of revolutionary ideas in Australia during this period caused what historian George Rudé describes as a 'sea-change', incorporating social, cultural and political shifts.[11] This was only possible through the continuous attempts by activists to reach an increasing 'coalition' of citizens. This chapter examines the composition of this 'coalition', and how it publicised the anti-war message across NSW throughout the war.

'TOWARDS A COALITION OF THE LEFT'

Although the burgeoning anti-Vietnam War movement in NSW was greatly influenced by CPA members, policies and ideology, the ALP dominates public memory of the conflict. This is, in large part, due to the ALP's support of the Moratorium movement from 1970 and the role of its leader Gough Whitlam in abolishing conscription after his momentous 1972 federal election victory. Both CPA and ALP members, many involved in the union movement and other protest organisations, influenced the changing character of the movement to differing degrees as the war progressed. They made substantial contributions, but if we shift our focus to the accounts of everyday protest action in the protest archive, we can see that AICD members expended more time and energy coordinating and promoting the movement than any other organisation.

The central role of AICD in NSW organising meant that the movement against the Vietnam War adopted protest tactics that had been developed by the existing Australian peace movement.[12] The Australian Peace Council (APC) had been formed in Melbourne in 1949, and by February 1950 had established a broad program of protest action, which included placing peace materials in local papers, running competitions, collecting donations, selling badges, working with other organisations, presenting guest speakers, and theatre.[13] During the 1950s, the peace movement was predominantly working class and associated with left-wing trade unionists, reflecting CPA influence within the formation of the APC and other pacifist organisations.[14] These were 'nomads of their present', according to Verity Burgmann, with aims and activities largely determined by their position within society.[15] The influx of broader socioeconomic groups changed the constitution of protest movements during the Vietnam War, meaning that techniques organically shifted to incorporate new viewpoints.

Existing organisations provided 'activist wisdom' about protest strategy and tactics to these new groups, while actively diverting their energies towards the Vietnam War.[16] Organisations such as the UAW, Women's International League of Peace and Freedom (WILPF), FPCA and members of the CPA and ALP were active within public protest and publicised the anti-war message in their leaflets, journals and pamphlets.[17] The CPA, in particular, provided 'ideological heritage' as it supported the formation of anti-war groups in the early years of Vietnam involvement.[18] The Victorian State Secretary Ralph Gibson called the CPA 'a driving force in the whole struggle', writing in January 1966 that growth in the protest movement was due to the 'skilful direction of CPA activists'.[19]

Members of the ALP left also began actively organising against the war from 1962. This caused tensions with the conservative NSW branch of the ALP, which feared involvement in the peace movement would hamper future electoral success. The Committee for the Implementation of the Geneva Agreement (Vietnam), formed at the 20th CPA Congress in June 1964 and soon after renamed Committee for Peace in Vietnam (CPV), was an early target of the NSW ALP. CPV was closely aligned with around 30 trade unions across the country and led by Reginald (Reg) Rickard, secretary of the Milk and Ice Carters' Union of NSW. In November 1964, the CPV sent Rickard and Alex McDonald, secretary of the Queensland Labor Council and a member of the Australian Council of Trade Unions (ACTU), to the International Conference for

Solidarity with the People of Vietnam against US Imperialist Aggression and for the Defence of Peace, in communist North Vietnam.[20]

Following this visit, Rickard and McDonald claimed that the CPV, which also included some ALP members, had 'organised mass demonstrations', provoking objections from NSW ALP leadership. On 29 January 1965, the NSW ALP declared that CPV policy was incompatible with its views, meaning that any CPV members in the party needed to resign within 14 days or forfeit their membership. This act nearly decimated the CPV but attempts within the left faction of the ALP to bypass the order resulted in the formation of AICD, which went on to coordinate activity by the CPA and the ALP, among other groups.[21]

Findlay claimed in 1968 that the CPA had intended to use the CPV as a 'co-ordinating agent' for its own ends, but CPV's failure in NSW led to a shift in focus onto the Vietnam Action Committee (VAC). CPA members were instrumental in setting up protest organisations in the early years of the war but were well aware that 'red-smearing', at what was then the height of the Cold War, was a risk to public appeal and could endanger the movement. The Party, to ward off any accusation of communist infiltration, limited its involvement to the strategic selection of leadership teams for new protest groups.[22] However, ASIO, which spent much of the Cold War exaggerating the communist influence on Australian society, believed the CPA 'worked incessantly to ensure that the protest movement's policies on the issues of the war develop along lines parallel with its own', and this seems to echo pronouncements by the CPA itself.[23] So while Findlay argues the CPA limited its role within the movement to 'sponsoring or encouraging' Australians to form organisations such as Youth Campaign Against Conscription (YCAC) and SOS, this simplifies a complex process that involved numerous points of view.

The CPA's coordinating role in the movement did not begin with the Vietnam War, nor was it a specifically Australian tactic. Leninist theory expanded on Marxist writings that emphasised the revolutionary potential of workers to create a 'coalition of the masses', incorporating the key worker–peasant alliance that would inevitably take power.[24]

21st CPA Congress, 1967

Noel Hazard/*Tribune* collection/MLSLNSW/courtesy SEARCH Foundation

Communist Audrey Blake explained that, from its establishment in Australia in 1920, the CPA formed a variety of 'fronts' 'to extend the space in which the Party could work'.[25] The CPA principle of collective strength continued to the Vietnam years. A party communication of 16 March 1965 about upcoming May Day celebrations exhorted members: 'In this year of building towards a mass Communist Party, May Day presents us with another target – to rally all Party members, supporters and workers, women, youth, children and pensioners to march for the militant demands of the Australian working people' – including an end to the war in Vietnam.[26]

CPA commitment to cooperation was accelerated after the 21st CPA Congress of 1967. Its report 'Towards a Coalition of the Left' emphasised that:

> Australia urgently needs a new social order. Only a united people, cooperating in all spheres of production, distribution and social life, can fully utilise new ideas and technology to create in our country abundance and security for all.[27]

The 22nd CPA Congress, three years later, continued the call for a 'new society' and a 'new state', incorporating 'cooperation' and 'self-management' through worker control.[28] CPA members Alec Robertson and John Grimshaw called for a broader acceptance of 'New Left' ideologies and methods of action to avoid the CPA becoming a party that 'tends to revert back to the past ... outside the mainstream of revolutionary action'.[29]

Nevertheless, the influence of the CPA within the anti-Vietnam War and anti-conscription movements decreased over time. CPA membership declined, from a high of about 22 000 members in 1945 to only 4500 in 1970, which is partly due to the beginning of the Sino-Soviet split from 1961. CPA members who were more closely aligned with Maoism, Trotskyism and libertarianism moved to a new, more radical organisation called CPA (Marxist-Leninist), which was never a popular choice within the broader left.[30] The year 1970 was also a hallmark for the CPA, as its steadfast focus on the Soviet Union caused a split that led to the formation of the Socialist Party of Australia, in December 1971.

CPA members believed that publicly tempering their approach and forming a 'coalition of the left' through a 'popular front' would attract non-communists, including unionists, ALP members, intellectuals and religious leaders, among others.[31] The party acknowledged that engaging in radicalism before the movement had majority support would hinder its overall aims – frustrating the militant left throughout the war.[32] In 1968, a short-lived, secretive group named Revolutionary Socialist Alliance (RSA) was devised by radical activist and teacher Denis Freney. Although Freney hoped to attract 'progressive' CPA members, he challenged the CPA for forming coalitions to 'passively adapt to the mood of the working class' by 'trying to become a party influencing the broadest possible layers of the masses'. RSA called for activists to 'fight, if necessary, for a whole period "against the current" to re-educate and reorientate the class'.[33]

One of the many infinitesimal disagreements within the movement arose when RSA attempted to rent an operational base in Sydney in 1969, a move thwarted by Bob Gould of the (largely Trotskyist) VAC, which considered the RSA coalition approach too close to the 'Stalinist' CPA. He signed a lease on the intended property before the RSA were able to secure it, 'crowing about how he beat the Stalinists yet again'. Although RSA essentially disbanded around this time, in 1970 Freney opened the radical Liberation bookshop in North Manly and became joint convenor of the Manly–Warringah Moratorium committee, alongside pacifist Quaker, WILPF and AICD member Phyllis (Phyl) Latona. In the same year, Freney rejoined the CPA and became a *Tribune* journalist, typifying the personal ideological shifts that activists could experience across the war years.[34]

While the CPA moved towards its 'coalition of the left' platform in the 1960s, the federal ALP leader Arthur Calwell was broadly supportive of the NSW Branch's attempts to distance itself from the anti-war movement. In the mid-1960s, he disapproved of any ALP involvement with peace organisations suspected of serving as CPA fronts.[35] His position created tensions in the party, especially as other federal ALP figures, such as Sydney's Tom Uren and Melbourne's Jim Cairns, frequently spoke to peace groups connected with the CPA. Calwell had stated in 1964 that he 'utterly and absolutely' opposed conscription, and from April 1966 called for 'protests and demonstrations from one end of the country to the other against conscription for overseas service'.[36] The prominence of anti-conscriptionists within the growing anti-war movement meant there was broad voter support for an ALP victory in the election of 26 November 1966, but the fears of many in the party that association with the left would cause electoral defeat came to fruition.[37]

Even though Calwell publicly aligned himself with the protest movement, AICD mostly supported non-ALP candidates during the 1966 election campaign, which reflected its connections with the CPA and other leftist activists. As a result, in the weeks after the devastating ALP defeat, the NSW ALP Executive banned members from participating in AICD activities.[38] Broad disillusionment with the election result fractured the movement, meaning that attempts by organisations like AICD to foster mass appeal slowed down and sole-group acts of radical protest became more common. This continued until the lead up to the 1969 federal election, and another ALP defeat, before a new, intensified phase of mass cooperation began, which culminated in the Moratorium campaign.[39]

By the Moratorium period, the ALP was firmly behind the movement. On 14 April 1970, less than a month before the first Moratorium of 8 May, Liberal Party Attorney-General Tom Hughes presented the Vietnam Moratorium Campaign Ministerial Statement in the Federal House of Representatives, which he hoped would convince anti-Vietnam War activists 'to reconsider their support and to withdraw from the position they have taken up'. In response, ALP Leader Gough Whitlam requested that the following statement be added: 'This House ... affirms the right of peaceful demonstration and the right of Australian people to express opposition to the war in Vietnam, as do the great majority of governments and peoples in the world'.[40]

The influence of AICD and similar organisations was so widely acknowledged that, in the same debate, the fervently anti-communist Hughes dismissed the motives of the movement for international cooperation and disarmament as:

> A well known and widely practised Communist tactic ... to invest with the aura of respectability activities designed to promote Communist ascendancy, by the process of persuading well-known people to lend their prestige and their support to unworthy causes that, by a process of calculated deception, are made to appear worthy.[41]

In this period some activists who were accused of communist sympathies took active steps to publicly disassociate from the CPA, so as to ensure ongoing popularity for the campaign. Two weeks after Hughes' comments, Jane Gray, secretary of the Northern Districts Vietnam Moratorium Group (NDVMG), wrote to the *Australian Financial Review*: 'it is obvious to all but those who do not wish to see that the influence of communist ideology in Australia is negligible', claiming that despite 'common ground' between the CPA and other groups, 'it does not follow that all of those groups are communists'.[42]

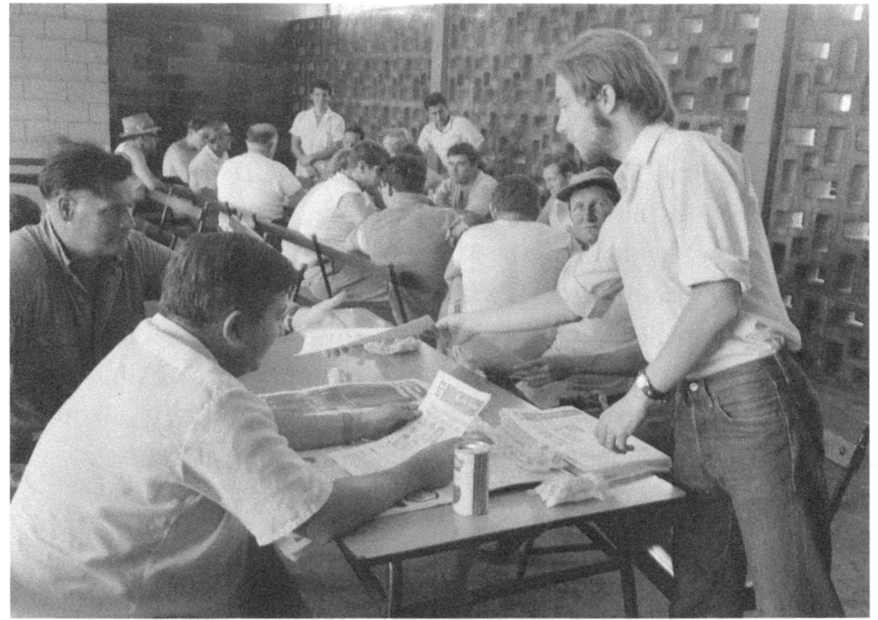

Distribution of AICD newsletter to workers, 1968

Noel Hazard/*Tribune* collection/MLSLNSW/courtesy SEARCH Foundation

Hughes' concern was understandable, as AICD was the central organisational influence on day-to-day anti-Vietnam War operations in the state. Its broad appeal provided an ideal meeting point between the various left factions existing in NSW during the war. This is not to say that tensions did not exist. The radical left, which included organisations such as VAC, Resistance and RSA, frequently disagreed with the 'traditional' left, represented by the CPA, AICD and some anti-war unions, and left factions of more conservative groups, such as churches and the ALP. In fact, during the war VAC labelled AICD a 'Stalinist' rival because some of its leaders were also CPA members.[43]

Despite such tensions, anti-war individuals and groups from across the country directed enquiries about the movement to AICD as the 'headquarters of all current bodies of anti-conscriptionists', and by 1968 its administrative efforts succeeded in facilitating a joint movement against the war.[44] More leaflets, letters, membership slips and posters opposing the war in Vietnam crossed the doors of its Parker Street and George Street headquarters in Sydney than in any other location in the state. A range of organisations, including YCAC, which was largely supported by ALP members, used the AICD office in Sydney as a base for regular meetings. AICD also took a 'major responsibility for the central organisation of the Moratorium', largely due to in-fighting among other groups, which I will discuss in Chapter Three.[45]

Put simply, it is impossible to quantify the breadth of AICD's quiet action during the war, but it will be apparent throughout this book, through continual references to AICD headquarters, members, collaborations, actions and publications.

THE ANTI-VIETNAM WAR ANTI-CONSCRIPTION ACTIVISTS' CONFERENCE

Although individuals and groups to both the left and right of the CPA largely disapproved of the 'coalition of the left' approach, the 26 November 1966 Liberal Party election victory, in which the ALP lost just under 5 and a half per cent of its primary vote, prompted a variety of organisations to move towards promoting a similarly democratic approach to collectively opposing the war.[46] Bitter disappointment turned to determination as anti-war activists who had actively supported Calwell's election campaign, as well as many who had not, realised that a strategic change was needed to more effectively reach the general public.

In December 1966, Bob Gould, whose group VAC had formed in 1965 in response to dissatisfaction with insufficient radicalism within the movement, wrote to a group of organisations in Australia and Aotearoa New Zealand to propose an Anti-Vietnam War Anti-Conscription Activists' Conference, aimed at forming a collective approach in opposing Vietnam.[47] Throughout the war, his Third World Bookshop at 35 Goulburn Street, Sydney, was the base for militant activists and the headquarters of Resistance, a group formed by Sydney University Labor Club (SULC) and VAC members.[48]

Gould made no secret of his opposition to the 'Stalinist' CPA and their specific methods in achieving a 'coalition of the left', and his militant left position caused him to express frequent antagonism towards other anti-war groups. Despite this, his central role in the organisation of the Sydney Anti-Vietnam War Anti-Conscription Activists' Conference places him at the forefront of the necessarily cooperative atmosphere that characterised many sections of the NSW anti-war movement.

Bob Gould, Barry Robinson of YCAC, and Geoff Anderson of AICD, were the joint secretaries of the Project Vietnam Committee (PVC), self-described as 'a Sydney Co-ordinating Committee which embraces a number of organisations involved in the campaign against the Vietnam War'. In early January they wrote to members that 'considerable response was received to this initiative from other states and country areas, and a widely representative cross section of significant activists in Anti-War Organisations have indicated their willingness to attend such a conference'. A few weeks later, PVC agreed to sponsor the conference, and an organising committee was elected that represented a range of anti-war organisations.[49] The membership of PVC alone reflects the movement's broader goal of a 'coalition', despite Gould's hesitance in this regard. While Gould and VAC organised some of the most militant responses to the conflict, YCAC was closely affiliated with the ALP, and had a left-wing, but less radical, approach to opposing the war.

The conference, held in Sydney from 27 to 30 January 1967, transformed the push for wider appeal into a movement-wide strategy. Its opening session was attended by 300 people, representing 50 diverse organisations, including the Vietnam Day Committee, Campaign for Nuclear Disarmament (Melbourne), the Postal Clerk and Telegraphists' Union, Queensland Peace Committee and SOS.[50] A major conference theme revolved around adapting organisational structures and protest techniques to a broader range of people, so as to attract a larger number of supporters to the cause.

Conference sessions positioned quiet protest as a central and essential facet of this goal. The opening lecture, 'The New Stage in the Vietnam War', acknowledged the need for a shift in techniques to respond to the specifically Australian landscape.[51] On Sunday 29 January, participants were instructed on 'Organising at the Work Shop Level', one of many sessions that outlined a range of methods to broadcast the anti-war message to the Australian population, including 'locality activity', carried out in such a way as to avoid the 'red smearing' experienced by 'older peace groups'. Solutions to this problem included the formation of an 'ad hoc Anti-Vietnam War Committee around some specific project or event' by non-CPA members – 'people beyond suspicion of redness' – meaning that 'reddened' peace activists could also be involved without attracting negative attention.[52]

A central contribution of the conference was the institution of a program of specifically quiet protest techniques, which foregrounded AICD as the central facilitator in NSW. The session 'Diversity in Peace Action' focused almost exclusively on instructing activists how to engage in effective quiet protest, including silent vigils, study groups, film screenings and lunchtime theatre. The session also shared ideas about radio and television advertisements; establishing anti-war education committees; inviting international anti-war figures such as Bertrand Russell or Jean-Paul Sartre to Australia; offering 'literature in a lighter vein for the uncommitted, e.g. in cartoon or comic strip form'; and even puppet shows. It also called for a 'central information centre in each capital city, like AICD in Sydney', acknowledging the organisation's central role.[53]

This program led to several key conference resolutions tied to the importance of quiet protest to attract mass support. The first, carried unanimously, set the 'next major organised phase of action against the Vietnam War' from Easter 1967, which included:

> Activities of a predominantly 'witness' or religious character, building up through literature distribution, cultural activities, teach-ins, canvasses ... activities in country towns, workshop meetings and other activities directed at trade unionists, local meetings, film showings and other activities, to a nationwide demonstration mobilisation.[54]

Although Gould and other radical leftists generally disapproved of the CPA 'popular front' approach, the passing of this resolution, at a conference Gould initiated, demonstrates his role in setting the terms of the movement from then on – not only in NSW, but in the whole of Australia. The commitment to varied protest tactics to increase public support illustrates not only the increasing membership of the movement, but also wider acceptance of its transformation. As the anti-war movement attracted more supporters, the degree of quiet protest within the movement increased, both in terms of administrative assistance to public activists and carrying out specific quieter tasks in opposing the war. The wider aims of education and outreach established during the Anti-Vietnam War Anti-Conscription Activists' Conference expanded in the later years of the conflict, particularly following the 1969 Liberal Party election victory and the next push towards mass appeal through the Moratorium campaign.

ATTRACTING THE 'NON-ACTIVIST'

Attracting a broader range of supporters was a worthy goal, but new techniques were needed to ensure its success. Most within the movement agreed this success depended on the attention and support of working class 'non-activists'. After the ALP federal election defeat of 25 October 1969, SULC, echoing calls in the wake of the previous election, declared that the 'way forward for the protest movement is not more of the same', but instead an 'attempt to relate our protest to the power structures of Australian society. More support must be sought from the working class' using 'new methods of communication'.[55]

Saunders calls the goal of creating a mass political strike against the war at this time 'little more than a pipe dream', partly due to the lack of working-class participation.[56] In 1980, Australian academic and writer Donald Horne, who described the Australian anti-Vietnam War protest movement as 'an alternative program for how to run things, produced by middle-class people who thought their way was better than that of the middle-class people then in control', connected this to the absence of a 'feeling of responsibility and involvement' in the working classes.[57]

Attributing lack of working-class support to a certain predisposition of character or individual beliefs and values was, even by this time, an outdated view.[58] Scholars like McPhail and Orum had written almost ten years earlier that examining 'individuals' immediate interactional environments' can show why the 'periodically unengaged' or those with less structured work responsibilities are more available for protest activities, and those with more demanding working lives are not.[59]

To understand the divide in protest availability we must acknowledge that time is not calculated or experienced in the same way across social and economic classes. 'Time poverty' is a 'time burden on the poor', affecting working-class families disproportionately, as they are less able to outsource domestic and other tasks or to engage in leisure or special interest activities.[60] The intersection of class and time poverty can also make it difficult for individuals within the working classes to see a clear vision of their future, which may impact their willingness or ability to engage in political activities that do not directly impact their lives.[61]

The 2022 World Values Survey, distributed in over 50 countries across the globe, asked citizens from a range of class backgrounds about their participation in and support for social movements. Its multiple-choice questionnaire enables simple analysis of the class basis of respondents alongside participation in protest actions. Of the 1813 respondents, 83.5 per cent were not university educated and, of these, only 18.8 per cent had attended a peaceful demonstration; 16 per cent had joined a boycott and 13.9 per cent joined strikes, but 52.1 per cent, 51.7 per cent and 49.3 per cent respectively of all respondents expressed willingness to be involved. A larger proportion had carried out quieter protest actions, such as donating to a group or campaign (47.3 per cent), contacting a government official (30.5 per cent) or signing an electronic petition (44.1 per cent).[62] While, in Saunders' words, the mass movement envisaged by the CPA and other organisations from the early years of the conflict 'was little more than a pipe dream', perhaps this was inevitable, simply due to the nature of class-based society which sees time calculated and experienced differently across populations.

REACHING THE MIGRANT LEFT

Australian society was more multicultural than ever before by the Vietnam years, due to the 1945 immigration drive instituted by Ben Chifley's ALP government and largely engineered by then Immigration Minister Arthur Calwell. Some migrant groups were more likely to sympathise with the anti-Vietnam War movement, depending on the political climate from which they had departed. The experiences of the Second World War and the communist defeat in the Greek Civil War of 1944–1949 saw many leftist Greeks take advantage of Australia's 'populate or perish' post-war migration policy. During the early years of the Cold War, Australia welcomed in droves of Greek 'New Australians', many of them communists, increasing the Greek-Australian population from approximately 15 000 in 1947 to 300 000 by 1970.[63] The influx of Greek communists to Australian shores from the late 1940s inevitably made them a target audience for the various anti-war campaigns of the Australian left.

The Vietnam War occurred during the takeover of Greece by the military Junta of 1967–1973, meaning that many Greek-Australian leftists were preoccupied by the situation occurring in their home country. The CPA's Greek-Australian Aristotle branch proposed a resolution during the 22nd CPA Congress of 1970 that focused not on Vietnam, but on the 'courageous and heroic struggle of the Communist Party of Greece which, under the most difficult conditions of illegality, works selflessly for the creation of a broad antidictatorial patriotic front for the overthrow of the dictatorship'.[64]

In the early 1970s, the Greek left saw its role as twofold: to 'participate in the numerous struggles of Greek people in Greece and elsewhere' and to 'help Greek immigrants fight for and assert their rights and solve the problems associated with the involvement of Greeks in the wider Australian radical left movement'.[65] Increased industrialisation during the post-war period took Greeks into factories, and therefore trade unions, but this was hampered by schisms within the Greek-Australian left itself, worsened by the Sino-Soviet split and the divided affiliation of Greeks between the CPA, CPA (Marxist-Leninist) and the

Youth Committee for the Restoration of Democracy in Greece demonstrate outside of the Greek Consulate, May 1968

Noel Hazard/*Tribune* collection/MLSLNSW/courtesy SEARCH Foundation

ALP, which played out in workers' clubs like Democritus in Melbourne, the Atlas Club in Sydney, and on the pages of the 'radical left's bible' *Neos Kosmos.*

Such groups made space for Greek migrant activists to gather and organise, resulting in closer relationships with the Australian left, most of which remain hidden from the protest archive.[66] More can be revealed by the minutiae of quiet protest, specifically the presence of the words 'Printed by Hellenic Herald' on a number of anti-war leaflets and posters published by VAC and associated groups. During the Vietnam years, NSW-based Greek newspaper *Hellenic Herald* (*Panellinios Kirikas*, now *The Greek Herald*) was housed at 216A Castlereagh Street, just steps away from the site of the current Consulate of Greece. From 1939 until early 1971, Alexander Grivas owned the *Hellenic Herald,* and his son, Sydney Anarchist Group and Seamen's Union of Australia (SUA) member Nestor Grivas, worked at the newspaper's offices.[67]

In 1962, Nestor offered up newly excavated basement space in his home at 72 Oxford Street, Paddington, as a meeting place for various radical left groups, where he would have almost certainly have met Bob Gould and others who made use of the *Hellenic Herald* printing press during the war.[68]

Greek migrants became more involved in the movement from 1966, when Liberal Prime Minister Harold Holt announced that migrants may be conscripted for service in Vietnam, prompting the formation of groups such as the NSW Greek Migrant Committee Against Conscription, Victoria's Greek Committee Against Conscription and the South Australian Greek Anti-Conscription Committee.[69] These groups were supported by AICD, who wrote to the federal government that 'migrant youth who in the past felt they were immune from army call-up and from being sent to Vietnam are now face to face with this distinct possibility' and called for the exclusion of migrants from the NSA.[70]

Australian activists also specifically targeted migrant groups as part of their appeal to the masses. The Newtown Moratorium Group translated a leaflet published ahead of the first Moratorium of 8 May 1970 entitled 'Stop Indo-China War' into Greek and Turkish, suggesting that migrants were associated with the group. In 1971 Newtown was included within the City of Sydney, with a population of 62 470, of which 1854 were born in Greece, meaning that Greeks comprised the largest single-country ethnic group in Sydney with the exception of English and Irish migrants.[71] Appealing to Greek migrants was a potentially fruitful venture for Australian activists aiming to create mass opposition to the Vietnam War.

In the weeks before the second Moratorium of 18 September 1970, the Newtown group held an International Folk Concert, including exhibitions of works by Australian artists, short talks on conscription and Vietnam, folk dances, as well as a performance by the famed Lambrakis Youth Choir, which was named after the left-wing Lambrakis Democratic Youth group formed by Greek activist and musician Mikis Theodorakis after the May 1963 assassination of leftist politician and athlete Grigoris Lambrakis in Thessaloniki.[72] Greek-Australians, like other migrant groups, were attracted to the anti-war movement by personal and political circumstances.

The rise and success of the anti-Vietnam War movement in NSW resulted from the efforts of a large number of supporters who represented a range of ideologies, classes and ethnicities. From the early years of the war, existing activist groups mobilised, their numbers increasing after the reintroduction of national service in 1964 and the devastating ALP electoral defeat of 1966 that prompted large-scale efforts to attract mass support to the cause. A focused examination of both quiet and loud protest during the war reveals that the strengths of the movement – particularly in NSW where the ALP left was not as prominent as in Victoria – lay in non-ALP organisations. The NSW movement could not have achieved the support it did without the adoption of a 'coalition'-based policy that reflected the CPA approach, or without the organisational dedication of AICD. But, as will be made clear in the remaining chapters of this book, although it is tempting to attribute the impact of the anti-Vietnam War movement to one or other of these parties or organisations, the historical archive shows us that all three played a crucial role in the success of the movement, and their membership was fluid and intersected. In fact, the CPA census of 1970 addressed this, asking members to 'name the one other mass movement or organisation in which you are most active'.[73] Countless individuals representing a range of ideological perspectives enacted both quiet and loud protest to achieve the goal of both ending the war and conscription. It is to this second concern that the next chapter turns.

CHAPTER TWO

FIGHTING THE NATIONAL SERVICE ACT

In the middle of 1968, the largely Trotskyist group Resistance printed a pamphlet for young men called *How Not to Join the Army*. In six pages, it suggested a range of methods to evade conscription, such as feigning alcoholism, homosexuality, drug addiction, mental illness, criminality, or neglecting personal hygiene:

> You have long hair? Good. Let it grow longer. Don't wash, stink, pick your nose, start a petition to make masturbation the National Sport. See how many four-letter words you can string into one sentence. Never wear shoes.

The pamphlet advised, 'good acting'll get you into a Government-run nuthouse' and suggested young men arrive at their medical examination 'rotten drunk', or 'don't arrive at all: call and apologize from the pub'. Despite its comical tone, the pamphlet contained practical and serious advice about conscientious objection to military duty, political opposition, and escaping the country. It also provided information about how to carry out 'service with sabotage', including arson on the battlefield, destroying radios and firearms, or dousing aircraft with acid.[1]

John Percy, then secretary of Resistance, has since said that 'an anarchist seaman', likely Nestor Grivas, supplied the pamphlet and 'gave us 20 bucks to print it'.[2] When the pamphlet emerged, Attorney-General Nigel Bowen ordered an inquiry to investigate whether any criminal offence had been committed by printing it.[3] Soon afterwards, Commonwealth Police raided Bob Gould's Third World Bookshop, then on Goulburn Street, Sydney, which also served as Resistance headquarters, and confiscated two typewriters, a Gestetner duplicating machine and some copies of the pamphlet.[4]

Percy later said:

> We had received a tip-off half an hour before the raid. So we phoned the TV stations, tidied up the headquarters, made sure posters advertising an upcoming teach-in on Vietnam were very prominently displayed, stashed away the bulk of the pamphlets and waited for the cops ... It was fantastic publicity. There we were on TV, there was our Gestetner getting carted out of the Third World Bookshop by the cops, there were the posters advertising the teach-in. Bookshop sales went right up ... We had to print tens of thousands more copies of the pamphlet.[5]

A few days after the raid, Percy was due to travel to the Australian National University (ANU) in Canberra for a research trip connected with his engineering studies at the University of Sydney. Two days prior to his departure, the *Canberra Times* reported that eight copies of 'a controversial pamphlet telling national servicemen how to sabotage military equipment' had been brought to Canberra by 18-year-old Sydney Arts student Liese Baker, and that Percy was printing 5000 more copies to distribute during his visit.[6] By the time Percy arrived on 27 June, the newspaper had revised the figure down to 500, and eventually, on 28 June, reported Percy had arrived with 250 copies and distributed them in exchange for 'donations' to Resistance, following a public talk at ANU. Percy was quoted as saying that the pamphlet was 'incidental to his own views and was partly frivolous, partly serious', but owned that it was 'intended to direct people towards sabotage'. He stated emphatically, 'I had a perfect right to publish, according to my own conceptions of right and wrong and democracy'.[7]

The activists involved in printing and distributing *How Not to Join the Army* used it to skirt sections of the *Crimes Act* that outlawed the

Police raid the Third World Bookshop, 1968

Noel Hazard/*Tribune* collection/MLSLNSW/courtesy SEARCH Foundation

incitation of young men to defy the NSA. This was a quieter method of protest, which would be echoed by the Committee in Defiance of the National Service Act in the coming year. When Percy was asked by the *Canberra Times* about the possibility of prosecution for his actions, he responded: 'If they have to prosecute a large number it will make the Government look even sillier'. The 11 July issue of ANU student newspaper *Woroni* explained:

> What people should do is laugh at the contents of the pamphlet, then look beyond the demagongish [sic] phrases to the motives behind its publication … Mr Percy never intended it to become a subject of national interest. He never intended "Nasho's" [national servicemen] to use its contents to disrupt the armed forces. What is more he would not like the Government to make a fool of itself or a scrapegoat [sic] of him by taking the matter to court.[8]

Although some, including the *Tribune*, viewed *How Not to Join the Army* as satirical, letters to the editor of the *Canberra Times* record that some residents were not amused.[9] Narrabundah resident K Matveev wrote that Percy and his ilk were 'going a bit far and take too much advantage of the freedom they enjoy in this country', arguing that in any communist country 'persons who even suggest publicly an idea of sabotaging the army will certainly be classed as saboteurs and traitors and as "enemies of the people"'.[10] Mrs J Davison of Narrabundah, whose husband served in the military, wrote to accuse Percy and others of treason, then wrote again to report that an anonymous caller had since telephoned her and asked 'What is the wife of a "professional killer" doing writing letters to the paper?'.[11] Mrs Glenice Doyle of Downer responded by saying how 'bitterly' she resented the anonymous caller's use of the term 'professional killer', ending her letter, 'I would like to add, for his benefit and others like him, that I have no telephone'.[12]

Crown Solicitor Harold Renfree, perhaps wisely refusing to be provoked, read the Commonwealth Police report about the raid but decided not to lay charges and ordered the equipment returned to

Resistance.[13] Undeterred, Resistance and various student organisations across the country continued to print the pamphlet, despite complaints in the Federal House of Representatives by Liberal Member for Evans and Presbyterian clergyman Malcolm Mackay in both September 1968 and March 1969 calling it 'seditious and scurrilous'.[14]

Resistance's publication of *How Not to Join the Army* was deliberately provocative but still constituted a quiet form of protest. The disproportionate response by political and law enforcement authorities increased its impact, allowing us to revisit the 'public performance' or 'political gimmick' advanced by Scalmer, which was usually achieved by intentionally loud and disruptive protest intended to draw attention to the cause, but could also be triggered by quieter actions.[15] The dramatic and very public responses by authorities to the pamphlet provide a way to reposition the quiet act, and allow us to rethink the binary common in popular understandings of activism that equate impact and true advancement of the cause with public protest.

In the wake of Menzies' reintroduction of national service in 1964, large numbers of Australians who would not be classed as 'activists' further expanded the movement by turning their attention to the Vietnam War and joining existing protest organisations, meaning that these types of quieter but impactful acts became more prominent.

CONSCRIPTION IN AUSTRALIA

The Vietnam War was not the first attempt by the Commonwealth Government to militarise members of the civilian population, nor was it the first time that the Australian population resisted conscription. Within six months of Australian Federation in 1901, the House of Representatives debated the need for a military training program to 'develop a healthy manhood in Australia'.[16] A compulsory cadetship requiring all males aged between 14 and 25 to complete military training was eventually instituted in 1911.[17] Despite an initial surge of recruits after Australia joined the British in the First World War in August 1914, Australian political authorities, and particularly Prime

Minister William 'Billy' Hughes, advocated young men be conscripted to strengthen the nation's contribution to the war. Unable to reach majority support within parliament to enact conscription, Hughes took the decision to the Australian public. His government introduced the War Census Bill in July 1915, proposing a register of able-bodied men aged 18–50, and by September a pro-conscription Universal Service League and union-based Anti-Conscription League had been formed.[18] Conscription referenda in 1916 and 1917 were narrowly defeated, after ferocious campaigns by a range of intersecting groups.

During the Second World War, Prime Minister Robert Menzies increased Citizen Military Forces (CMF) numbers, adding them to the fighting force within Australian territories. In 1943, succeeding Prime Minister John Curtin extended CMF service overseas in the South West Pacific area. Menzies returned to government in 1949 and, two years later, established a National Service Training Scheme which required all 18-year-old men to engage in 14 weeks of full-time military training and three years of part-time CMF service. It lasted until November 1959, before it was abandoned.[19]

When Menzies reintroduced national service on 24 November 1964 it was not a novel concept to the Australian population.[20] However, the opposition it provoked in Australian society reflected the active, sometimes violent, anti-conscription campaigns of 1916–17. Without Menzies' reintroduction of conscription or his announcement that conscripts would be sent to Vietnam in March 1966, an act that was narrowly opposed in opinion polls in both 1966 and 1967, the scale of anti-Vietnam War activity in Australia would not have reached the heights it did.

During the Vietnam War, men turning 20 were required to register for National Service by completing a registration card available from post offices and government offices – those who refused to register could be fined and immediately called up. Following this, a ballot, or 'lottery', was carried out through the random selection of marbles placed in a barrel, each of which was printed with a number corresponding to a particular birth date. Those whose number was called were required to report for military duty of up to two years in the Regular Army.

Although over 60 000 men were conscripted into the Army in this way, fewer than one-third of those served in Vietnam. This was partly due to exemptions allowed under the NSA for various groups of men, including religious ministers or members of full-time religious orders, theology students and, if the courts agreed, absolute pacifists. University students were able to defer their service until after graduation.

From 1965 to 1972, over 800 000 men turning 20 registered for national service, 63 000 were called up into Australia's defence forces and about 19 000 of these were sent to Vietnam. Of the around 60 000 Australians who served in Vietnam approximately 521 were killed and over 3000 wounded.[21] Almost 14 000 men who did not want to serve in the military or in Vietnam refused to register. Not even a quarter of that number were prosecuted, so failing to register was an effective way to avoid military duty, despite the potential financial implications – it was illegal to employ any person who had defaulted on the NSA.

Some young men quietly objected by writing letters to the government upon registration, including Michael Matteson, who has stated since the war: 'I was against conscription and I would have no part of it'. Matteson was eventually imprisoned for publicly resisting conscription, as will be discussed later in this chapter.[22] Rowan Cahill wrote a reasoned statement of his opposition to the war and conscription on the reverse side of his registration form, which included: 'The action of the allies in Vietnam, the decimation of the people and the land, represents a crime against humanity. I will not be party to this crime'.[23]

Men who did not satisfy the exemption requirements were required to report to an induction centre for duty. Failure to do so was punished by two years in prison, unless the conscript could prove in court that he was an absolute pacifist, and a legitimate conscientious objector. Although the NSA formally incorporated changes to the original *Defence Act 1903* that allowed non-religious pacifist conscientious beliefs, it was difficult to demonstrate conscientious objection without a history of religious belief and practice. Even religious non-pacifists whose conscientious objections were solely to the Vietnam War were refused

VIE NAM
STOP
LOTTERY
VIE NAM
STOP
Conscript
LOTTERY
VIE NAM
STOP
Conscript
LOTTE
VIE NAM
STOP
Conscript

Student protest against conscription in Broadway, Sydney, 1969

Noel Hazard/*Tribune* collection/MLSLNSW/courtesy SEARCH Foundation

in court, because for much of the conflict the NSA only provided for exemptions for opposition to all war.[24]

In total, around 1200 men were accepted as conscientious objectors but their reasons for claiming this status varied widely, and court decisions appeared arbitrary. Some viewed their opposition to conscription as a personal decision but did not disagree with the NSA; some thought the Vietnam War, or war as a whole, was immoral; and others disagreed with the coercive nature of the system.[25] Some non-compliers appealed to the humanity of the court, such as Martin Tuck of Gordon, who stated, 'I ask the members of this court to judge me not in your official capacities but also as a fellow human being, for this must ultimately be your decision as well as mine – how long must young men like myself go to gaol in order to be free?'[26] As draftee David Pepperell has reflected since the war, 'It seemed pretty weird to be fighting for freedom when you were actually being forced into it'.[27]

Between 250 and 300 Aboriginal men fought in the Vietnam War, although in some cases their conscription was problematic. The construction of Aboriginality by Australian governments in the context of the White Australia Policy led to complicated applications of the NSA. Mervyn Eades did not register due to laws that excluded Aboriginal enlistment, but still was required to appear in the Perth Court of Petty Sessions and was fined for avoiding registration. He was classed as non-Aboriginal under the NSA, despite being accepted as Aboriginal by his own community and within the state of Western Australia where he lived.[28] Although some Aboriginal men were opposed to conscription, a range of organisations, with a variety of ideological standpoints, felt that calling up Aboriginal men was a way to oppose discrimination or the implied allegation that Aboriginal men were inferior to non-Aboriginal men. Groups who advocated for Aboriginal civil rights, such as the Federal Council for the Advancement of Aborigines and Torres Strait Islanders, agreed with groups that took an assimilationist stance, such as the Returned Services League (RSL), which insisted on Aboriginal participation in all responsibilities placed upon non-Aboriginal people.[29]

Although most who publicly opposed conscription came from the broad left, it is not possible to generalise about the ideological composition of the movement. Objections to national service could be found in a range of quarters, with Governor of New South Wales Sir Roden Cutler, a Second World War veteran and Victoria Cross recipient, expressing doubts in August 1972 about the 'efficacy' of conscription, claiming that 'logical objections can be raised' to its legitimacy.[30] The broad constitution of the anti-conscription movement is best illustrated by an advertisement in the *Australian* on 29 June 1968, organised by Sydney's Citizen's Committee Against the NSA 1968 Amendments. It contains hundreds of names separated into occupations, including the arts, business, commerce, agriculture, clergy, education, students and librarians. Several signatories to the Statement of Defiance written and promoted by the Committee in Defiance of the National Service Act were original Liberal Reform Party members, representing former Liberal Party voters. Some of these organised and raised funds for the 29 June advertisement.[31]

This chapter makes no attempt to provide a comprehensive overview of the NSA or anti-conscription movement, as it has been so effectively discussed, including in Bobbie Oliver's excellent *Hell No! We Won't Go! Resistance to Conscription in Post-War Australia* (2022) and Carolyn Collins's *Save our Sons: Women, Dissent and Conscription During the Vietnam War* (2021), the story of SOS, an organisation that was central to most quiet forms of anti-conscription protest.[32] Rather, this chapter shares ways that anti-conscriptionists quietly worked together to create the storm against conscription in NSW during the Vietnam War.

ATTRACTING PUBLIC SUPPORT FOR THE MOVEMENT

The anti-conscription movement is best viewed as a collective effort by Australians of different classes, occupations, religions, political ideologies, ages and genders. The long-term connections developed and solidified through this movement enabled the unprecedented size of the Moratorium movement. The fight against the NSA began in 1964 and increased in size after the March 1966 announcement that men called up for duty could be sent to Vietnam. At this time, the Australian Labor Party (ALP) turned its attention to the issue of conscription, which served to legitimise the movement in the eyes of many Australians.

Labor's Gough Whitlam is remembered for abolishing conscription upon his election as Prime Minister in 1972, but in 1964 the ALP did not take a collective anti-conscriptionist stance.[33] During the ALP split of 1955, fervently anti-communist members, who were largely influenced by conservative Catholic figure BA Santamaria, broke off to form the ALP (Anti-Communist), which was soon renamed the Democratic Labor Party.[34] The Sino-Soviet split that began in 1961 led to a similar fracturing within the CPA, meaning that when Menzies reintroduced conscription, less rigid boundaries existed between the ALP and CPA, opening up broader political participation in the anti-conscription movement. These shifts coincided with ALP Leader Arthur Calwell, from 1964, opposing conscription in Vietnam, and calling for 'protests and demonstrations from one side of the country to the other against conscription for overseas' in 1966.[35] ALP politicians became active in the anti-conscription movement, such as Senator for South Australia and national president of the Operative Plasterers' and Plaster Workers' Federation of Australia, Jim Cavanagh, who in 1971 placed draft evaders and resisters within a heroic and masculinist frame by asking in the Senate: 'What alternative is left to our youth but to rebel? Are they not following the tradition set by their forefathers? Are they not great examples of Australia's heroic manhood?'[36]

Although some ALP members consistently opposed conscription throughout the war, including Calwell who decried a scheme that sent young men 'to fight and die in a cruel, filthy, brutal, unwinnable war in Vietnam mangrove swamps', many of these members did not oppose any alliance with the US or involvement in Vietnam, as they thought it best for Australia's national interest.[37] Despite disunity within the party causing 'publicly displayed turmoil over Vietnam and conscription', ALP members who joined the movement against conscription gave it a 'respectable' face, and helped attract a large number of Australians who had very little understanding or experience of activism.[38]

Religious groups added to this respectability, countering press and political portrayals of activists as young and unruly. Religious involvement in the movement existed before the reintroduction of conscription but increased in both scale and scope after Menzies' announcement of November 1964. In October of the same year, Anglican bishops Cranswick of Hobart, Moyes of Armidale and Garnsey of Melbourne sponsored a Congress for International Cooperation and Disarmament in Sydney that attracted 670 supporters.[39] Anglicans at the 1968 Lambeth Conference of the Anglican Communion resolved to 'uphold and extend the right of conscientious objection' and were joined by other denominations in their stance.[40] By 1970, at least 78 parishes or churches across NSW, including Church of England, Baptist, Methodist, Presbyterian, Lutheran, Catholic, Church of Christ, Congregational and the Salvation Army, had expressed an opposition to the war or conscription.[41]

A range of unions adopted anti-conscription stances at the outset of Australia's involvement in Vietnam. The Australian Railways Union, for example, sent a telegram to Prime Minister Harold Holt in 1966:

> Australian Railways Union desire enter vigorous protest decision your government conscripting Australian youth for overseas military service without sanction of people who should be given opportunity determining their attitude by way of referendum. Those whom you are forcing to serve in overseas areas entitled same consideration as Menzies and yourself enjoyed when you were eligible for military service.[42]

In November 1969, the ACTU Executive adopted a resolution urging unions to increase their opposition to the conflict and conscription, demanding the federal government withdraw all troops from Vietnam and declaring, 'We call on all trade unionists to register the greatest and most effective protest possible to end this shocking violation of human rights and to demand an end to this war in Vietnam without further delay'.[43] The continuous integration of respectable dissenters within the anti-conscription movement was crucial to the increasing support it received throughout the war.

BILL WHITE AND THE NSW TEACHERS FEDERATION

When Harold Holt announced in March 1966 that Australian conscripts could be required to serve in Vietnam, Sydney schoolteacher and conscientious objector William Phillip Orrick 'Bill' White was defending his own stance against military service. The extent of quiet but active opposition provoked by White's case was remarkable for its time, occurring relatively early in the war, before the Australian public had become accustomed to the new type of public demonstration.

White applied for registration as a conscientious objector in November 1965, declaring: 'Man's chief purpose is to live – therefore the taking of human life is wrong and unjustifiable. I cannot with a clear conscience kill a person, or be part of an organisation that is able or willing to kill or make war'.[44] He outlined his moral opposition to conscription and the Vietnam War based on an objection to 'war itself as a national and international policy' and to the right of the state to conscript a person.[45] His wife Claire (née Seale), who married White on 6 January 1967, said that, for Bill, serving in the military 'would have been denying his own humanity', as 'he didn't want to be part of a killing organisation'.[46]

On 20 December 1966, White appeared in court, where his case was dismissed, and he was ordered to serve in the military by performing non-combatant duties. On 22 March 1967, White appealed this decision, which was again dismissed, leading to a call-up notice on 18 July. Under the NSA, employing a person who resisted conscription merited a fine of $200, which meant that White's subsequent refusal to present for duty resulted in his dismissal by the NSW Education Department and physical removal from his teaching classroom at Denistone East Primary School in northern Sydney. Fifty women and children, including students at Denistone East and a range of religious ministers, demonstrated outside the court on 3 August when he was charged with refusal to comply with the NSA, forcing adjournment of the case.

White's treatment galvanised other teachers. On 29 September, teachers at Sir Joseph Banks High School in Revesby held a lunch-hour

Bill White at an anti-conscription demonstration and draft card burning, 22 July 1966

Noel Hazard/*Tribune* collection/MLSLNSW/courtesy SEARCH Foundation

meeting about White's dismissal, and their representative Peter Meehan wrote to the NSW Teachers Federation (the Federation) demanding they take stronger action by finding suitable employment for White, and that if government reprisals occurred, they should 'fight such proceedings'.[47]

The Waterside Workers Federation (WWF) also supported White, placing him within a long tradition of Australian masculinity and activism by writing that he was 'proving himself in that course as one of the real Australians of the mould of Peter Bowling', a unionist, waterside worker, Australian Socialist League member and activist. To the WWF, White was like 'the men who defied authority at Eureka and others who upset the powers that be in the historic conscription struggles of 1917'.[48]

Before his case could be revisited, White reapplied for registration as a conscientious objector, which was again rejected, then on 17 November was formally sentenced to 21 days in jail. Illustrating the extent of support for White, the AICD 1966 'Xmas Get Together' included a

'Toast to Bill White' as a 'special feature of this informal gathering'.[49] SOS committee member Glenys 'Glen' Tomasetti, a folksinger and poet, wrote the celebrated 'The Ballad of Bill White' in support. Its original lyrics declared that White would 'never comply until they break him down … What kind of proof do judges need that this man's case is true?'[50]

White continued to appeal for conscientious objector status from prison and it was eventually granted on 23 December 1966 by a court that was undoubtedly impacted by the weight of anti-conscriptionist support within society. This support not only came from activists who threw themselves in front of police cars on the day of his arrest and kept vigil outside White's home before his imprisonment, but also the hundreds who wrote letters of support or who donated funds, as well as journalists who wrote daily reports about his case in the final months of 1966. White's Certificate of Discharge, held in the Mitchell Library, tells us he was enlisted as a Private on 17 November 1966 and discharged on 23 December of the same year, with only 12 days of effective service in the military as a trainee and no time spent overseas.[51]

On the day White achieved victory in court, Les Waddington, then honorary secretary of the Ex-Services Human Rights Association of Australia (ESHRAA), wrote to White's parents to congratulate them on his release from prison. He placed White within the tradition of Australia's long-term campaigns against military action: 'Surely this episode will be recorded in Australian history, and could well mark a turning point in official and private minds towards the non-militaristic approach to world conflicts'. The day after White's release from prison, Bill Muir of Penrith, who had served in the Fourth Battalion of the Australian Imperial Force from 1915 until 1918, sent 'hearty congratulations on your win against military dictatorship'. Muir said White's 'battle for freedom is a historical point in Australian affairs which will live long', before mentioning that he himself voted against conscription while fighting in the trenches in France.[52] On 18 February 1972, Field Librarian Hunt wrote with similar sentiments on behalf of the Mitchell Librarian Gordon Richardson to request the donation of White's letter archive to the State Library of NSW.[53]

Anti-conscription activists meet arresting police outside the White family home in Gladesville, 22 November 1966

Noel Hazard/*Tribune* collection/MLSLNSW/courtesy SEARCH Foundation

Other supporters, including parents of White's students and his teaching colleagues, formed the Bill White [Conscientious Objectors] Defence Committee (BWDC) in August 1966 to aid White 'in whatever ways possible', as well as to campaign for amendments to the NSA and assist other conscientious objectors. After White won his case, the BWDC reported a bank surplus for which they thanked 'thousands of well wishes, donors and supporters'. From this time, they turned their attention more squarely on other young men who refused to fight for the same moral reasons as White, reporting in April 1967, for example, that they had sent funds to four young men from Western Australia, Victoria and NSW.[54]

The strength of support for White becomes tangible when one opens the two boxes of William Phillip Orrick White papers held by the Mitchell Library. Masses of cut-off slips from BWDC fundraising leaflets spill out, inscribed with amounts of donations: $1, $2, $20. Some include short notes, such as Mrs P Hermann of Drummoyne's – 'I do hope you will be successful'. Others are attached to longer letters of support: $6 from Anglican Reverend William Childs of Cessnock on 13 September 1966; $13 from the CPA Eureka Youth League on 20 December; and fifty dollars – representing almost $800 in 2026 – from Mr JB Henderson of Corral, sent through the Methodist Central Mission on 7 October.[55]

BWDC secretary Pat Ruffels and treasurer Nancy Short noted where donated funds had been banked and when receipts were returned – representing a time-consuming example of quiet protest. Support for Bill White comprised many hundreds of hours spent in private homes or organisational offices and filled activists' days, weeks and months. Stepping back and observing these types of supportive activities, predominantly carried out by women, through the archive, expands our understanding of the extent of activism that took place away from public streets, parks and squares.

White's actions reverberated throughout the Teacher's Federation, increasing quiet protest activity by both schoolteachers and students across the state, through continual meetings, petitions, and letter writing. In November 1965, the same month that White first attempted to register as a conscientious objector, the Federation passed a series of resolutions objecting to the removal of NSA provisions that had allowed teachers to defer national service until after their first year of teaching – a change that negatively affected their ongoing employment opportunities and financial security. On 22 November, it raised the 'proven serious shortage of teachers' and limitations on class sizes to appeal for the exemption of young male teachers from the draft. On 4 December, it passed a further resolution pledging that 'forceful and continuing protests be made against the practice of calling up young teachers for compulsory military service'.[56]

In July 1966, Sydney's *Telegraph* reported that the Federation was seeking legal advice about White's case as it believed 'teachers should be exempt from National Service because they were more important to the community as teachers'.[57] In September 1966, the Federation resolved to write to Minister for Education and Science Charles B Cutler that NSW could not afford to lose the 300 teachers who were projected to be drafted in 1967, as 'teachers are performing as vital a service to the community as teachers in religious orders in private schools who are exempt from military service'. On 11 February 1967, over one month after White was released from prison, the Federation passed a resolution supporting the continuing employment of White within the Department of Education with 'full continuity of the service and salary progression as is any other National Servicemen who has completed his obligation under the National Service Act and has returned to teaching'.[58]

The Federation remained active throughout the war, its members forming a Teachers Vietnam Moratorium Group in early 1970 that unanimously supported the Moratorium's general aims to force withdrawal of all Australian troops from Vietnam and repeal the NSA. On 'Teachers' Day' of 5 May, three days before the first Vietnam Moratorium, they added quiet protest tactics to the cacophony of mass protest by wearing black armbands and Moratorium badges, holding periods of silence through the school day, staff meetings, film screenings, silent lunchtime vigils, teacher–student discussions and Teachers' Moratorium posters on school grounds.[59]

COOPERATION AS ANTI-CONSCRIPTIONIST PRACTICE

The case of Bill White proved a testing ground, in many ways, for broadening cooperation between individuals and organisations in supporting young men to avoid or resist conscription. The events surrounding the imprisonment of journalist and draft resister Simon Townsend further illustrate the effectiveness of a joint effort against conscription. Townsend, known to Australians as the host of the children's show *Simon Townsend's Wonder World* on Network Ten from 1979 to 1987, attempted to register as a conscientious objector soon after registering for national service in 1965, but was refused by a judge who felt he was 'not sincere'. After refusing to take a medical examination, he was imprisoned for one month in Long Bay Gaol in Sydney. He reapplied for exemption from the NSA, which was again refused. In February 1967, Townsend refused to take a military medical examination and in March did not report for military duty. On 15 May, he was charged in the Special Federal Court and imprisoned again.

On 19 May Townsend wrote a letter to the Abolish Conscription Campaign (ACC), led by Ella Outhred, criticising the hypocrisy of a system that refused to accept his expressed pacifism, and reporting that he had been allocated eight prison guards who woke him up every two hours for his 'well-being'. ACC organised a 'major protest' for 10 June 1968 which included a march from Liverpool Station to Ingleburn Military Camp in southwest Sydney, where Townsend was imprisoned. Soon afterwards, Townsend applied again for registration as a CO, which was eventually granted on 14 June 1968.[60]

Between his first and second attempts to achieve CO status, Townsend formed Sydney's Conscientious Objectors' Group (COG) with Carol McLean, Greg Barter and Pat Ruffels, aiming to 'provide a meeting place for COs where they may, through discussion, clear up their own ideas and questions on conscientious objection in preparation for court cases'. COG met regularly at the Friends Meeting House on Devonshire Street in Surry Hills, which was loaned to them by the pacifist Quakers, who believed that conscription was 'an enforced training of young men to kill their fellow-men' and 'a negation of those religious principles to which we claim adherence as a Christian nation'.[61] On 24 August 1966, COG thanked Quakers Carol and Dr Dougald McLean, a psychiatrist at Parramatta Psychiatric Hospital, for opening the hall each week and preparing the tea, coffee and biscuits. The McLeans were to extend their own quiet anti-conscriptionist protest in 1969 when they purchased 100 acres of land in Kangaroo Valley, approximately 150 kilometres south of Sydney, to build a 'serene sanctuary' for conscientious objectors.[62]

COG claimed that 'pacifist, peace and anti-conscription groups exist for wider purposes' that transcended the simple need for strong collective opposition to conscription. Cooperation within the anti-conscription movement was a precursor to the strategic coordination

Abolish Conscription Campaign demonstration for Simon Townsend, 19 May 1968

Noel Hazard/*Tribune* collection/MLSLNSW/courtesy SEARCH Foundation

of the Moratorium movement – as an example, the Manly–Warringah Committee for International Cooperation and Disarmament, which in July 1969 sponsored a Conscription Teach-in organised by 'a group of young people in this area' at the Collaroy Beach Surf Club Hall, was reconstituted as the Manly–Warringah Moratorium Committee in early 1970.

The Sydney University Labor Club (SULC) specifically mentioned the tactical objective to garner mass support when reporting on a July 1968 Citizens–Students No Conscription Meeting in Victoria Park:

> Although most of those present were familiar faces from the front lawn meetings, there were a significant number of local residents and should be continued. Glebe is obviously an advantageous area for starting this kind of campaign not only because of the large student population, but also the relatively progressive nature of the residents i.e. strong Labor area and many are Trade Unionists. It is only by experience gained in running such

> meetings will we determine a formula for successful community agitation over issues like conscription.[63]

The National Campaign Against Conscription (NCAC) is one example of mass quiet coordination in practice. On 14 January 1969, a NCAC NSW working committee discussed quieter methods to muster a collective force against the NSA. Anti-conscriptionists and conscientious non-compliers would become involved in acts of protest such as pamphlet publication, public forums alongside AICD, a collective deputation to Canberra, discussions between non-compliers and unionists, the seeking of prominent figures to speak out against conscription, press cooperation, as well as a conscript hunger strike.[64] NCAC's 1969 leaflet 'Why Register for National Service?' emphasises the multi-faceted nature of existing supports for young men wishing to avoid the draft: 'If you intend not to register, there are people and groups who will actively support you', followed by a list of Conscientious Objectors Advisory Committees in NSW – based in Parramatta, Caringbah and Armidale, Victoria, South Australia, Queensland, Tasmania, Western Australia and the ACT, as well as discussion groups in NSW, Victoria, South Australia and the ACT. The leaflet was signed by a range of draft evaders, draft resisters and their supporters. The breadth of NCAC's quiet activities and their cooperation with other individuals and organisations is best demonstrated by the many methods listed to oppose the draft in its 9 February 1969 newsletter, including meetings, vigils, leaflet distribution, discussion, arrest and supply of transportation.[65]

ESHRAA, formerly the Ex-Services Association of Australia (ESAA), illustrates how this cooperation transcended political ideology. ESHRAA began when a group of Sydney-based ex-servicemen gathered in 1966 to discuss 'fatuous and defamatory' statements made by RSL National President Sir William Yeo about Bill White, whose father Phil was an ESHRAA committee member.[66] The original ESAA Statement of Policy referred to the United Nations Charter and the Universal Declaration of Human Rights in stating: 'We believe that National Service for home defence should not involve conscription

ESHRAA meeting, May 1969

Noel Hazard/*Tribune* collection/MLSLNSW/courtesy SEARCH Foundation

for foreign wars or the coercion of genuine conscientious objectors to war, or to any particular war'. Here, they also emphasised their position as a 'humanitarian, non-sectarian and non-party political' group that did not oppose war in all its forms but merely objected to overseas conscription.[67]

ESHRAA was no friend of the RSL. Its first president, Allan Ashbolt, was a well-known journalist and executive producer of the ABC's *Four Corners* television show, but was temporarily suspended from the ABC in 1963 for producing a decidedly anti-militaristic investigative report on the RSL's role as an anti-communist 'political pressure group'.[68] When Martin Leslie 'Les' Waddington replaced Ashbolt, he was expelled from the RSL on account of his involvement in the peace movement.[69] Waddington said in a 1990s interview, 'In those days the RSL had a "beer and boys" mentality. You didn't get many enlightened conversations and there was an automatic assumption that members would support any war that came along'. Challenging the common belief that any opposition to the war or conscription originated on the left, Waddington said:

ESHRAA members march in AICD rally, 15 November 1966

Noel Hazard/*Tribune* collection/MLSLNSW/courtesy SEARCH Foundation

> I opposed Vietnam from the start because I believed we were being told official lies about what was happening. I was not a communist and I never even considered myself Left-wing; but expressing those views meant I was bound to come into conflict with the main body of the RSL.[70]

In November 1966, ESHRAA published a list of its provisional objectives in its newsletter *Conscience*, including press representation on the Vietnam issue and furnishing 'regular meeting places equipped with social amenities and facilities for cultural and recreational activities of ex-service persons and their families'.[71] Cooperation with other protest organisations, including the Victorian Ex-Servicemen's Protest Committee, SOS and Youth Campaign Against Conscription (YCAC) was mentioned, as were quiet protest techniques such as wearing a black ribbon or a black V (for Vietnam), silent vigils and anti-conscription study groups. They appealed to members for administrative and technical assistance, including loans of equipment such as typewriters, as well as donations of money or time to help with increasing mail.[72]

By January 1971, ESHRAA could proudly write to members:

> This Association was started four-and-a-half years ago by a group of ex-service people who shared a concern for the immoral and dangerous course Australia's foreign policy was taking. We felt that the RSL had abandoned its original ideals and a new organisation was needed to carry the torch of conscience in the community ... We believe we have already accomplished something of value. We believe we have helped, and are helping, to check Australia's drift towards authoritarianism. We do what we can to help the courageous, conscientious young men whose moral identity brings them into lonely conflict with a system loaded against individual rights – a system sustained by public apathy and ignorance.[73]

'DON'T REGISTER' TO DRAFT COUNSELLING

The number of campaigns to support young men of conscription age increased as the war progressed and became more radical over time. 'Don't Register' campaigns were particularly successful in drawing together anti-conscriptionists in quiet protest, and led to other actions, including the Committee in Defiance of the National Service Act's Statement of Defiance and their establishment of Draft Counselling Centres.

The 'Don't Register' campaign's aim was similar to the Committee in Defiance – to breach the *Crimes Act* and obstruct legal action towards draft evaders or resisters. Launched by Students for a Democratic Society (SDS) in early 1969, it was inspired by discussions held at the National Conference of Non-Compliers in Melbourne in December 1968, organised by Melbourne and Sydney University SDS anti-conscription committees. Through 'Don't Register', SDS aimed to impel men turning 20 to avoid registering for national service. The chair of Sydney SDS Mike Jones was charged with incitement on the campaign's first day, indicating the impact of quiet protest.[74]

COG had provided a physical space where conscientious objectors could discuss their views and gain advice, which developed into Sydney's Advisory Committee for Conscientious Objectors (ACCO). They met every Wednesday night in the Friends Meeting House, where a team of advisors including ACCO secretary Carol McLean, Outhred, Ruffels, Methodist clergymen Ron Page and Norman Webb, and student unionist Sean Foley, carried out one-on-one interviews with young men.[75] Also involved was University of Sydney Professor of Zoology Charles Birch, who was 'a willing source of counselling for people who wanted to not be caught up [in the war] ... in a very un-ego-gratifying way', according to former colleague, the physicist and ecologist Lord Robert May.[76]

As the war progressed, this type of personalised anti-conscription quiet protest increased. On 8 September 1969, the original 72 signatories of the Statement of Defiance agreed on the formation of a Draft Resistance and Counselling Service. One week later, this decision was endorsed at an AICD meeting, which sent out a notice entitled 'Australian Draft Resistance (in formation)' to trade and student unionists, academics, religious leaders, non-compliers and organisations including SDS, Quakers and SOS, proposing a meeting to be held at the AICD offices at 587a George Street on 23 September.

Anti-conscriptionists and potential draft resisters were encouraged by the Committee in Defiance to take a 'pledge to resist', which cited the Geneva Accords, the Nuremberg and Far East War Crimes Tribunals, the Treaty of London and the UN Charter in support of their actions to breach the *Crimes Act* by 'seeking to frustrate the implementation of all conscription legislation'. This pledge stated: 'We refuse to become involved in any form of military or para-military conscription and we regard all authority that seeks to impose such conscription as immoral and illegitimate'. AICD framed the cooperative nature of quiet protest as crucial to the success of the cause: 'Such a project, seen as making real the Statement of Defiance pledge to "encourage, aid and support" non-compliers, could only be effectively organised as a cooperative venture involving all main anti-conscription groupings'.[77]

The Draft Resistance Counselling Centre (DRCC) was based at AICD headquarters with centres in other parts of the state, including Haymarket. The purpose of its Draft Counselling Service (DCS) was:

> To provide each young man facing conscription with the information and assistance most appropriate to his personal viewpoint and circumstances. Counselling aims to supply the individual with relevant information concerning the provisions of the National Service Act and its administration; offer advice on the best course of action available to him; and, where necessary, refer him to religious, medical and other specialist counsellors.[78]

Similar centres were also established in Melbourne by the Centre for Democratic Action, in Canberra by CONTRA and in Adelaide by Provo, an anarchist organisation originating in the Netherlands that used non-violent tactics to provoke violent responses from law-enforcement authorities.

Organising such a large-scale endeavour creates mountains of forms, leaflets, letters and other notices. Only by analysing these items together can we clearly see the everyday routine of quiet protest, and the real time and energy spent organising this specific facet of the multi-modal anti-conscription movement. One DCS advertisement of 1970 asked supporters to complete a registration form and return it with a fee that was used to fund hall rental, printing material and postage. These activities all required donations of time and energy by an individual or group of activists. Counsellors were recruited through a roster questionnaire asking them to select preferred centres, dates and times. Again, an individual or group decided on the content of the form which, when finalised, was widely distributed. Completed questionnaires received by AICD saw these or other activists creating a viable roster. Added to this were supporting activities including brochure or poster creation and display, anti-conscription automobile broadcasts and general fundraising.[79] While one-on-one counselling was undoubtedly the most visibly impactful facet of DRCC operations, hours and days of quiet protest were required to make this service possible, even just in one centre in one area within one state.

The DCS brochure *The Ins and Outs of Conscription* lists all possibilities for objection, evasion, non-compliance or resistance within a step-by-step guide to registration and conscription. It explains the differences between active public resistance and 'going underground' or leaving the country to avoid conscription.[80] Various groups held public events to communicate these ideas, such as an iteration of the Draft Resistance and Counselling School organised by ACCO, AICD and SDS at the Musicians' Club Auditorium on Chalmers Street, Sydney, which aimed to 'undertake an in-depth examination of the development of draft resistance in Australia', plan future draft counselling, and possibly establish a Sydney Draft Resisters Union (DRU).

Such forums produced the SDS 'Fill in a Falsie' campaign. In 1970 and 1971, SDS distributed instructions directing activists to obstruct national service procedures. One suggested method was to appropriate registration forms from local post offices and the Department of Labour and National Service (DLNS):

> There is no law against collecting them ... Get a form for yourself, brother, son, friend; any excuse you can think up – but get Forms! It is quite easy to ask for several forms at the one P.O. Go back several times, some people have made as many as twenty trips to the one P.O. Organise a car trip around your local area to collect them ... Register your local fascists ... Minister of religeon [sic] could collect ten or twenty for his church group ... teacher at a Teacher's College can collect bulk.[81]

They also suggested telephone disruption, by phoning the DLNS for 'advice' or prank calling: 'Whenever you pass a phone booth, stop and dial the National Service Dept. and walk out leaving the phone off the hook. This blocks one line for thirty seconds after the phone is answered'.[82] As this type of disruption was classed as a criminal offence, a 1971 instructional leaflet for the Fill in a Falsie campaign was 'Authorised by Mickey Mouse for the Disneyland Liberation Front (Australia)' and specified: 'For tactical considerations related to the Commonwealth Crimes Act, these proposals do not necessarily represent the opinion of anyone living, dead or confused'.[83]

DRAFT RESISTANCE

In the latter half of Australian involvement in the war, individual conscripts took a more militant approach through the Draft Resistance Movement (DRM), initially formed in Melbourne by radical left members of the youth organisations such as YCAC in 1968 but inspired by earlier COs, including Bill White. Cases of open draft resistance did occur before the beginning of the DRM.[84] On 8 March 1966, conscript and YCAC secretary Barry Robinson attended the Sydney DLNS offices after he received his call-up notice, where he was asked to show his draft card. Robinson responded by stating that he had burnt it, then refused to accept a new registration form or draft card. The following day, SULC challenged the federal government:

> The next move lies with the Department of Labour and National Service. Barry could get 100 days of goal for refusing to produce his draft card to a departmental officer, but it is debateable [sic] whether the Government would be prepared to face the torrent of criticism that the gaoling of a 20 year old political offender would unleash.[85]

The DRM similarly focused on open non-compliance of the NSA to impel political authorities to imprison draft resisters, writing: 'the DRM has not been formed to oppose conscription, it has been formed to wreck it. We are opposed to the war in Vietnam and we intend to resist the conscription of Australian youth for this war by all available means'.[86] In April 1968, Sydney anarchist Michael Matteson and pacifist Chris Campbell, both draft resisters, joined their Victorian counterparts who had travelled to Sydney on a 'freedom ride' to protest outside Holsworthy prison to support imprisoned conscientious objector Denis O'Donnell.[87]

Five months later, in September 1968, Matteson and seven other young men from Sydney who had defied the NSA, including Sean Foley, Geoff Mullen, Simon Townsend, jackaroo Lenard Truscott and the 21-year-old triplets David, Robert and Hugh Mowbray, formed a group called The Unconscriptables which 'was open to all those young men who face civil gaol because of a responsible and conscientious decision not to comply with the National Service Act'.[88] Mullen, who had been imprisoned for refusing to attend a military medical examination, stood as an independent candidate for the seat of Wentworth against Liberal Minister for Labour and National Service Leslie Bury in the 25 October 1969 federal election. Although Mullen was defeated, his stand produced a flurry of quiet support by anti-conscriptionists, including members of Citizens against the National Service Act, such as fundraising, door-to-door interviewing, letterboxing, poster-printing and sticking, public meetings, manning polling booths on election day, typing and duplicating.[89]

The DRM was short-lived but staged a series of public actions. On 20 June 1970 the Draft Resisters' Union was established by 45 draft resisters following a conference at La Mama Theatre in Carlton, Melbourne. DRU activists intensified their defiance against the NSA, to put pressure on the federal government to increase prosecutions and provoke more public opposition to conscription. DRU was established in August 1970, based in Newtown and led by draft resister and University of Sydney Student Representative Council member Ian Davis. Potential members were asked to complete a detailed questionnaire asking whether resisters had refused to register, been sent a medical call-up notice, fined or jailed, or had lost employment due to draft resistance, and their specific reasons for non-compliance. Its final question was, 'Do you wish your draft resistance to be made public? Or do you wish to be a "silent" non-complier?', showing that both quiet and not-so-quiet resistance were integrated into DRU tactics.[90]

One facet of the draft resistance campaign was the establishment of an 'underground', which was, according to draft resister Michael

Hamel-Green, 'not an underground where you disappeared, but where you confronted the police and their power to arrest you. We developed community support and showed the government could not enforce the scheme, even if it wanted to'.[91] The 'underground' was a network of safe houses provided by activists who were willing to quietly support draft resisters by offering accommodation, food and safety while they were evading police capture.[92]

Those who wished to make their non-compliance public engaged in activities intended to provoke political and law enforcement authorities into action. Matteson held underground press conferences and appeared on ABC's *This Day Tonight* during his 14-month period of evasion in 1972. Twice he came close to being captured by police on University of Sydney grounds. On 24 April 1972, two Commonwealth police handcuffed themselves to him while he was travelling in a car driven by Jim Crouch, who drove into the university grounds. Matteson shouted for help and was surrounded by around 1000 students, who freed him.[93]

On 15 May 1972, Brian Childs was arrested in Sydney by the Commonwealth Police for failing to register, then refusing to pay the resulting fine. Three days later, four Sydney draft resisters – Jim Dixon, Chris Stanley, Bob Wood and Bruce Clarke – arrived at Parliament House in Canberra to present 'accurate figures on draft resisters in Sydney', where Wood was arrested. On 21 May, a group of draft resisters appeared at Long Bay Gaol to protest the imprisonment of Childs and Wood, where Mike Parsons offered himself up for arrest, but was ignored by police.[94] Through such daring acts, DRU hoped to draw attention to the arbitrary nature of NSA enforcement and the ultimate illegitimacy of the conscription scheme.

These and other public acts also meant resisters and their supporters spent significant hours engaged in quiet protest. On 26 November 1972, just over a week before Whitlam would be elected prime minister and repeal the NSA, DRU released a policy statement demonstrating the extent of the group's vision, and challenged the ALP to put into action its public anti-conscriptionist stance: 'If the ALP is sincere in its opposition to conscription then the demands will be readily granted'. These demands included the immediate repeal of the NSA, the return of ASIO files to draft resisters, as well as removal of employment discrimination and conviction history for all arrested or charged resisters. Beyond this, DRU asked for the section of the *Crimes Act* used to convict anti-conscription activists be abolished, compensation to all draft resisters for costs incurred while evading arrest, and public inquiries into the 'illegal and extra-legal activities' of the Attorney-General, his department and the Commonwealth Police in enforcing the NSA, as well as the Liberal Party role in Australian involvement in Vietnam and the conscription scheme.[95]

In the same year, DRU released the statement 'Illegal Harassment; The Attorney General's Law and Order', which accused the Attorney-General, DLNS and Commonwealth Police of the assault of Matteson and Sandy Thomas, phone tapping, megaphone theft, the curbing of free speech and illegal entry, which included 4am raids on allies who had refused to pay fines for incitement. They also compiled a list of Commonwealth police officers considered a danger to draft resisters, with names and photographs, stating: 'The Law is being shown more and more clearly to be the Government's tool for the protection of its policies and the suppression of its opponents'.[96]

The DRU list of demands and its extensive research into conscription legislation and process points to the involvement and assistance of a broader network of allies, many of whom were women, which formed the backbone of the quiet protest movement. Women were responsible for much of the administrative work of draft resistance, particularly surrounding the 15–16 September 1970 and 18–19 September 1971 National Conferences of Draft Resisters in Sydney and Melbourne. Despite their vital role, women did not have voting rights in DRU meetings, while men – even those who were not draft resisters or were under conscription age – did. Activist Sue McCulloch recalled:

> We were not really passive, but women did tend to take a secondary role. We were listened to in a very peripheral way. If we had noticed it at the time we would have been a lot more angry about it, but none of us knew better. We were just so involved in the greater cause. We spent an inordinate amount

of time demonstrating, handing out leaflets – writing them or getting them printed.[97]

DRU necessarily existed in the shadows, due to the seriousness of the consequences for non-compliance, and must be defined by its focus on quiet protest, as well as its more public flouting of the NSA and the authority of law enforcement that relied on daring public appearances by draft resisters. These created moments of 'theatre', to adopt Scalmer's conceptualisation, that drew attention to the cause and created mayhem – quite literally, when police chased Matteson through ABC studios.[98] Such moments were not possible without enormous efforts by non-compliers themselves, as well as droves of family, friends and other supporters.

Although Australian involvement in the Vietnam War provoked noteworthy opposition within society as soon as it began in 1962, the reintroduction of conscription in 1964 and the extension of overseas service to conscripts in 1966 spurred the transformation of this opposition into a mass anti-war and anti-conscription movement. As the war progressed and Australian combat involvement deepened, these movements became larger and more interconnected. The anti-conscription movement would not have been as impactful without a combination of quiet and loud protest activities by COs, draft evaders, draft resisters and their allies, who represented a broad range of ages, ideologies and classes. This intensified cooperation had existed before the war, but not to the extent seen during Vietnam. Activist tactics and strategies against the Vietnam War would be amplified from 1970, when countless hours spent by activists on quiet protest activities to build the largest mass public protest in Australia culminated in the Moratoriums.

CHAPTER THREE

THE INFRASTRUCTURE OF THE MORATORIUM CAMPAIGN

On 25 November 1969, 36 activists representing peace groups from across Australia attended a national consultation in Canberra to discuss the feasibility of organising a Moratorium to End the War in Vietnam.[1] Their model was the 15 October Moratorium in the US, in which two million Americans demonstrated for an end to the war, and the 500 000-strong march on Washington DC that had taken place on 15 November. Association for International Cooperation and Disarmament (AICD) secretary Geoff Anderson was one of the 36 who attended the national consultation, and upon his return he and a group of other activists began to plan a Vietnam Moratorium Campaign (VMC) for NSW.

AICD's newsletter of 2 December 1969 celebrated the US Moratorium as the 'largest mass demonstration in American history' and said 75 federal ALP politicians supported the organisation of an Australian iteration. AICD hoped that such an event would expand to 'all major community groupings, such as the Universities, staff and students, senior secondary students, Churches, Trade Unions, cultural, professional and community groupings', who would 'not only sponsor the project but organise their own particular contribution to the Moratorium programme'. They urged supporters to 'take the earliest available opportunity to discuss with interested colleagues ways and means of establishing effective Moratorium support committees in your sphere of work or locality'.[2]

The Moratorium campaign was able to build on the level of cooperation already established through the anti-conscription movement using a dedicated policy of decentralisation. This meant targeting suburban and rural communities on the ground. AICD focused on attracting broad support across NSW, seeking strength in unity between organisations reflecting diverse ideological standpoints. This localised approach created a culturally and ideologically diverse mass of Australians who were able to act in unison to oppose the war. This strategy, that aimed to 'diversify and decentralise' the anti-war movement, would ultimately attract a crowd of up to 60 000 supporters in NSW to the Moratorium rallies. The VMC's pursuit of an 'open and inclusive coalition placing the breadth of participation before the coherence of ideology' meant that the Moratorium was 'as much an organisational as political phenomenon'.[3] The honorary secretary of the Moratorium Legal Committee, Leo Martin, wrote after the second Moratorium that 'VMC is the broadest organisation this country has ever known'. He thought the primary reason for its successful growth was 'the fact that individuals have been able to put aside their differences, so that maximum impetus is given to promoting the main aims of the VMC'.[4]

The campaign was named 'A Moratorium Against Business as Usual to End the War', and the disruption of 'business as usual' took place in public and private, or loud and quiet, ways. The main events, the Moratorium rallies of 8 May 1970, 18 September 1970 and 30 June 1971, were unprecedented in scale. City streets across the country filled as up to 200 000 protesters marched in opposition to Australian involvement in the Vietnam War in the first rally, made more impressive by comparing Australia's population of 12.5 million with the US that had more than 200 million people. The overwhelming visual spectacle created by the first Moratorium was followed by smaller but powerful second and third events.

The Moratorium was a very new type of protest, which brought not only loudness and noise to Sydney and other cities and towns, but also public quietness. The campaign produced a public manifestation of protest that had never before been seen in Australia and was matched by an unparalleled level of quiet protest. Activists incorporated protest tactics such as sit-ins and other forms of discussion into the Moratorium rallies and created enduring memories for participants and observers of mass actions that brought 'incredible stillness' to public spaces.[5]

Once Geoff Anderson returned from Canberra, AICD called an open meeting in Sydney for 'citizens from the community at large', on 17 December, to share the resolutions from the national consultations. Here, conversations between activists led to the formation of the Vietnam Moratorium Campaign New South Wales (VMC), and its central NSW Moratorium Coordinating Committee (MCC). Not all were pleased with this ostensibly democratic process. Militant groups were concerned that the national consultation did not allow for fair representation of all organisations and ideologies. Resistance, worried about continuing AICD control, insisted on a distinct VMC identity, which was only possible through the establishment of a separate Moratorium office.[6]

Shortly afterwards, the VMC established its headquarters in the Boilermakers–Blacksmiths Society Hall at 232 Castlereagh Street, less than ten minutes' walk from AICD's George Street office, underscoring the links between the two. From these rooms, a torrent of quiet protest was instituted and organised.

The first mass meeting of Moratorium sponsors was held at the Teachers Federation Auditorium at 300 Sussex Street on 9 February 1970. It created a detailed plan for VMC and locality group action. A page of actions distributed after the meeting listed petitions; churches tolling bells; approaches to university administrators, church leaders, editors, publishers, mayors, community leaders and the RSL to talk about the Moratorium; advertising in newspapers; selling buttons; posters and stickers; vigils outside jails for arrested draft evaders or resisters; conducting mourning processions; encouraging overseas protests; screening films; church candlelight parades; radio advertising and call-ins; holding shopping centre motorcades; meetings; debates; teach-ins; canvassing door-to-door; letterboxing; leafleting markets, shopping centres, railway stations, bus terminals, laundromats, factories, department stores and sporting fixtures; study groups; high

Vietnam Moratorium Campaign New South Wales press conference, March 1970

Noel Hazard/*Tribune* collection/MLSLNSW/courtesy SEARCH Foundation

school debates and teach-ins; campaigns to write letters to politicians; lunch-hour discussions; planting a tree of life; one minute of silence at 11am every Friday until the Moratorium; black arm bands; shop committee and union sponsorship of the Moratorium; stopping work; as well as businessmen and employers closing their office, shop or factory for the whole day, half the day or one hour.[7]

The hesitance of radical activists did not subside. They believed the AICD, which in their minds represented a too-moderate CPA, had devalued the anti-war message and decreased the efficacy of the movement by decentralising and democratising within the Moratorium campaign. Brisbane university student Brian Laver and Darce Cassidy, a former University of Sydney student and 1965 Freedom Rider, produced a booklet called *The Communist Party is behind this Moratorium – way behind*, with a photograph of Laver being restrained by CPA figures during the first Moratorium of 8 May 1970 on the cover. The booklet criticised the CPA for diluting its message, turning its back on the worker–student alliance and aligning with the ALP in promoting the Moratorium.[8] These charges were later condemned by prominent

Victorian CPA members Bernie Taft, Laurie Carmichael and John Sendy, who feared they would 'repel people of good will who want to get down to the job'.[9]

On 22 June 1970, an open letter criticising AICD's role in the first Moratorium and proposing to reconstitute the campaign was distributed anonymously at a Moratorium Sponsors' meeting. It alleged the original agreement to establish a 'politically neutral office' was 'subsequently frustrated by AICD' because AICD wished to control the narrative and events of the Moratorium campaign. In response, AICD members, including VMC convenor Ken McLeod, Bruce Gordon, Ken O'Hara, Beverley Dunnett and Geoff Anderson, wrote a seven-page statement entitled 'The facts about AICD's role in the Moratorium'. This document declared:

> The Moratorium is not an organisation: It is not an office in Liverpool Street, or in George Street, or in Goulburn Street. It is not AICD or Resistance. It is not the Secretariat or the Committee. It is not even the 100–200 people who attend Sponsors' Meetings. It is several thousand individual Australians who, in a thousand ways and for a thousand reasons believe the Indo-China War to be perhaps the greatest obscenity of our times, regard Australia's involvement in Vietnam as a matter of personal responsibility, and condemn military conscription in the context of that war as immoral. The REAL Moratorium is a movement of people, a very diverse and broadly based campaign built upon a coalition in action of some 150 separate organisations and over 2000 individual sponsors. At the very centre of this campaign are three mutually agreed principles: non-exclusion, non-imposition and decentralisation. It is around these principles that the previous success of the Moratorium was constructed, and it is from them that its future development will grow.[10]

The statement also outlined the history of the VMC, listing secretariat members and their broadly representative affiliations, including Resistance (Sue Thornton), Women's Liberation (Sandra

Hawker), Sydney University Labor Club (Hayden Thompson), AICD (Bruce Gordon), trade unions (Phil Sanford), Committee in Defiance of the National Service Act (Marian Hill) and Carol McLean from the Society of Friends, or Quakers.

The statement also addressed the demands for a centralised office, and outlined the role of AICD within the Moratorium campaign:

> Since May 10th AICD has had to accept, again by default, total responsibility for the continuing administration of the Moratorium – all postings, all receipting and accounting, all records and filing, all correspondence and all printing of minutes, Agenda, business papers etc have been done by AICD. No one has challenged this and no other organisation has offered to assist ... Surely it is ludicrous to propose the setting up from scratch of new facilities that are already available within the movement. If AICD or any other organisation has the necessary facilities and is prepared to make them available, then it would not seem unreasonable for the Moratorium to use them.[11]

This statement appeared to silence the critics, at least publicly. Three months later, in September, at a Moratorium Sponsors' meeting in the Irish Association Hall at 64 Devonshire Street, Surry Hills, Denis Freney moved that the Moratorium office at Castlereagh Street close and the VMC move to the AICD building. The motion was carried.[12] Ultimately, the radical left disapproved of the broad coalition that was gathered for the Moratorium campaign and viewed the decentralisation of protest actions as a 'right wing attempt to dilute the movement's radicalism'.[13]

DECENTRALISING THE MORATORIUM CAMPAIGN

Cultural memory of the Moratorium movement in Australia focuses on the mass rallies, which are often characterised as an organic groundswell of public opposition, with little attention paid to the meticulously organised and planned hours, days and weeks of discussion, lobbying, writing and fundraising necessary to corral so many towards the campaign.[14] Such understandings were evident during the campaigns. In a vote by ACTU leadership on their support for the Moratorium, ALP NSW Vice President John Ducker opposed, stating the campaign was 'confused, divided and unable to work efficiently'.[15] While there was some division, activists across the country produced a vast amount of Moratorium infrastructure in the first few months of 1970 that was so effective ALP Federal President Tom Burns declared that if Moratorium organisation had instead been directed towards the ALP's 1969 federal election campaign, they would have won.[16]

AICD's statement listed three overarching principles that guided the Moratorium campaign: 'non-exclusion, non-imposition and decentralisation'. Of these, according to Maddison and Scalmer, decentralisation was the 'ruling principle'.[17] Mobilisation within social movements is successful if it occurs at a range of levels, usually by national leaders who form local groups that, in turn, recruit individuals. Multi-level organisation of this sort will only succeed if social networks are strong, meaning that it is often necessary to work alongside established groups, such as churches and unions.[18] The success of such networks relies on activists being firmly embedded within existing communities.[19]

The 2013 Hands Off Melbourne's Estates (HOME) campaign provides a recent example of how strong community bonds can powerfully advance broader social movements. When the Victorian Government, then led by Ted Baillieu of the Liberal Party, proposed erecting private apartments on public housing land in Fitzroy, tenants within the Atherton Gardens Residents Association occupied Department of Human Services offices to draw attention to maintenance neglect in the estate, and arranged petitions, letterboxing, mass public meetings, rallies and street stalls to oppose the plans. HOME approached a group of unions for support, which was given in principle, echoing the Green Bans, when unions in Sydney and other cities stopped work to bolster community campaigns against excessive development and the loss of heritage and worker housing.

These community actions forced the government to indefinitely delay its building plans.[20]

The work of developing community bonds and laying the groundwork for the first Moratorium rally in NSW, scheduled on 8 May 1970, began months ahead of the event. The coordinating committee that had been appointed on 17 December 1969 oversaw VMC strategy across the state and marshalled the large number of sponsors that aligned themselves with the Moratorium. These sponsors were individuals, existing protest groups, or new networks, often suburban or regional Moratorium committees, whose role was to devise and carry out tactics best suited to their local communities.

From March 1970, the VMC prioritised solid cooperation: 'We should not allow the movement to be divided along any lines, either age or political, as this only tends to weaken the whole movement'. By then, the list of Moratorium sponsors included 950 individuals, 69 organisations and 27 local committees, as well as regional groups in Newcastle, Wollongong and Armidale. They were managed by a secretariat, which began to meet with sponsors in early 1970.[21]

The records of the regular meetings between the secretariat and sponsors allow us to chart the ways the secretariat shifted its constitution and strategy in response to the increasing demands of the campaign. Meticulous minutes contain long lists of the actions needed to communicate the Moratorium's message to the general population. The March 1970 secretariat report illustrates the magnitude of quiet activity, at the state and local level, listing printed material and Moratorium ephemera that was already available for sale, including 2000 posters, 100 000 informational brochures, 100 000 leaflets for letterboxing and street distribution, 15 000 stickers and 500 information kits with material for speakers' notes. Later it added postcards featuring a drawing by cartoonist Bruce Petty, 2000 badges, 20 000 black armbands, 15 000 car stickers, and postage-stamp stickers for envelopes, most centrally designed or donated by well-known artist-activists. Ahead of the second Moratorium of 18 September, a professional poster competition, publicised through the VMC's media and promotions sub-committee's 'propaganda campaign', generated striking visuals.[22] This merchandise was distributed and sold across the state, including in Denis Freney's North Sydney Liberation store, and a Moratorium shop was set up at VMC headquarters on Castlereagh Street, where the VMC convenor worked full-time, along with a 'small army of volunteers'.[23]

The VMC organised a program of radio and newspaper advertisements to publicise the Moratorium and encouraged local committees to raise funds for publicity in local papers. They also established a weekly news sheet, *Out Now*, which eventually appeared in August 1970, prior to the second Moratorium. It aimed to spread information about the war and the Moratorium campaign, but was short-lived, with its third and final issue published on 10 September 1970. It did, however, draw from international campaigns, publishing informative articles about activism such as 'Organising Protest' by US activist Saul Alinsky who had, alongside Cesar Chavez, organised the 1965–1970 Californian migrant grape pickers' strike. Alinsky argued for strong leadership as well as local and diverse activist groupings within social movements.[24]

The secretariat also ran services to disseminate information, providing press clippings and abstracts of articles; a talk back radio panel; a 'letters to the editor' panel; copyrighting services; preparing advertising and feature articles; and providing general assistance for churches, trade unions, suburban and independent newspapers and journals wishing to publish material. They reprinted and sold articles by prominent thinkers such as American historian Gabriel Kolko, linguist and philosopher Noam Chomsky, and the co-editor of San Francisco's 'revolutionary New Left' magazine *Leviathan*, Peter Wiley. The secretariat also recruited volunteers who were able to translate Moratorium leaflets into Spanish, Italian and Greek. This publicity was such a mammoth task that the secretariat recommended the appointment of a part- or full-time public relations officer.

By 24 April 1970, the list of necessary organisational tasks had increased exponentially. The VMC closely communicated with police, before and during the Moratorium, and it recruited medical student volunteers to provide first aid at the main rally. An entertainment committee worked on a program of events and the Arts Vietnam committee took responsibility for music and arranged amplification. The finance committee recruited and supervised volunteers who would collect donations from rally attendees. Another group of volunteers liaised with international speakers, which included Greek anti-Junta activist and London University Lecturer in Social Science Mark Dragoumis, US Special Forces (Green Berets) Sergeant Donald Duncan, US Army GI Joe Miles and US activist Nancy Rubin. Phil Sanford, who had been deported from the US for his involvement with the American chapter of Students for a Democratic Society, took charge of babysitting at the rally and recruited volunteers, predominantly from the Young Friends (Quakers). By the third Moratorium in June 1971, this had expanded into a dedicated rally child-minding centre.[25]

DECENTRALISATION IN ACTION

AICD member and historian Beverley Symons has written about the importance of inclusivity within the Moratorium movement, and the way general slogans were created to attract 'ordinary people in the suburbs', not just 'the little Left political parties and groups and the radicals'.[26] These efforts were decidedly successful, as by 27 April 1970, 43 local Moratorium committees had been established, representing more than 50 Sydney suburbs and areas as well as Newcastle, Blue Mountains, Canberra, Wollongong, Armidale, Cooma and Wagga Wagga.

Added to these were over 75 organisation-based committees, representing not only existing anti-war and student groups, political parties and unions, but also included the Arab–Hebrew Joint Action Committee, Actors and Announcers Equity, Olympia Jazz Band, Original Old Age and Invalid Pensioners' Association, Committee of Clergy for Participation in the Moratorium and the Callan Park Group Vietnam Moratorium Campaign.[27] The geographical and occupational range of these groups show us the extent of Moratorium infrastructure, and the wide range of ages, religions and classes within the movement,

VIETNAM MORATORIUM CAMPAIGN, 587 George Street, Sydney (GPO Box 161).

CHILD-MINDING CENTRE, JUNE 30TH

As you know, the third National Moratorium against the War in Vietnam will be held in all states on WEDNESDAY, 30TH JUNE. The Moratorium Co-ordinating Committee has decided to organise child minding facilities during the afternoon, to assist those parents who may otherwise find it difficult to participate in the Moratorium.

The Child-Minding Centre will be in the A.E.U./Boilermakers' Society Hall, 232 Castlereagh Street (near Cnr. Bathurst St., opposite Fire Station), between the hours of 1.00 p.m. - 5.00 p.m. (We only have the hall booking till 5 p.m., so it is essential that children are collected by then).

We are presently enlisting a team of both men and women to look after the children, and we invite any people wishing to assist in this way to notify us on 26.6201, or return the form below.

Parents wishing to use this service, are asked to fill out and return the form below AS SOON AS POSSIBLE. You will appreciate the importance of us having early knowledge of how many children we will be looking after, also the range of ages. Particularly in the case of babies and toddlers, we will need to be advised of specific details about your child's requirements, re feeding and sleeping arrangements etc. We would contact you further if we needed any more information.

Parents are asked to provide smocks, or old clothes, favourite toy or book, pencils etc. We will endeavour to provide materials for varied activities, including finger painting, drawing, story-telling & reading, building-block games etc. We will also provide light afternoon tea for the children.

All enquiries re the Child-Minding Centre should be made to Beverley Dunnett on 26.6201.

I wish to have my child/chidren cared for at the Child-Minding Centre, Wednesday, 30th June.

CHILD'S NAME/S: ....

....

AGE/S: ....

ADDRESS: ....

....

'PHONE: ....

I wish to volunteer to help look after the children at the Child-Minding Centre, Wednesday, 30th June.

NAME:

....

ADDRESS: ....

....

'PHONE: ....

PLEASE RETURN TO: CHILD-MINDING CENTRE, V.M.C., GPO BOX 161, SYDNEY, 2001.

Admission form for VMC Child-Minding Centre, 1971

Communist Party of Australia records/MLSLNSW/
courtesy SEARCH Foundation

challenging the popular conception of the rallies as a spontaneous outpouring of opposition to the war.

The success of decentralisation can be partly attributed to the continuous messaging of smaller groups that encouraged a united and diverse front against the war. An open letter of 14 August 1970 written by Catholic David Mallick and Congregationalist John Munson urged religious Australians to attend a range of silent vigils, meetings or other Moratorium events: 'We do not ask you to agree with the declared position of the Moratorium or that you become in any way identified with it ... We do ask you to consider and express your own understanding of the Christian approach to peace and war'.[28] The Railway Moratorium Committee wrote in its May 1971 bulletin that 'actions of all types are required', sharing that 'a group of Railway Christians are now praying for an end to the war as their way of speaking out'.[29]

In a letter to Moratorium sponsors dated 1 September 1970, just over a fortnight before the second rally, the VMC confirmed its commitment to its approach of community engagement and decentralisation: 'Central organisation can only provide a framework within which such a movement can find its expression. Ultimately the success of the Moratorium must depend upon the personal commitment of each individual supporter'.[30]

ORGANISING IN THE SUBURBS: THE NORTHERN DISTRICTS VIETNAM MORATORIUM GROUP

On 24 February 1970 at a private home in the suburb of Beecroft, 22 activists gathered to form the Northern Districts Vietnam Moratorium Group (NDVMG), which aimed 'to get people to sponsor the Moratorium and take part by shutting down shops, schools, universities etc. on 8th, to get publicity against the war in Vietnam, to make people think'. At this first meeting, Bill Leslie of the Teachers Federation and VMC explained the structure and intentions of the Moratorium, and the group formed a central committee and sub-committees for finance, publicity, leafleting and contacting churches, 'including the Catholics'. The group agreed on a range of planned actions, such as contacting local headmasters to arrange lunchtime meetings at schools, holding public meetings in Hornsby Plaza shopping centre, organising weekly press releases and distributing materials sourced from AICD.[31]

Attendees at this first meeting had full lives and specific reasons for participating in the Moratorium campaign, but these were not always articulated. Tenno Koolberg, who became the group's treasurer, had migrated from Estonia in 1926 and was fined in the Liverpool Police Court in 1940 for failing to register as an alien. He studied Mechanical Engineering at Sydney Technical College, then from 1943 served in the Royal Australian Air Force (RAAF) during the Second World War, prior to his naturalisation in 1946.[32] His RAAF application tells us that he had participated in amateur football, hockey, running, swimming, boxing and wrestling in Estonia. When he was appointed NDVMG treasurer, he was managing a career in accounting alongside active membership of the Western Suburbs Amateur Water Polo Club team – he would later be integral to the formation of the Australian Union of Senior Swimming International (Masters Swimming Australia).[33] Koolberg's individual history of energetic public service translated into an eagerness to contribute to the movement through quiet protest and represents one of many individual stories of quiet activism within the administrative protest archive.

Local Moratorium groups were key to raising the enormous sums of sponsor fees and donations that were needed to sustain the VMC campaign. In March 1970, the NDVMG asked supporters for 50 cent donations to purchase space in the *Hornsby Times*, which ran an advertisement in the following month asking:

> Isn't it time we helped put an end to death and destruction? Join us in calling for the immediate withdrawal of Australian forces from Vietnam and repeal of the National Service Act – it's our way of expressing opposition to young Australians being forced to kill and be killed in a war against people that offer us no threat and wish us no harm.[34]

The following is a draft copy of an advertisement we hope will apear in local papers. To finance it each signatory is asked to donate 50 cents. To indicate your willingness to participate in this worth-while project, please sign and print your name on this sheet and return it with your donation of 50c. Perhaps you have friends who would also be prepared to sign?

DRAFT COPY

ISN'T IT TIME WE
HELPED PUT AN END TO
DEATH AND DESTRUCTION.

Join us in calling for the immediate withdrawal of Australian forces from Vietnam and repeal of the National Service Act -- it's our way of expressing opposition to young Australians being forced to kill and be killed in a war against people that offer us no threat and wish us no harm. The majority of Australians now want Australia's troops withdrawn; only 40% (according to the latest Gallup Poll) are still in favour of our presence in Vietnam.

Signature ....

Name in Full ....

Suburb ....

Please find 50c. enclosed

NORTHERN DISTRICTS VIETNAM
MORATORIUM CAMPAIGN

Please tear off this coupon

A MORATORIUM AGAINST BUSINESS AS USUAL TO END THE WAR

Please return to Jane Gray 40 Hannah St., Beecroft

Northern Districts Vietnam Moratorium Campaign, March 1970

People for Nuclear Disarmament/MLSLNSW

From this ad, the group collected names, addresses and signatures of new supporters, as well as more 50 cent donations, enabling it to buy space in the *Northern District Times*.[35]

The NDVMG archive reveals the more personal impacts of locality organising for the Moratorium. One unnamed supporter who wrote to NDVMG secretary Jane Gray to apologise for their lack of communication said they were overwhelmed by 'four Moratorium groups making demands on my time, plus some personal business not unconnected with the National Service Act, all of which left me little time'.[36] Others wrote to express discontent, such as a Mr Hordern who complained to Gray that the group was trying to 'unduly influence' his son, causing dissension in the family. Gray apologised but cleverly used the opportunity to attract additional support, writing: 'Before you judge the situation too hastily why don't you come along yourself to a meeting or call and see me – I would be very happy to re-assure you!'[37]

The NDVMG also held creative events to raise funds, including essay, poetry and music competitions. Gray sought prizes from noted authors Colin Thiele, Geoffrey Dutton, Thomas Shapcott, Nancy Keesing, Judith Wright, Thomas Keneally and George Johnston, among others, asking them 'Do you feel you could associate yourself with us by donating one of your books with a signed inscription indicating your concern?'[38] The poetry competition required entrants to pay a small fee to submit their poems for judging by a panel that included poet Nancy Keesing and University of Sydney Professor in English Leonie Kramer. On 8 August 1970 the group held a music competition at a Moratorium concert at the Methodist Church Hall in Beecroft, which cost 50 cents to attend. Compositions included 'Destruction' by 16-year-old Ann Martin, using the pseudonym 'Insignifico'; 'Anti-Conscription Blues' by 17-year-old Michael Fine; 'Prayer' by 17-year-old Megan Rodger (using the pseudonym Lucy van Pelt); and 'Tjurunga' by 18-year-old Ernest Gallagher, who chose the rather inventive pseudonym 'Captain Cook'.[39]

Brass bands and children prepare for the First Moratorium to End the War in Vietnam, George Street, Sydney, 8 May 1970

Noel Hazard/*Tribune* collection/MLSLNSW/courtesy SEARCH Foundation

QUIETNESS WITHIN THE MORATORIUM

Although quiet protest was key to the success of the Moratorium campaign, the power of the public rally was crucial, as declared at a March 1970 Moratorium sponsors' meeting: 'It is extremely important that the greatest numbers of people be brought together at the one time. The movement as a whole will be judged by the size of the major events'. To attract more support, the campaign had to appeal to quieter activists who might engage in localised activity but were reluctant to protest publicly due to the very real fear of violence or red-smearing. To help quieter protesters feel safe at the first Moratorium rally, the VMC resolved to 'include an orderly march with brass bands. To people not used to demonstrating, this will give them confidence that they are participating in a respectable patriotic activity'.[40]

Full-page advertisements in the *SMH* listing prominent anti-war individuals and organisations that supported the Moratorium were intended to foster that same confidence. The advertisement published on 7 May 1970, one day before the first Moratorium rally, categorised hundreds of names into occupations, including housewives, artists, writers, businessmen, architects, teachers, clergy, trade unionists and journalists. This approach aimed to increase public identification with the movement by showcasing its diversity and, ultimately, reduce any fear of participation.[41]

Quiet and non-traditional protest was also incorporated into Moratorium rallies. The 8 May rally included a 'front lawn' meeting of students and academics at the University of Sydney, a similar meeting for professionals and white-collar workers in Sydney's Central Business District, and an evening prayer vigil at the Hyde Park Pool of Remembrance. On the following day, local groups handed out publicity materials in suburban shopping centres and on 10 May the 'Vietnam and Conscience' Forum was held at the Lyceum Theatre on Pitt Street, followed by a performance of *Old Botany Bay* by actor and director Peter O'Shaughnessy, folk musician Marian Henderson and director Richard Brooks.

The unprecedented success of the first Moratorium strengthened the determination of activists. Contemporary estimates place the crowds across Australia as 200 000-strong, with up to 60 000 in Sydney, although NSW newspapers, crossing a spectrum of ideological perspectives, printed significantly smaller numbers. The *SMH* reported 20 000 people and *Tribune* estimated 25 000, which may be more accurate assessments.[42]

The VMC resolved on 8 June to repeat the event in September 'in the same spirit as events on May 8', noting the crucial role of quiet protest and emphasising 'education and publicity, particularly through trade unions and among workers'.[43]

Activists sit and stand during the First Moratorium to End the War in Vietnam, 8 May 1970

Noel Hazard/*Tribune* collection/MLSLNSW/courtesy SEARCH Foundation

WITHDRAW ALL TROOPS NOW
VIETNAM MORATORIUM
NO RIGHT TURN
BUSES EXCEPTED

Executing such an ambitious program required continuous fundraising efforts. On 7 September, the VMC calculated that additional donations of around $5000, equivalent to almost $75 000 in 2026, were required to ensure the 18 September Moratorium did not operate at a deficit.[44] Only $4000 was raised, and Ken O'Hara wrote to sponsors to appeal for donations in early October.[45] It is not easy, with minds locked in the present, to comprehend the real-world impact of those finances in 1970, but the quantity of promotional and other materials that passed through the VMC office in early September conveys a clearer picture. On 7 September, the office held 60 000 copies of *Out Now*'s second issue and expected 100 000 copies of its third issue would arrive by 10 September. It had 75 000 leaflets on the history of the war, 20–30 000 leaflets in Greek and Italian, 40 000 high school leaflets, 75 000 trade union leaflets, and were expecting an incoming order of 20 000 badges, 20 000 stickers and 10 000 posters.

LAW AND ORDER

The second Moratorium, on 18 September 1970, repeated the combination of loud and quiet protest, with vigils, prayers, speeches and forums by a variety of groups. The following day, Gough Whitlam, Victorian VMC Chair Jim Cairns and ACTU President Bob Hawke held an ALP Moratorium public meeting at Sydney Town Hall.[46] Such events were aimed at attracting fearful activists and were a measured response to a fervent 'law and order' campaign waged by the Coalition government that aimed to both weaken the Moratorium movement and gain political capital ahead of the November Senate elections.[47]

Liberal Prime Minister John Gorton had drawn battle lines on 26 March 1970, when he referred to activists' plans for the first Moratorium as 'storm trooper tactics', and alleged that Jim Cairns had issued a 'call for anarchy'.[48] In Victoria, the clear support of the ALP for the Moratorium countered these political attacks. In NSW, however, state ALP President Charles Oliver had undermined public support for the first Moratorium by claiming the VMC was controlled by the CPA.[49]

The NSW-based organisers of the Moratorium quietly resisted this narrative. As mentioned in Chapter One, Jane Gray wrote to the *Australian Financial Review* to condemn its linking of anti-war beliefs with communism, saying 'In the government coalition we have a dedicated band of zealots ready to hurl charges of "communist line" or "communist dupes" at anyone who opposes the government's inept policies'.[50] Gray was conscious of the need to avoid alienating non-activists, so was 'gravely disturbed' when sponsors resolved to invite representatives of the communist NLF and Revolutionary Provisional Government of South Vietnam to attend the Moratorium. She wrote that her group had attracted community support in good faith that 'there was no basis upon which the traditional "smear" campaign could be founded', and she believed that 'the decision will only create opportunities for discrediting the campaign without any compensating advantages'.[51]

Although the second Moratorium is frequently discounted in public memory due to conflict that led to around 200 arrests in Sydney, many have insisted the violence was not started by activists, as Liberal Premier Robert Askin and the media alleged, but by police. As *Tribune* reported, 'police planners selected Sydney and Adelaide to stage massive intimidatory violence against the growing Moratorium movement ... the plans of violent police repression were applied with a clockwork precision that spoke eloquently of weeks of planning and careful briefing'.[52]

Many within the movement had anticipated repression. Two days before the rally, UNSW student newspaper *Tharunka* wrote of the Askin government's '"law and order" syndrome', and his grant of additional powers to police: 'The Liberal Party is trying to create an atmosphere of anarchy by embarking on a policy via the Police Department of making demonstrations appear more violent than they are by increasing the number of arrests'. Writing that 'anarchy is inevitable if law and order becomes a means of perpetuating the strong', they urged activists to 'play it cool at the Moratorium, don't let the Liberal Party win the State election on a law and order issue'.[53]

A VMC meeting held at the University of Sydney on 23 September discussed legal support for those arrested and considered collective action against police violence. They asked 'people with information and/or

Police apprehend an activist at the Second Moratorium, 18 September 1970

Noel Hazard/*Tribune* collection/MLSLNSW/courtesy SEARCH Foundation

allegations of police brutality, or information relating to removal of police identification badges' to write to Askin or state ALP leader Pat Hills to urge the Premier to establish a Royal Commission to investigate the matter.[54] On that same day, Jane Gray wrote to Askin:

> Contrary to your statements that the marchers were a 'scruffy rabble', or words to that effect, we believe if we had not been a reasonable, intelligent and self-controlled crowd the tactics used by the police could well have produced hysteria and panic with the resulting possibilities of real tragedy ... It was an illuminating but shocking experience for many of us middle aged

> people. No wonder the intelligent and concerned young people in our society are becoming alienated. We are ashamed it happened in Australia and believe you should be also. Whether the police acted under your directives or under those of the Commissioner of Police should be made clear.[55]

On 29 September, Syd Einfeld, the deputy leader of the NSW Opposition and ALP Member for Bondi, who had personally processed the migration applications of Holocaust survivors to ensure they would be welcomed to Australia, questioned Askin in the NSW Legislative Assembly. He asked why 200 people were arrested in Sydney, when only four were charged in Melbourne, and demanded Askin 'publicly state his Government's support for the Universal Declaration of Human Rights, particularly article 20, which states, "Everyone has the right of freedom of peaceful assembly and association"'. Askin replied that 'the Government has no objection whatever to parades, demonstrations and activities signifying dissent', as long as they 'are carried out in lawful fashion and providing that they do not unduly interfere with the rights of other citizens'. He referenced NSW ALP President Charles Oliver's disassociation from the Moratorium as evidence of its lawlessness, claiming 'the organisers declared that they were going to break the law' by proceeding with the Moratorium in the absence of official approval and 'the police did a pretty good job in watching law and order and looking after the interests of the law-abiding public'.[56]

The VMC responded with a press statement on 30 September, providing detailed evidence that the Moratorium secretariat had 'made repeated attempts to meet with the Police Commissioner' and that 'on every occasion these approaches were either ignored or rebuffed'. VMC representatives Ken McLeod, Bill Leslie, Bruce Gordon and Professor Max Deutscher finally secured a meeting with Police Commissioner Norman Allan on 17 September, at which they were unexpectedly asked for 12 separate applications for permission to hold the rally, which necessitated 12 separate interviews. Despite spending many hours engaged in these interviews, shortly before midday on 18 September, the day of the main rally, Allan informed the VMC its application was not approved, citing possible traffic issues. As a result, the rally was held 'illegally', but the VMC insisted that 'it was the Police Commissioner, not the Moratorium organisers, who consistently and obstinately refused to participate in any discussion concerning arrangements for the Moratorium'.[57]

THE NATIONAL ANTI-WAR CONFERENCE AND BEYOND

Political roadblocks did not deter the VMC from its goal to expand support through decentralisation. On 11 October, the Moratorium committee was dissolved and the secretariat expanded 'into a more representative body to be known as the NSW Co-ordinating Committee', containing members from 'locality groups, trade unions, universities, industrial and occupational groups and youth'. One week later, this new committee presented a draft of a program for future actions acknowledging that 'the Moratorium Campaign has been highly successful and has in fact been the principal action and organisational focus of the anti-war movement in Australia' but members wanted to 'consolidate this potential mass movement by developing actions of a more continuous and diverse nature'. Future actions were to be significantly quieter, with a focus on 'educational activities', 'organisational development' and 'promotional activities' that aimed to create continuing support for the cause, rather than peaks during Moratorium rallies.[58]

The attention to educational activities was not a new development. As early as 8 June 1970, the VMC Committee had discussed the need for 'an international anti-war conference on peace and independence in Indo-China between all interested sections of the anti-war movement in Australia', 'to stimulate great discussion of these issues in Australia'.[59] These plans came to fruition on 17–21 February 1971, when the National Anti-War Conference was held at the Teachers Federation Auditorium on Sussex Street, sponsored by the VMC National Coordinating Committee, and led by Ken McLeod. It featured four international speakers, including University of Paris political scientist Philippe

National Anti-War Conference, 17–21 February 1971

Noel Hazard/*Tribune* collection/MLSLNSW/courtesy SEARCH Foundation

Devillers, US Army veteran organiser Michael Uhl, Save our Soldiers and *Leviathan* editor Peter Wiley, and Bala Tampoe of the Sri Lankan Trotskyist Lanka Sama Samara Party. Its brochure emphasised the need for public education to move the movement forward, as well as to set the agenda for its next phase:

> Through the Moratorium, a real mass national anti-war coalition has been built, involving more people and having a greater impact on the community than ever before. In the process of building this coalition and of developing a truly mass dimension, the anti-war movement has changed in many significant ways. New modes of action have emerged, new approaches to organising developed, and new areas of support opened up.[60]

Like the Moratorium, the National Anti-War Conference was the culmination of almost ten years of anti-Vietnam War organisation in NSW. The conference was both an example of quiet protest and a forum for activist groupings to share quiet protest tactics. It was a bold act by the Moratorium campaign after the aggressive demonstration of 'law and order' during the September 1970 rally and illustrates the persistence of activists who sought solutions to key public issues.

Looking to the present emphasises the usefulness of such forums for discussing and formulating responses to social justice issues. In January 2025, Queensland University of Technology's Carumba Institute, headed by Mununjali and South Sea Islander woman Professor Chelsea Watego, sponsored the National Symposium Unifying Anti-Racist Research and Action. The purpose of the event, occurring amid public debates about the nature of pro-Palestinian protest, was to develop strategies to address institutional racism and anti-colonialism, but the *Australian* framed it as divisive. The unjustified accusations of racism that were directed towards conference speakers echoed the claims of pro-Vietnam War advocates that the Moratoriums were violent, and similarly show how powerful such discussions can be.[61]

A major theme of the 1971 National Anti-War Conference was 'Strategies and Tactics: The Directions of the Anti-war Movement', and many papers presented perspectives on quieter forms of protest. Melbourne Catholic activist Val Noone spoke about 'Building a wider community of resistance'; Federal Pacifist Council of Australia member and *Peacemaker* editor Vivienne Abraham discussed draft counselling; and VMC National Schools Organiser Ted Marr presented ideas about local and school-based organising.[62] Marr articulated the importance of quiet protest most clearly, emphasising the need for 'thousands of backyard activists' who do their 'best work' in contexts such as 'universities, factories, working-places in general, local communities and schools – in fact any situation where a number of people are brought together and have something in common'. He affirmed the need for continued decentralisation:

> We can no longer sit back and expect all the demonstrations and large turn-outs to be organised for us by the few 'activists' at the top ... Only with close-knit dynamic local groups keeping up the momentum of the anti-war movement in their districts will the movement broaden its base.[63]

Denis Freney's paper 'The Youth Revolt in Suburbia and the Anti-War Movement' concurred:

> While the central Moratorium office and work is vital, and must also take renewed interest in the youth and the adaptation of its propaganda and literature to the youth revolt much, much more than at present, it is a vital necessity for the local groups to also tackle the problem, independently and directly at their own level.[64]

The organisation of this national conference, and the time and energy required to arrange keynote speakers and conference papers, set up registration and finances, print posters and flyers, and provide a location and accommodation, is another example of administrative quiet protest. The invitees included members of the general public and specific Australian organisations, as well as overseas guests from the US, Britain, France and Japan. All activists were welcome to submit papers for publication and purchase at the conference, and some were selected to present. Groups sold literature in the foyer, where sandwiches and refreshments were also for sale. Attendees were also directed to the surrounding Spanish, Greek and Chinese restaurants, as well as the Teachers' Club located in the building.

Interstate and country guests were hosted via a billeting service, in which local supporters provided free accommodation in their homes. The volume of paperwork required to match the needs and schedules of delegates with hosts was extraordinary.

The conference was expected to cost $10 000 to $15 000, equating to as much as $190 000 in 2026. Adults paid $8 for attendance, undergraduates and apprentices $5, secondary students $3, pensioners $2 and all were invited to make additional donations. Organisations could bring three delegates for $25, and Moratorium groups were able to bring as many as six delegates for $40. The funds raised supported the conference, and a series of 'decentralised pre-conference discussions, forums, debates, meetings, etc. in jobs, local areas, schools and universities' for 'supporters of the present movement and thousands of workers, students and others not already involved'.[65] Newcastle Trades Hall Council Workers' Club sent $250 with a letter expressing their commitment to intensified decentralisation of the Moratorium campaign, stating that they 'fully support the aims and decisions of the Anti-War Conference' and 'will be giving assistance to our local committee both financially and we hope by active participation in the various activities which are being organised in our district'.[66] Fred Olsson, who sent $75 to AICD for Moratorium organisation, was already looking ahead to the next rally, which was now planned for June.[67]

A Moratorium sponsors' meeting held at the Waterside Workers Federation Hall at 60 Sussex Street on 24 January 1971 announced nationally coordinated actions were planned for 30 April, May and June. The meeting emphasised the centrality of localised activities to the campaign, proposing the establishment of a Moratorium 'STUFF' shop in North Sydney, as well as a 'Folk Concern' organised by the Sutherland Shire Students' Moratorium Group and a swinging and folk-singing event held by the Outer Western Moratorium Group.[68]

The final Moratorium of 30 June 1971 attracted only 10 000 people in Sydney and 20 000 in Melbourne, yet *Tribune* reported that 'the Australian total of demonstrators was the biggest yet', claiming the success of increased decentralisation and localised activity had achieved long-held aims to incorporate workers into the broader movement.[69] Union involvement had been an aim of the Moratorium campaign from June 1970, when locality groups were encouraged to visit factories to spread the word, and an entire morning of the National Anti-War Conference had been devoted to trade union participation.[70] These efforts meant that on the day of the final Moratorium rally, waterside workers, seamen and other maritime unions 'closed the port of Sydney' by stopping work on all 16 Australian ships for the day. Seven thousand Boilermakers–Blacksmiths Society members stopped work in Sydney, with another 3000 in Newcastle and Wollongong. More railway workers stopped work at the Chullora workshops than in previous Moratoriums and builders' labourers working on the Sydney Opera House walked off. The Amalgamated Engineering Union, Australasian Society of Engineers, and Federated Engine Drivers and Fireman's Association joined, and in Newcastle BHP steelworkers at the basic oxygen plant and 30 other workshops downed tools. High school students intensified activities in Wollongong by also participating in the stoppages.[71]

Decentralisation, partly a practical response by the VMC to the increased emphasis on 'law and order' by political authorities who had been eager to disparage the movement, had steered the campaign in a productive direction.

The Moratorium campaign came to an end after the July 1971 federal government decision to withdraw Australian troops from Vietnam, in line with the US policy of Vietnamisation that abandoned its South Vietnamese allies and resulted in a North Vietnamese victory. Draft resister Bob Scates, who was released from prison shortly after Whitlam repealed the NSA in December 1972, called the Moratorium a 'turning point when we ceased to be a minority of youthful revolutionaries seeking to overthrow society; we became a respectful group of humane anti-war people whose stand was respected by the general community'.[72] This increased respectability was undoubtedly due to continuous efforts by central organisers to attract public support by adopting a less radical or extremist front, as well as a program of decentralisation that saw unprecedented action – both quiet and loud – during all three Moratorium events. The overwhelming success of the Moratorium campaign across NSW could not have occurred without the many thousands of hours of quiet organisation by activists in living rooms, offices and auditoriums.

CHAPTER FOUR

FINANCING THE PROTEST MOVEMENT

In May 1965, the largely Trotskyist Australian Students' Labor Federation (ASLF) met in response to the escalated bombing of North Vietnam during Operation Rolling Thunder. There, they devised a campaign to raise funds for the National Liberation Front (NLF).[1] Also known as the National Front for the Liberation of the South, the NLF was established by North Vietnam in 1960 to direct Vietnamese communist (Viet Cong) forces in their overall goal to defeat the South Vietnamese military and reunify Vietnam under communist leadership. In September 1965, the University of New South Wales (UNSW) Students Union Council considered a proposal to 'donate £10 to start a fund for medical aid for the Vietnamese National Liberation Front'. The proposal was ultimately dismissed, probably because the students feared possible legal repercussions of financing an enemy force.[2]

In March of the following year, the Sydney University Labor Club (SULC), headed by the Vietnam Action Campaign's (VAC) Hall Greenland, announced the establishment of a Medical Aid for Vietnam Fund:

> The peace movement in Sydney has so far confined itself to downtown demonstrations and meetings and to the advocacy of negotiations. This activity has kept the Vietnam debate open and highlighted opposition to the war – but no more.[2]

The fund was launched within a fortnight and separated into two sections: one providing aid to victims of US bombing in Vietnam, and the other sending funds to the Viet Cong for medical supplies, via the International Red Cross or the World Council of Churches in Hong Kong.[4]

Three students responded by anonymously distributing a leaflet entitled 'The Case Against Medical Aid for Vietnam' across the University of Sydney, alleging that sending medical aid 'on political grounds' was 'ill-considered or dishonest'. SULC's response was firm:

> Every Australian citizen is contributing to Medical Aid for Australian Aggression through Federal taxation, but the people who really need our help, the people who are among the poorest and most downtrodden on this earth, are not getting it. The ALP Club intends to see that they do get some help, and we hope that this will be more than a token ... in the long run there is only one solution: STOP THE WAR AND LET THE VIETNAMESE PEOPLE GOVERN THEMSELVES.[5]

By 20 April, the Fund had received $100, but almost solely for victims of US intervention. The prospect of providing medical aid to the NLF had, according to SULC:

> Provoked unbelievably violent opposition. This opposition is motivated by a mixture of irrational anti-communism and infantile jingoism. The cry of 'traitor' comes easy to these people and the fact that medical aid to the NLF is not legally treason of course makes no difference to them.[6]

In June 1966, SULC received a letter from NLF representatives in Moscow directing them to send the $240 received in donations to South Vietnam via the Soviet Red Cross, either as direct funds or to send quinine for malaria treatment, or emetine for dysentery.[7] The fund grew steadily.

In May 1967, the ASLF held another conference of university Labor clubs and every attendee resolved to raise 'medical, financial and other aid' for the NLF.[8] Soon afterwards, Labor clubs at Melbourne, Monash, Wollongong and ANU also resolved to begin fundraising, although Wollongong's fund never eventuated.[9] The Monash University Labor Club (MULC) in Melbourne appointed a steering committee, which on 14 July announced its intention to follow the lead of SULC and separate its fund into two: one 'unspecified (expression of support and solidarity)', and the second to provide medical aid for civilians in NLF areas. The fund faced widespread disapproval, and although MULC insisted the money sent through their 'unspecified' fund 'would not be used for military purposes', its critics were dissatisfied. The Victorian Government sent 'political police' to the homes of MULC members to investigate.[10] One of these was Michael Hyde, who argued the action aimed to:

> Prompt people to think – and it worked … when we sent money to the NLF it was reported in the press, and people who otherwise may not have cared about the war were driven to think about it … People were dragged slightly towards the Left by those actions or at the very least, began to think about the issues.[11]

The controversy at Monash University is more prominent within public memory than SULC's actions. This may be due to the heavy-handed legal response to MULC fundraising, after the group openly defied a 31 August 1967 declaration by Vice-Chancellor Louis Mathieson that collecting for the NLF on university grounds was illegal, by setting up a medical aid collection stand in the foyer of the Union building. Days later, on 9 September 1967, the *Defence Forces Protection Act 1967* (Cth.) imposed a maximum fine of $2000 or 2 years in prison, or both, for sending aid to the NLF, the North Vietnamese Communist Party or the North Vietnamese Government, although this did not apply to general aid organisations such as the International Red Cross.[12] The law was supported by both the Liberal Party and the ALP, but some ALP parliamentarians disapproved of a law that opposed humanitarian care. Senator for Tasmania Justin O'Byrne said at the second reading of the Bill on 7 September that 'a lot of hoo-ha has been spoken about bullets bearing the name of a university club crashing through the bodies of Australian troops'. He mentioned that both Melbourne and Monash University Labor Clubs intended to provide medical aid for the country as a whole:

> Apparently if compassion comes from the International Red Cross or the Australian Red Cross it is respectable, but if it comes from somebody else then it is a criminal offence ... I sometimes wonder to what lengths the Government will go in order to score a political point. In seeking to impose the tremendous penalties set out in the Bill and in classifying humanitarianism as treason the Government has transgressed some of the basic qualities of a democratic society.[13]

MULC shared O'Byrne's opinion of the Act, which they believed 'is not really intended to protest our defence forces but to repress opposition to the Government at home'. In response to their actions, Prime Minister Harold Holt delivered an address on campus, on 11 September, during which a student cheekily handed him a copy of the *Thoughts of Mao Tse-tung*. When MULC sent $100 to Lord Boyd Orr's British Medical Aid for Vietnam Committee for medical supplies to be provided on their behalf to the Liberation Red Cross of South Vietnam, the Commonwealth Police visited the homes of some of its members.[14]

The UNSW student paper *Tharunka* monitored the situation at Monash with interest, and reminded readers on 5 September that 'the Sydney dailies were feeling chagrined by their failure to make the sensation out of the NLF issue that the Melbourne dailies had achieved ... After all the idea did originate in Sydney with the Medi-Cong appeal some eighteen months ago'.[15] In July 1967, SULC reported it had sent some of the $520 it had raised to the Australian Red Cross 'after some equivocation and hesitation', and to the Bertrand Russell Peace Foundation. Both 'undertook to pass our donations on to proper parties', and stated their plans to expand the work of direct financial aid to Vietnam.[16] The 'equivocation and hesitation' indicates some disagreement within SULC, some perhaps advocating for a more tempered approach to quell any possible public or political consequences for funding the NLF directly, or through the Soviet Red Cross.

The decision to send a portion of the funds to Bertrand Russell's foundation was particularly controversial. In 1966 and 1967, the British philosopher and Nobel Prize winner headed a people's 'International War Crimes Tribunal', largely funded by North Vietnam, in which 25 notable global figures interviewed 30 individuals, including American military personnel, to investigate the legality of US actions in Vietnam. Russell was joined by French philosophers Jean-Paul Sartre and Simone de Beauvoir, who had both been active in opposing French colonialism in Algeria and Vietnam. Sartre had covertly written the preface of French communist Henri Alleg's 1958 account of torture by French forces in Algeria, *La Question*.[17]

This International War Crimes Tribunal remains influential among Australian activists. On 7 February 2025, a People's Inquiry into Campus Free Speech on Palestine began to 'document the censorship, repression, and harassment faced by students, academics, and staff advocating for Palestine across Australian universities'. It attracted prominent supporters, such as Australian Greens Senator for NSW Mehreen Faruqi, along with students, academics, the Jewish Council of Australia, and the Australian Palestine Advocacy Network (APAN). APAN has said it was inspired by the 1966 Russell Tribunal, 'where academics, activists, and public figures came together to investigate American war crimes in Vietnam because official bodies refused to'.[18]

Likely encouraged by the support for SULC's Medi-Cong appeal, University of Sydney's Student Representative Council Committee for Vietnam Civilian Medical Aid began raising funds in October 1967 for medical assistance to be sent through the International Red Cross, which was permissible under the Act. Its convenor John Blount wrote in *Tribune*: 'Since all parties to the war have disclaimed any intention of harming any civilians in either [North or South] Vietnam we feel that a non-partisan humanitarian appeal of this nature can and should be supported, regardless of political views and affiliations'.[19] Not all were content to temper their approach. When studies recommenced in February 1968, Denis Freney boldly urged students to 'JOIN US AND DEFY THE LAW' by supporting 'the victory of the Vietnamese revolution led by the National Liberation Movement' and providing 'fullest possible solidarity and aid to the NLF and North Vietnam'.[20]

Outside of universities, the prospect of aiding North or South Vietnamese communists was unpopular. Most Australians supported the war effort at this time, and Findlay calls the 'Aid for the NLF' campaign 'the protest movement's greatest failure', because instead of provoking support for the anti-war movement as intended, it 'generated a wave of public revulsion'.[21]

Michael Hyde writes that the activists refused to acknowledge this disapproval:

> It did fleetingly occur to me that treason was not something to trifle with. Left-wingers, progressives and unionists in other countries had been executed on the charge. From the perspective of our government (and from that of most of the Labor party as well), we were, after all, openly supporting an enemy of Australia, so it logically followed that we were traitors. But we never accepted that logic. We felt we were acting in the best interests of the Australian people. In a way, we argued, we were more patriotic than those who carried around their nationalism like a neon sign.[22]

Deprived of attention by the Commonwealth Government's reluctance to prosecute the matter and highlight this 'new way of acting politically', activists stopped talking about this appeal and it was not mentioned after 1968.[23]

Others found ways to send medical funds to the NLF and North Vietnam. AICD Vice President and *Anglican* owner Francis James frequently claimed to have sent money to North Vietnam and spoke at a October 1967 'MedicAid to the NLF' event in Melbourne about sending medical aid 'through the Red Cross to the National Liberation Front

Freda Brown and Jean McLean after returning from North Vietnam, July 1969

Noel Hazard/*Tribune* collection/MLSLNSW/ courtesy SEARCH Foundation

of South Vietnam'.[24] AICD sent a five-person delegation representing South Australia, Victoria, NSW, ACT and Queensland to Hanoi in June 1972 to examine the 'question of medical and reconstruction aid programmes' and see what was needed for the Vietnamese in terms of support.[25] The following month, ANU political scientist Bruce McFarlane began raising money for Medical Aid to Indochina, as a response to the 'American saturation bombing of liberated Zones in South Vietnam, Laos and Cambodia' which 'altered the ecological balance of the countryside'. It included a 'Quinine Appeal' to address the resulting outbreak of malaria.[26] Such efforts continued after the war, when rebuilding efforts were a primary consideration of Australians who were concerned about their nation's contribution to the devastation of Vietnam.[27]

Freda Brown, president of the Union of Australian Women (UAW), vice president of the Women's International Democratic Federation (WIDF), and a CPA member, caused controversy when she visited North Vietnam in 1969 at the invitation of a delegation of Vietnam Women's Union members. There she met with Melbourne Save Our Sons (SOS) leader Jean McLean, and during their ten-day visit the two delivered $100 of medication to the NLF. Although Brown was careful to obtain a receipt for the medications to avoid any charges of providing financial support to the NLF, the donation still contravened the Act, and McLean was questioned upon her return to Australia. Undeterred, Brown returned to Vietnam in the same year with cash to support the rebuilding of schools and hospitals, framing this trip as a 'challenge' aimed at the federal government.[28]

While many who became involved in fundraising for the NLF or the Vietnamese people also attended public or louder protests, the collection of moneys to support victims of war and military forces, or to fund the anti-war and anti-conscription movements, was approached strategically, to appeal to a broad cross-section of the state's population. This chapter focuses on the various fundraising campaigns that took place in NSW during the Vietnam War, from raffles and barbecues to public lectures and bookselling. Activists also withheld money, through tax resistance and boycotts, and funded legal services to activists arrested for public disturbance or other charges throughout the war. Fundraising efforts became increasingly creative, reflecting the need to appeal to a variety of Australians to achieve the many aims of the anti-war movement.

FUNDRAISING AS A FORM OF PROTEST

Participation in a social movement can be quantified by time and energy supplied through labour, or by the amount of capital spent on movement actions. Historian Melanie Oppenheimer's extensive work on the history of voluntarism emphasises that 'political protest and advocacy are forms of volunteering' and 'the anti-war movement was predicated on people's commitment, their advocacy and unpaid labour, just as the social welfare, environmental and sporting movements were'.[29] Persuading people to spend time away from work, family and other responsibilities is difficult, so most movements raise funds to expand their activities or, like many protest organisations during the Vietnam War, adopt a multi-layered approach to encouraging participation.[30] AICD understood that active protest was not available to all, particularly those with disabilities, work and other responsibilities or age-related concerns, so it requested different forms of practical help to cater to people with a range of abilities. While preparing for its Vietnam Lobby Day of 25 March 1969, AICD asked supporters unable to travel to Canberra to enact 'other types of action', including endorsement of Lobby Day, organisational help, AICD membership, or 'a special donation to AICD to assist in defraying overall promotion and organisational expenses'.[31]

This versatility was a constant feature of AICD appeals for help, financial or otherwise. In 1972, as public enthusiasm for the anti-war movement decreased because of the impending Australian withdrawal from Vietnam, the August Mobilisation Committee, which included Anglican Reverend John Beer, Carol McLean, Les Waddington and Geoff Anderson, distributed a leaflet on the importance of voting for the ALP in the upcoming federal election. The back page of the four-page leaflet included a cut-off slip headed 'How you can help' and listed protest actions that required less effort. These included joining mailing lists, distributing leaflets, or attending a meeting on the topic of voting, and asked supporters to 'give as large a donation as you can now. To mobilise for peace costs money'.[32] Raising funds was crucial for ongoing AICD operations: 'You may not be aware, that assuming a maximum renewal of subscriptions, the resulting income would not maintain the association for more than three months of the year'.[33]

Social movement theorists have long confirmed that the number of people participating in a protest event is always far smaller than the total number who agree with its goals.[34] A movement must aim,

MEMBERSHIP SUBSCRIPTIONS ARE DUE 1/4/71

PLEASE HURRY YOUR RENEWAL. WE WILL BE STRUGGLING TO KEEP AFLOAT TILL YOUR RENEWAL ARRIVES. SOME REASONS FOR OUR NEED OF YOUR URGENT RESPONSE ARE INDICATED BELOW.

MORATORIUM

OVER THE PAST 12 MONTHS, AICD HAS CONTRIBUTED MAJOR AND CONTINUOUS SUPPORT TO THE MAY AND SEPTEMBER MORATORIUMS AND THE RECENTLY CONCLUDED ANTI-WAR CONFERENCE.

OUR CONTRIBUTION OVER AND ABOVE REIMBURSED EXPENDITURE HAS FAR EXCEEDED THE CONTRIBUTION OF ANY OTHER OF THE 200 SPONSORING ORGANISATIONS.

TO INSTANCE BUT ONE EXAMPLE, THE SALARIES OF ONE FULL TIME STAFF MEMBER (KEN MCLEOD) AND SEVERAL PART TIME MEMBERS (BEVERLEY DUNNETT AND BRUCE GORDON) REPRESENTS A CONTRIBUTION OF MORE THAN $5,000 OVER THE PAST TWELVE MONTHS, AND NOW WE BEGIN TO MOVE INTO MORATORIUM 1971.

EQUIPMENT

OUR TYPING AND DUPLICATING EQUIPMENT IS LONG OVERDUE FOR REPLACEMENT. AS A CONSEQUENCE ITS INEFFICIENCY PLACES A GREAT STRAIN ON OUR TECHNICAL STAFF WHO HAVE TO PRODUCE A MASSIVE AMOUNT OF WORK AT HIGH PRESSURE FOR PROLONGED PERIODS.

IMMEDIATE REPLACEMENT OF SOME OF THIS EQUIPMENT IS THEREFORE AN URGENT MATTER: A MINIMUM OF $1000 WILL BE NEEDED.

LIBRARY EDUCATION & RESEARCH

OUR LIBRARIAN, MRS. DAWN GIETZELT, WHO HAS BEEN WORKING FOR TWO DAYS A WEEK FOR A VERY NOMINAL SALARY FOR SEVERAL YEARS PAST HAS REPORTED THAT THE VOLUME OF WORK NOW BEING HANDLED BY THE LIBRARY DEMANDS THE EMPLOYMENT OF A FULL-TIME WORKER. WE PROPOSE TO CANVASS THE AVAILABILITY OF A SUITABLE PERSON TO WORK FULLTIME AT AN EARLY DATE. MRS. GIETZELT WILL BE CONTINUING TO ASSIST THE LIBRARY BY CONTRIBUTING HER SERVICES ON A VOLUNTARY PART TIME BASIS.

THE ENCLOSED MATERIAL WILL INDICATE FURTHER IMPORTANT ACTIVITIES WHICH OUR EDUCATION COMMITTEE WISHES TO INITIATE OVER THE COMING MONTHS.

ALTHOUGH ALL WORKSHOP INSTRUCTORS WILL BE CONTRIBUTING THEIR SERVICES VOLUNTARILY THE PROGRAMME WILL OF NECESSITY INVOLVE SOME EXPENDITURE SUCH AS HIRE OF FILMS, PROJECTORS, ETC.

THIS BY NO MEANS GIVES THE WHOLE PICTURE, BUT HOPE IT WILL SUFFICE TO ENLIST A PROMPT RESPONSE TO OUR APPEAL FOR URGENT RENEWAL OF YOUR SUB.

YOU MAY NOT BE AWARE, THAT ASSUMING A MAXIMUM RENEWAL OF SUBSCRIPTIONS, THE RESULTING INCOME WOULD NOT MAINTAIN THE ASSOCIATION FOR MORE THAN THREE MONTHS OF THE YEAR. WE WOULD THEREFORE WELCOME ANY ADDITIONAL CONTRIBUTION YOU MAY BE ABLE TO INCLUDE WITH YOUR SUBSCRIPTION.

(Supplement to AICD Newsletter, March 1971)

TEAR OFF, FILL IN AND RETURN IN ENCLOSED ENVELOPE.

AICD membership 1971:72

RATES: $5 YEARLY GENERAL.
$2 STUDENTS, PENSIONERS.
$10 ORGANISATIONS.

ENCLOSED:
: SUBSCRIPTION $.........
: DONATION $.........

AICD newsletter, March 1971

CPA papers/MLSLNSW/courtesy SEARCH Foundation

then, to convince those who agree with the cause to become involved by emphasising the benefits of participation, one of which is broader identification with a movement they agree with.[35] The Ex-Services Human Rights Association of Australia (ESHRAA) established two categories of membership to increase numbers, support and funds: associate membership for non-service people at $1 per year, alongside full membership for ex-military personnel at $2 per year.[36] This enabled ESHRAA to attract financial support from Australians who identified with the ex-service community that opposed the Vietnam War and conscription, as well as veterans who, owing to their wartime sacrifices, felt a sense of exclusivity.[37] These types of expansive fundraising tactics were not new to the Vietnam War period, but the intensity of feeling against the war and the number of supporters attracted to the cause meant that they were continuously tested and refined throughout the conflict.

A key method used by protest groups to raise funds was membership or sponsorship, and many included a cut-off slip in organisational newsletters, newspaper advertisements or other publications that prospective members could fill in and return, preferably with a donation or membership fees. The need to raise funds for the movement was a constant pressure, meaning the protest archive is filled with letters, leaflets, meeting minutes, advertisements and other documents appealing for financial support. Some collections include everyday receipts, as well as the vital cut-off slips and accompanying notes that allow us to see who was contributing to the movement. The AICD records held in the Mitchell Library include receipt books with donations as low as 20 cents (around $3.50 in 2026) or membership fees of $2 per annum, which entitled members to a monthly newsletter, bi-monthly journal, use of their reference library, and assistance with speakers or literature.[38] These slips are key to understanding the motivations or circumstances of the quietest activists.

Such everyday records are scarce in the archive. Founder and editor of the current affairs journal *Voice* from the 1950s, Harold Levien, wrote *Vietnam: Myth and Reality* in 1967, a short booklet addressing various 'myths' peddled by the federal government about the Vietnam

War.[39] On the back page of the booklet, Levien included a cut-off slip to be returned for further information, which does not appear in the listing of the Levien collection held in the Mitchell Library, limiting possible findings by eager historian or curious activist.[40] Yet these types of records reveal so much about how activists understand protest, and how public-facing or louder aspects of the movement are prioritised over quieter, but similarly essential, forms of protest such as fundraising.

I do not intend to castigate activists for their failure to keep receipts. For organisations such as AICD that were able to rent offices, as well as smaller groups who operated from private homes, keeping records beyond the period required for tax purposes was unlikely, owing to space limitations, or an aversion to clutter. Also, although some activists were paid for their time, most quiet protest occurring during the war was carried out by volunteers. Oppenheimer emphasises the gendered nature of such volunteering – men did the more 'active' work in the anti-Vietnam War movement, whereas women did more of the laborious administrative or clerical work.[41] Such work was perhaps more likely to be unpaid because as 'women's work' it was – and in many spheres continues to be – viewed as 'support' rather than 'activism'. Some such volunteers may have not been in a position to make decisions about the conservation of the records they were receiving, creating or distributing.

To diverge from the historian's constant preoccupation with the preservation and accessibility of records, those that do exist within the extensive anti-Vietnam War protest archive reveal much about the tactical ways protest organisations framed their need for volunteers, members and funds, as well as the effort required to raise funds. Organisations handled numerous donations, each of which – in the days before online banking and instant EFT transfers – required bank visits, individual deposits and the posting of separate receipts to contributors. Many smaller groups would engage in hierarchical fundraising, meaning they also collected money for larger groups or organisations, such as AICD or VMC. During the imprisonment and court cases of Bill White, the Bill White [Conscientious Objectors] Defence Committee received donations from SOS, Eureka Youth League and the Federal Pacifist Council of Australia, as well as religious groups such as the Anglican Parish of St John's in Cessnock, Methodist Central Mission, and the Christian Fellowship Association, among many others.[42]

Illustrating this process, Geoff Anderson of AICD wrote to the secretary of the Waverley Peace Committee (later Waverley Peace Group) Frank Graham, on 8 March 1966, asking if the group could 'once again take part in the current appeal for finance to enable us to further step up our activities in this cause so vital to Australia and the whole of the human race, the cause of world peace'. The committee conferred with its members, who pledged a total of $78. On 29 March 1966, Anderson again wrote to Graham, providing receipts and receipt numbers for four separate payments, each of which had necessitated travel to nearby banks.[43]

SOS was tactical in its fundraising efforts, clearly realising the importance of knowing your audience. According to long-term SOS Melbourne member Joan Coxsedge, SOS aimed to appeal to its 'largely middle-class support base', whose members were 'happy to attend meetings, write letters, organise fund-raising ventures among their well-heeled friends'.[44] Some who were new to activism found it less challenging to participate in quieter protest, at least until they became more comfortable operating in an activist space. The 1966 SOS leaflet 'Conscription is Wrong' used its message that 'every woman, every voter, has a responsibility to think deeply about conscription and Vietnam' to attract members, and included a cut-off slip on its back page for those interested to provide their details and donate 'towards costs of mailing', appealing to even those who had little to spare.[45] Mrs Myers of Avalon Beach sold stamps in the April–May 1971 SOS Sydney newsletter to raise funds.[46] SOS was not the only group that devised fundraising campaigns specifically catered to their audience. The Annandale–Petersham Moratorium Group raised funds through wine bottling to appeal to middle-class constituents who perhaps were less likely to get involved in protest in a more overt way.[47]

The Bradfield Anti-Vietnam War Committee, based on Sydney's North Shore, ran raffles, sold books and leafletted to raise funds for both AICD and its own activities, asking supporters for financial assistance to letterbox 5000–10 000 copies of a 'hard-hitting leaflet' during the 1968 Christmas period.[48] In 1969, the group suspended its activities, 'believing that the USA and its allies, including Australia, did genuinely mean to withdraw their troops and end the war in Vietnam'. In April 1970 it resumed fundraising for the Moratorium campaign and pledged support to the VMC, writing to members:

> Finance is urgently required to cover postage, stationery, roneoing costs, hire of halls, for meetings we hope to organise ... any money above our requirements will be donated to the Moratorium Campaign Committee to assist them with salaries of officers, rent, bringing speakers from overseas for the planned final mass gathering etc.

It also suggested a membership fee of 50 cents to 'help with future correspondence and/or donation to help in other activities which you yourselves may suggest', recognising that outreach activities could not take place without financial support.[49]

Hierarchical fundraising was often also a transnational affair. The US International Committee of Conscience on Vietnam (ICCV) was formed when the *New York Times* published its statement to political and military authorities that said, 'The horrors that your planes and massive firepower are inflicting on the people of Vietnam are beyond any moral or political justification'. By August 1967, this had been signed by approximately 10 000 clergymen worldwide. Its Australian Branch Committee, presided over by Methodist Minister Alan Walker, Presbyterian Gwyn Miller as secretary and Anglican Clive H Norton as treasurer, wrote to ministers and priests from a range of denominations asking them to sign the statement and join 120 Australian clergy who had joined the ICCV. It also asked for a donation of two dollars to 'allow us to communicate with you from time to time, giving information which may come to us', financing the Australian branch and strengthening the ICCV internationally.[50]

Organisations were clear in public communications about the vital role of funds to ensure their survival and aid the cause as a whole.

ICCV Vigil for Peace, Canberra 1967

Noel Hazard/*Tribune* collection/MLSLNSW/courtesy SEARCH Foundation

In its 20 June 1966 *Conscience* newsletter, ESHRAA wrote: 'In our present embryo stage of development, we need infusions of cash to help us keep going – to pay for stationery, postage, phone bills, hire of meeting rooms etc'.[51] Possibly the most direct appeals for funds, certainly due to their fervour and constancy, came from Vietnam Action Committee (VAC), which was open with supporters about 'financial embarrassments' caused by overcommitment to printing, mailing or otherwise distributing publications, and resulting debt. Supporters could not help but be aware of VAC's continuously precarious economic position. As early as December 1965, VAC declared on the front page of its newsletter: 'V.A.C. IN DEBT ONCE AGAIN', after printing a total of 70 000 copies of their first leaflet 'Why are we fighting in Vietnam?'. Those on VAC's 3000-strong mailing list were urged: 'Unless you want the Bailiffs in at V.A.C. please keep those donations rolling in'.[52]

VAC leaders were also expert at incorporating the cut-off slip to beseech supporters for funds. In a letter sent with the second issue of its journal *Vietnam Action*, Hall Greenland, Steve Johnston and Bob Gould laid out the costs incurred by a Sydney demonstration of 23 March 1966 at which ALP leader Arthur Calwell spoke. VAC paid over $700 for this rally, including postage of over $500, as well as costs of placards, silk-screened posters and hall hire, but due to torrential rain were only able to collect $415 on the day. Adding printing costs of $2000 and $900 for other expenses put VAC in desperate need of funds, which necessitated a cascade of cut-off slips on the last page of its letter. The range of suggested actions included selling copies of *Vietnam Action*, purchasing and distributing leaflets, donating either to the Vietnam Action Promotion Fund or general VAC funds, and sending a gift subscription.[53]

One way that VAC participated in cooperative fundraising was by distributing Bertrand Russell's case for an International War Crimes Tribunal and, after receiving a request to participate, planning an 'Australian hearing'.[54] Soon after, a notice to members declared that 'VAC NEEDS FUNDS URGENTLY' due to a 'temporary financial embarrassment' caused by the delay in payments for printing and distributing 30 000 copies of Eric Norden's 1966 leaflet *American Atrocities in Vietnam*. The VAC's 'embarrassment' was intensified by recent costs of $400 for its latest newsletter, $800 for leaflets, as well as for printing and distributing Bertrand Russell's 16-page pamphlet *War of Atrocity in Vietnam*.

VAC's eagerness constantly pushed it to the edge of insolvency, but at no point did it slow its enthusiastic spending. In 1969 it employed a part-time typist and an organiser 'to cope with our increased tasks', encouraging supporters to 'keep those donations rolling in'.[55] Gould shared in a 1974 interview that the VAC list had as many as 18 000 members in 1969 and 'between the cost of mailing and telephones the actual activists eked out a very scanty existence … all through the period myself and a couple of others worked full time and really lived on our own resources'. In Gould's case, this included the income brought home by his schoolteacher wife.[56]

SOCIAL FUNDRAISING

People are more likely to participate in protest activities if they are already embedded in 'everyday networks' of activism based on relationships with family, friends, work colleagues or neighbours. Although shared values and beliefs about key issues are important, action is often reliant on social networks creating emotional attachments that increase the possibility of participation and can prevent departure from the movement.[57] Fundraising initiatives, combined with 'spontaneous and self-organized' social events, such as parties and neighbourhood picnics, can create a solid base of close-knit activists. Vietnam-era protest groups knew this from past experience.[58] At the height of the 1950s panic around communism, when many in the peace movement were accused of leftism and support was more difficult to retain, everyday actions like social events, raffles and bazaars shored up support.[59] These efforts continued into the Vietnam War, when the strength of opposition to Australian involvement meant that activists from a range of areas, ages and classes became involved in the movement, and formed social networks.

Smaller groups regularly organised parties or barbecues to mark particular events. The Canterbury District Peace and Disarmament Committee celebrated its third anniversary in May 1965 with 'a very festive birthday party' in the home of Mr and Mrs Roy Kirby in the suburb of Punchbowl, with entertainment by 'top artists', including folk singers and soloists as well as dancing, games and refreshments, for only 5 shillings per person. Many such parties included a small charge to either cover costs or for broader fundraising purposes.[60] The Bradfield Anti-War Committee invited 'members and friends' to its December 1967 'social' in the Roseville garden of Mrs Roy Whitfield. The group had 'discussed at odd times the holding of a social but with the pressing job of being "Anti-Vietnam War", this rightly had a low priority. But after an active year, the executive decided we deserved one evening of relaxation and enjoyment'. A cover charge of $1 was requested, to pay for liquid refreshments, but guests were encouraged to 'bring your own meat to cook'.[61] Many similar events can be found in the protest archive, including the earlier mentioned Caravan against Conscription party of 1968 organised by the Rex Hewett Committee. In the same year, a Fairfield Peace Committee barbecue raised funds for AICD with a talk by Reverend John Beer and folk singing by Silvia and Tom Salisbury 'of "Reedy River" fame'. Resistance strategically organised parties after key events, such as the 13 April 1968 Radical Youth Movement forum and the 1968 May Day March.[62]

Resistance also organised larger-scale events, such as annual camps in rural NSW that included lectures on a variety of topics and the opportunity for socialising.[63] Similarly grand was the 1 May 1965 Peace in Vietnam Reception Cruise on the USS *Vancouver* organised by the Women's International League of Peace and Freedom (WILPF). This event, in the same month the HMAS *Sydney* departed Port Jackson with the 1st Battalion, Royal Australian Regiment (1RAR) for Vũng Tàu, was aimed at middle-class women who were unsure how to show their opposition at such an early stage of the war.[64]

VAC held a range of parties throughout the war, both at the Third World Bookshop on Goulburn Street and in private homes. On 23 October 1965, guests were instructed to 'bring your own grog' to a party in Woollahra.[65] High School Students Against the War in Vietnam, which was also based in the Third World Bookshop space, organised a party in 1969 at 67 Glebe Point Road near Broadway, telling guests to 'Bring your friends and bring your own … ', the last word intentionally omitted to avoid drawing attention to underage drinking. The group's purpose in holding the party was made clear in the invitation: 'We want to keep in touch and get the movement together', with a 40-cent charge to cover costs.[66]

During the Moratorium period, activists were encouraged to make use of social networks to broaden the message as far as possible, which is reflected in the increased variety and purpose of such events. On 5 December 1970, the Western Suburbs Moratorium Group organised a 'Bar-B-Que' with film night in a private home at 32 Waratah Street, Croydon Park, to attract new members. Guests were not charged an attendance fee, but were encouraged to bring their own steak and refreshments to watch the American anti-war film *In the Year of the Pig*, followed by a talk by former headmaster of Macquarie Boys High School and AICD committee member William Gollan.[67]

Liberal Reform Group and later Australia Party member Claire Ray reminisced about the diverse groups that gathered at the fundraising barbecues she held at St Anne's, the private hospital she established in Killara. At one 1970 event, there:

> Would have been a hundred at least. Locals and people from the network. And they paid to come ... There were people there from all walks of life: there were atheists, there were born agains, there were the traditional lot, there were others ... but they all got on well together. Nobody sort of worried about it. It was an incredible mix of people.[68]

Some with excessive work or family responsibilities lacked the capacity to attend social events organised by anti-war protesters, so other entertaining forms of 'everyday fundraising' were arranged, including raffles. AICD's Trade Union Committee held a 'Guessing Competition' in March 1967 that asked participants to fill in the missing words: 'Stop ... in Vietnam'. Tickets were sold for 10 cents each or 20 cents for 3, with the prize a transistor radio valued at $100.[69] The Moratorium Christmas Competition held by VMC in 1970 offered two Christmas hampers worth $50 and $30 as prizes and required entrants to fill in the missing letters: 'ST-P T-- W-R'.[70]

Selling books, booklets and journals spread the message while raising money for the cause, following a resolution made at the 1967 Anti-Vietnam War Anti-Conscription Activists' Conference to focus on 'literature distribution'.[71] Gould's Third World Bookshop, Freney's Liberation store, the offices of organisations such as AICD, which had an established reference library, and ad hoc stores set up during the Moratorium all sold anti-war publications. AICD regularly distributed lists of Australian and overseas publications that it held in its Sydney office, such as Jim Cairns' 20-page pamphlet *Vietnam: Is it Truth We Want?* and journalist Wilfred Burchett's *Vietnam: Inside Story of the Guerrilla War*.[72]

Third World Bookshop, 1965

Noel Hazard/*Tribune* collection/MLSLNSW/courtesy SEARCH Foundation

Gould opened the Third World Bookshop in 1967, the first of 12 attempts 'to establish a sustainable presence in the Sydney bookshop trade', which culminated in his final premises at Gould's Book Arcade on King Street, Newtown, where its façade is still visible to passersby. In Rowan Cahill's 2011 *Labour History* eulogy for Gould, he said Gould opened bookstores to ensure that the 'fragile' past did not 'disappear' or appear 'proscribed', and to provide activists with the knowledge required to engage in meaningful activism.[73] An advertisement from 1967 gives a sense of the space, describing 'a new kind of bookshop in Goulburn Street ... owned and operated by the Vietnam Action Campaign', that carried 'the widest range of radical literature Australia's ever seen' on topics as broad as Buddhism, anarchism, guerrilla warfare, feminism, capitalism, prison reform, colonialism, trade unionism and Black power.[74] In 1969, VAC said the 'Third World Bookshop has now become a focal point in Sydney ... As well as carrying the most comprehensive range of literature on Vietnam, the shop caters to the radical's taste in books and music generally'.[75] Professor Gary Foley has discussed the role of Gould's bookstore in supplying Redfern Black Power movement members with literature about anti-colonialist and revolutionary concepts.[76] Gould was a formidable and memorable member of the anti-Vietnam War movement – activist Margo Moore remembered the 'years and years' she spent 'going along to Vietnam Action Meetings' where 'nobody actually spoke to you except Bob Gould, who has this wonderful capacity to remember everybody's name and actually talks to people'.[77]

Groups with fewer resources opened collaborative stores. In May 1971, Community Aid for Peace converted an 'airy "attic" of a shop' into a 'shop-cum-public relations centre' including an art gallery and reference library, at 280 Pacific Highway, Hornsby, where Community Aid Abroad sold handcrafts and clothes, and Another Mother for Peace sold jewellery, bumper stickers and peace stationery. The groups viewed the store as 'a very important protest from a public relations point of view', asking for 'immediate financial help' to help set it up and pay their first rental payment of $31 per week.[78]

TAX RESISTANCE AND BOYCOTTS

War itself is a moneymaking venture. Much of the $218.4 million contributed by Australian governments to the Vietnam War from 1962–1972, comprising up to 4.5 per cent of gross national product (corresponding to over $2.6 billion in 2026), was funnelled back into Australian businesses.[79] This figure does not include the purchase of 'military hardware' that saw the total spent on the Vietnam War estimated by the CPA at over $1.13 billion (more than $15 billion in 2026), which it compared to the 'inhuman' increase of old age pension in 1970 from $15 per week to $15.50.[80] Some louder protests during the war were aimed at opposition to war-profiteering, including a July 1970 raid to post up anti-war slogans at the Sydney Stock Exchange led by *Tribune* editor Alec Robertson.[81]

Some activists expressed their objection to the vast sums spent on the war by withholding a percentage of their annual income tax debt equivalent to the proportion of government spending used for fighting in Vietnam. Tax resistance in the form of 'non payment of taxes, or withholding the part of taxes corresponding to military expenditure as a form of protest', was first discussed by activists on a national scale at the 1967 Anti-Vietnam War Anti-Conscription Activists' Conference, but consensus was not reached on a formal campaign.[82] Some carried out such actions individually. On 24 March 1968, Mrs MJ Holmes of Mosman wrote to the Deputy Commissioner of Taxation: 'for some years, I have paid under protest that portion of my income tax which is used for the Vietnam War … I have decided that I must do more, and that I will refuse any longer voluntarily to give the Government tax money for furthering its policy in Vietnam'. She sent the same amount to the Australian Red Cross to aid war victims in South and North Vietnam, writing:

> My withholding of tax money is obviously no more than token, but it is the only course open to me even remotely comparable with refusal to register under the National Service Act, a course which if I were a young man of military age, I should feel obliged

Activists taking over the Sydney Stock Exchange, 1970

Noel Hazard/*Tribune* collection/MLSLNSW/courtesy SEARCH Foundation

> to adopt. It is a patriotic duty to dissent by word and deed from policies which one believes to be both morally wrong and contrary to the interest of Australia.[83]

Holmes was not the only person who felt this way. The singer Glen Tomasetti also withheld a percentage of her taxes to protest the war, likely influenced by similar acts by American folk singers, including Joan Baez.[84]

Tax resistance was also proposed – unsuccessfully – as part of the Programme for the Continuing Moratorium Campaign presented at a 11 October 1970 VMC sponsors' meeting. Ken McLeod believed this was an impractical form of resistance:

> Such activity, aimed to organise large numbers of people to refuse to pay a proportion of their taxes equivalent to the percentage of war expenditure, ignores the fact that most wage earners in Australia pay tax by deduction. It also ignores the fact that few wage earners would be prepared to indulge in activities which would result in an enquiry into their tax returns over previous years.[85]

Withholding money through boycotts, a well-established method of pressing for political change, may have appealed to risk-averse citizens without the time or inclination for loud protest.[86] This method did not prove entirely popular during Vietnam, although some organisations proposed ideas. ESHRAA laid out two plans that aimed to reduce financial and labour investment in the commercial press, which persisted in projecting the government line on Vietnam. The first would provide for 'locally arranged groups', or people in workplaces such as schools, hospitals and factories, to purchase daily papers, 'making it unnecessary for staff members to buy their own', causing an overall 'depression of sales'. This would, in turn, be amplified by a concurrent boycott of major advertisers. Less viable, and perhaps also a little absurd, was 'a complete black-out on volunteered press releases and letters from [anti-war] organisations and individuals', causing a 'deepening silence' and imbalanced view of the war, which reduced press credibility.[87] Ultimately, as will be discussed in Chapter Eight, groups in the movement continued to use state and national newspapers to widen their reach.

USING LEGAL AVENUES TO PROVIDE FINANCIAL SUPPORT

Political opposition to the unprecedented use of loud protest tactics during the Vietnam War led to the introduction, amendment or reinterpretation of laws surrounding 'law and order' and national service to quell the noise created by activists across the country. Resisting political challenges to democratic protest generated significant legal costs and saw lawyers provide some of the more robust and impactful quiet support for those arrested for their activism. While Chapter Six discusses court-based voluntarism by members of the general public, here I focus on pro bono representation by lawyers themselves, which is frequently hidden within the machinery of larger organisations or groups.

The Inter-Church Committee on Peace in Victoria 1968 brochure *Note for the Conduct of Cases for Conscientious Objectors* provided advice for conscripts across the country about their right to object, how to request non-combatant duties, and legal procedure in conscientious objection court cases.[88] Similarly, the DCS brochure *The Ins and Outs of Conscription*, which had an initial print run of 50 000, provided legal options to young drafted men at all stages of the conscription process and supporters, as did the associated DRCC.[89] Legal experts evidently provided much of this information, but were not named.

Some organisations served as conduits between lawyers and activists. After the June 1971 Moratorium rally, Berenice 'Berry' Buckley wrote to the VMC with information to assist it to be as effective as possible in providing legal or other help after arrests. Buckley was the tireless secretary of the NSW Council for Civil Liberties, which was founded by her husband Ken in objection to the public use of excessive police force. She wrote that notice of arrests was frequently received too late to allow for meaningful legal response, so outlined bailing procedure and asked for at least seven days' notice if observers were required at demonstrations. She also requested that a lawyer sit by a telephone at the time of each rally to answer any queries and that VMC arrange for lawyers to be available at police stations.[90] To this day, the NSW Council for Civil Liberties urges legal practitioners to register with them to 'assist on the right to protest', and provides legal advice to anyone preparing to stage a rally or protest about how to keep within these laws.[91]

From its formation in August 1965, VAC set to work addressing its dissatisfaction with the lack of loud protest by quickly organising public demonstrations in 'a remarkable reactivation of the public sphere'.[92] A string of arrests at the second Martin Place Anti-Vietnam

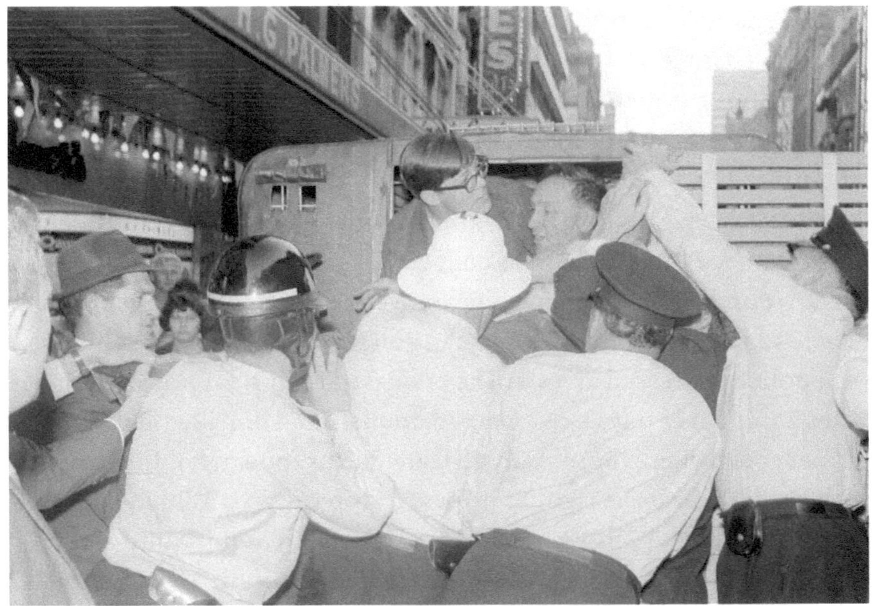

Police putting activists into vans on Martin Place, Sydney, 22 October 1965

Noel Hazard/*Tribune* collection/MLSLNSW/courtesy SEARCH Foundation

War Demonstration, organised by VAC on 22 October 1965, triggered formal legal responses by NSW activists to police opposition, including fundraising and direct representation. Most Australians at the time disapproved of any public demonstration, let alone those led by radical Trotskyists, meaning that police force against protesters would not attract much criticism. Increased arrests meant increased court time, necessitating legal representation.

The rally began at 5pm, and within half an hour more than 500 demonstrators had gathered, along with smaller counter-demonstrations by supporters of the war. Anti-war activists avoided these groups by peacefully marching along Pitt Street from Martin Place to Central Station but were blocked at the Pitt Street intersection by a slew of police and police vans. In response, 300 to 400 demonstrators sat down in the middle of the road, a tactic used at many public rallies today. This bold act attracted more police and led to 51 arrests, including

CPA General Secretary Laurie Aarons, for such charges as 'obstructing the free passage of a person', 'participation in an illegal procession', 'assaulting a police officer', 'resisting arrest' and 'using offensive language'. A group of men were placed into a police van and began chanting '1-2-3-4 we don't want war' while rocking the van from side to side. Others walked to Wynyard Park where over £100 (equivalent to more than $3300 in 2026) was collected to aid the campaign against the war. Around 150–200 people then moved to the Central Police Station, where supporters sat outside playing guitars as lawyers were summoned and police processed arrests. They released their final prisoner on bail after 2am. Three days later, many demonstrated outside the Liverpool Street court where those charged were due to appear, holding placards that read 'Defend the right to protest', 'Stop the war: Which is worse – blocking traffic or killing people?' and 'Demand inquiry into arrests'.[93]

A group of activists established the Vietnam Demonstration Defence Fund (VDDF) to raise legal funds of approximately £500 (equivalent to more than $16 000 in 2026) to pay fines in relation to this demonstration and provide legal representation in court cases that ran until February 1966. Lecturer in Economics and VDDF Chairman-Treasurer Dr John Child sent out a brochure to supporters, printed by the *Hellenic Herald*, acknowledging that while 'not everyone will necessarily agree with the policy of the Vietnam Action Committee … we hope all will agree that the right of peaceful public demonstration on matters of vital public importance must be defended at all costs'. VAC's ideological standpoint was evidently so unpopular that a note was added to the list of academics and unionists printed on the brochure saying they 'do not necessarily agree with the policy of the Vietnam Action Committee'.[94]

Undeterred, VAC announced in its next newsletter that 'Vietnam protests must go on', organising a rally for 14 December. By this time, 30 protesters had appeared in court for either obstructing traffic or using abusive language during the October demonstration, most receiving a £5 fine (more than $160 in 2026). VAC wrote that 'the Defence Counsel have put up an excellent showing in the Court, and have scored several legal victories, the most spectacular one being the dismissal of the charges of resisting arrest and assaulting a policeman, which were laid against Miss Kathleen Grimshaw'. It shared the rousing arguments used by barrister Jim Staples, who described the 22 activists who appeared in court on 22 November as 'serious people, exercising their right as a minority to express their point of view' and 'as they did not own newspapers or other mass media, they had no other outlet than a public demonstration'. Staples appealed to the court: 'if demonstrators were placed under any penalty that might hinder their future right to express a minority viewpoint it would place serious limitations on their democratic rights'.[95] Staples was paid by the VDDF but his willingness to put himself at risk of criticism by defending these activists was in itself a bold act of quiet protest.

On 7 March 1967, VDDF told supporters it had helped 11 activists who had been arrested during US President Lyndon Johnson's Australian visit in October 1966, but the funds raised had not covered legal costs, which had escalated after more arrests during the January 1967 visit of South Vietnamese Air Vice Marshal Nguyen Ky. The VDDF expressed continuing commitment to legal aid:

> In a democracy worthy of the name the people have a right to peaceful public protest against the policy of the government. In the exercise of that right, incidents are bound to occur, and there is a risk of arrest. The Committee feels strongly that people should not be deterred from participating by fear of heavy legal expenses. We intend therefore to continue to raise funds for this purpose.[96]

In late 1967, Child was replaced as president of the VDDF by Alec Fisher. Jack Mundey, secretary of the Builders Labourers Federation, spent a period as acting secretary-treasurer of the VDDF in 1967, and provided his union's building at 535 George Street, Sydney, as the VDDF base.[97] Funding was, however, hard to come by. On 3 July 1967, Child wrote to AICD about the VDDF's 'desperate financial straits' and present commitment to another $500 of legal costs, and asked whether AICD would mind returning $50 previously donated

Activist apprehended during President Lyndon B Johnson's visit to the Art Gallery of NSW, October 1966

Noel Hazard/*Tribune* collection/ MLSLNSW/courtesy SEARCH Foundation

by VDDF.[98] Four months later, Child and Fisher wrote a letter to thank supporters for the $800 total funds received in the previous year, and seek more support to fund appeals in the Magistrates Court for activists which had 'in several cases, resulted in a conviction being quashed, or the penalty reduced'. They wrote: 'By helping to defend people arrested in these demonstrations (sometimes on very slender evidence of misconduct) we believe that the Demonstration Defence Fund is doing an important job'.[99]

Throughout the war, activists sought legal advice for a variety of protest acts that drew the attention of political authorities and resulted in arrests. In 1970, convenors of the Manly–Warringah Vietnam Moratorium Committee, Phyl Latona and Denis Freney, were charged with publishing an 'obscene publication' and summonsed to appear in the Central Court of Petty Sessions on Liverpool Street. On a leaflet advertising the 8 May Moratorium, the Committee had reprinted a well-known image of an American GI holding up the remains of a Vietnamese boy's body, with the statement:

> The photo on the front of this leaflet was taken by a photographer, Bunyo Ishikawa of the major Japanese daily, ASAHI SHIMBUN. It shows the horror of the war. We do not apologise for publishing it. The whole war – and not just incidents like the My Lai massacre – is an atrocity.

Shortly before their 10 November court appearance, Latona and Freney distributed a statement saying that the VMC 'fully supports the decision of the Manly–Warringah Moratorium Committee to publish this photo', and that it had been published by Moratorium committees across the country, as well as in the *Tribune*.[100] They declared: 'If this photo is judged "obscene", then the actual act itself, which resulted in this horror, is a thousand times more obscene', labelling the war 'genocidal in nature'. In declaring that the 'political bankruptcy of the Gorton government is exposed by this charge', Latona and Freney pointed to the illogicality of political objection to a violent photograph, but not the violence itself.[101]

Demonstration about obscenity, 1970

Noel Hazard/*Tribune* collection/MLSLNSW/courtesy SEARCH Foundation

Soon afterwards, Freney was questioned by detectives about whether he had placed the 'obscene' leaflet on teachers' desks at his place of work, Mosman High School. Latona was also questioned, as was the company who printed the leaflet, Comment Publishers. The Waterside Workers Federation (WWF) Sydney branch executive provided Latona and Freney with legal support and openly challenged the NSW Liberal government to prosecute them for publishing the image in their *Special Branch News*. While Latona and Freney's case was being heard, WWF representatives and other supporters distributed the issue outside the courthouse in Liverpool Street, calling for full backing of the two defendants and others for opposing the war, which they said was the 'real obscenity'. The tokenistic nature of such charges was made clear when presiding Judge Lewer dismissed the case and discharged Latona and Freney.[102]

As arrests increased, particularly after the second Moratorium rally in September 1970, the VMC formed a Moratorium Legal Committee, 'as a result of police action and the threat of the "Law and Order" bill'.

In late 1970, its honorary secretary Leo Martin wrote to Moratorium sponsors that 'we need to prepare ourselves for the unexpected' and pointed to the need for additional funding, which was administered separately from the VMC: 'Obviously, sacrifices have to be made, financial as well as time ... any sacrifice we make is insignificant compared with the sacrifices made by the Vietnamese people in their struggle for national independence'. His letter was accompanied with a book of raffle tickets for sponsors to sell, the prize a Christmas hamper. Martin's decisive statement that 'we should see Court activities as an extension of the protest against the war in Vietnam' clearly shows that he considered legal support a quiet form of activism, and undoubtedly vital to the cause.[103]

Protest histories rarely highlight time, energy and funding as key elements of social movements, and discussions of money, accounting, banking and receipts can seem mundane. In reality, however, a continuous flow of money was needed for the anti-war and anti-conscription movements to run. Economies of protest movements are highly creative stories that emphasise everyday, and extremely human, aspects of activism. They also tell us much about how protest exists and thrives within a democratic and capitalist society. The next chapter progresses from a discussion of finances to focus on the necessarily corporeal nature of both loud and quiet activism by exploring direct uses of the activist body in crafting imaginative contributions to the movement.

CHAPTER FIVE

ACTIVIST BODIES

After hearing about New York's Angry Arts Week, which ran from 29 January to 5 February 1967, Sydney activists decided to run their own Arts Vietnam Week, and scheduled it for October 1968. Roger Milliss introduced the idea to readers of the *Tribune*: 'There's never been anything like Arts Vietnam before, with its art exhibition, poetry reading, string music recital, evenings of folk music, jazz and rhythm and blues and its "patchwork quilt of attitudes and realities" presented by some of Sydney's leading stage and TV actors'. This was, he thought, 'indicative of the deep unease running right through Australian society over the horrifying war of destruction in which Australia has become involved'.[1]

Arts Vietnam was another way activists could legitimate protest, as it included artists who were respected members of society, including revered painters Russell Drysdale, Arthur Boyd and Ian Fairweather; poets Robert Fitzgerald, AD Hope and Judith Wright; composers Richard Meale, Peter Sculthorpe and Nigel Butterley; and actor Peter O'Shaughnessy. Folk singer Marian Henderson predicted the event:

> Mightn't have much effect on government policy, but at least it should make people – all sorts of people – respect the protesters and try to understand why they feel as they do … After all, if you were rich enough to afford a Drysdale and you learned that Russell Drysdale was right against the war, it'd make you want to find out why, wouldn't it?[2]

On 9 October 1968, the ALP's Deputy Leader of the Opposition Lance Barnard highlighted the event in the House of Representatives, asking Liberal Prime Minister John Gorton whether he was aware of Arts Vietnam, the 'season of drama, music, poetry and painting', which included 'some of Australia's most distinguished artists'. He stressed the respectability of the participants, asking Gorton if he would 'concede that those who dissent from the Government's Vietnam policy include many of the most thoughtful and creative members of society?' Gorton responded: 'I cannot see any reason whatsoever why citizens who wish to express a particular point of view should not adopt this kind of method ... however wrong and misjudged I think that point of view may be', and reiterated his general view of protest as including 'violence, disrupting traffic or attacks on individuals or property'.[3]

Although Arts Vietnam was considered to represent a new type of protest in Australia, its combination of art and social activism reflected earlier communist-led efforts to integrate art into political traditions in the decades before the war. In the early 1930s, Andrei Zhdanov, secretary to the Central Committee of the Russian Communist Party, insisted that cultural production needed to incorporate the working classes as both subject and audience to effectively rally the population. CPA members were encouraged by this pronouncement to use their 'creativity as a political tool' to mobilise the general public to the leftist cause, leading to the formation of the Workers' Art Club (WAC) in 1932. In 1945, CPA leader Harry Gould reaffirmed the need to 'unite art and science with the labour movement', leading to the establishment of groups such as the Society of Realist Art, the People's Choir and the WAC theatre group, later known as the New Theatre.[4]

Artistic and cultural activism was considered a necessary facet of traditional protest events from the early years of the Vietnam War. A Youth Campaign Against Conscription (YCAC) newsletter of August 1967 said it was 'heartening to see the participation of academics, clergy and Australian artists in such numbers' in a recent Sydney protest, declaring that 'YCAC welcomes these new elements, and the associated broadening of the movement'.[5] As the war progressed, arts-based approaches were integrated to a larger extent in protest actions, often

Musical performances during Arts Vietnam Week, October 1968

Noel Hazard/*Tribune* collection/MLSLNSW/courtesy SEARCH Foundation

inspired by events in the US. This included the Moratorium campaign, which was well placed to harness past lessons about the value of creative activism. Many artists became involved in the rallies, and from the very first Moratorium of 8 May 1970 these events included a range of cultural activities, including 'pop and protest concerts', film screenings, street theatre and folk singing. Following the success of the first Moratorium, the decision was made across the country to 'go in for culture in a bigger way' for the second event on 18 September 1970, including events such as a mass meeting on UNSW Kensington campus lawns featuring musical performances and guerrilla theatre.[6] The October 1970 Draft Program for the Continuing Moratorium Campaign asked sponsors to compile 'a list of folk singers, poets, artists etc. who are available to assist Moratorium functions'. It also offered a portfolio of prints of six drawings, with works 'reproduced with artists' permission as a contribution to the Moratorium' from artists Russell Drysdale, Roderick Shaw, Louis James, Brett Whiteley, Tony Woods and Roy Dalgarno, for sale at $6 per set.[7]

A variety of artists chose to 'use and deploy their bodies in specific ways to achieve their political goals' during the Vietnam War. This practice held – and continues to hold – significant social and political power.[8] Its potency was demonstrated in February 2025 when, amid the ongoing political and public tensions over Palestine, the Australian Government's arts funding body Creative Australia revoked the selection of Lebanese-Australian artist and former Palestinian refugee camp community arts worker Khaled Sabsabi and his curator Michael Dagostino as representatives at the Australian Pavilion of the 2026 Venice Biennale. In the same week, news broke that the National Gallery of Australia (NGA) had covered up Palestinian flags that were part of the SaVĀge K'lub Te Paepae Aora'i artwork 'Where the Gods Cannot be Fooled'. In the fallout, the only visual artist on the Creative Australia Board resigned and protesters demonstrated outside the NGA. Sabsabi and Dagostino wrote: 'Art should not be censored as artists reflect the times they live in' and National Association for the Visual Arts Executive Director Penelope Benton said, 'when artists and their works are censored, it creates an environment where difficult topics are avoided, weakening the ability of the arts to spark important conversations and challenge perspectives'.[9] In May 2025, the Monash University Museum of Art, having followed Creative Australia's lead by suspending a group exhibition featuring Sabsabi's work, reversed its decision. In July, Creative Australia apologised to Sabsabi and Dagostino and reinstated them as Venice Biennale representatives. In October 2025, Creative Australia awarded Sabsabi a $100 000 grant for a solo exhibition at Adelaide's Samstag Museum of Art, which will also feature his exhibited Venice Biennale artwork.[10] Viewed from any angle, these events and actions tell us much about the influence of art within social movements.

Artists, including musicians, actors, dancers, writers, poets and filmmakers, strategically used their bodies as 'texts' to communicate political messages during the Vietnam War, in forums such as demonstrations, theatre productions, public lectures, concerts and games.[11] Protesters used their bodies to display the message by wearing anti-war or anti-conscription clothing, badges and armbands. The presence of silent bodies at vigils and within court rooms was powerful. Conversely, people created absence using their bodies, communicating dissent through walk-outs or strikes. This chapter focuses on the popularity of corporeal activism, beyond traditional protest marching and sit-ins, to explore the ways bodies became essential tools of social change.

SONGS AND MUSIC

Music, particularly folk music, was the most common artistic accompaniment to anti-Vietnam War protests. The use of songs and lyrics to communicate political messages, as well as to 'enjoy and celebrate collective identity', has a long history both internationally and within NSW – labourites began performing political songs in the open air on Sydney's public Domain in the late colonial period.[12]

The anthems beloved in trade union and communist circles began to develop a local flavour in the twentieth century. In 1944, New Theatre members formed the Unity Singers, and in the same decade Hilda Lane founded the Sydney People's Choir, part of the NSW Guild of Choirs. In the 1950s, a New Theatre production of the play *Reedy River* about the 1891 shearers' strike, originally staged in Melbourne and accompanied in Sydney by revivalist bush band The Bushwhackers, marked the 'crest of a wave of nationalist interest in folk and bush music'.[13] Young people were also exposed to music as political practice in the same period during Eureka Youth League school holiday camps which included singing and folk dancing.[14]

Vietnam-era protest organisations understood that music was a political entity and could attract the non-activist to the cause. On 28 November 1965, a coalition of groups including the Victorian ALP, Victorian Campaign for Nuclear Disarmament, Vietnam Day

Committee, Congress for International Cooperation and Disarmament, Melbourne University Folk Music Club, YCAC, and Blackburn Women for Peace held a free concert entitled 'Folk Songs with a Message – Songs of Peace and Love' at Melbourne's Myer Music Bowl. The groups collectively insisted 'there is a need for far greater intellectual and also spiritual understanding of the vistas opening up before youth … to this end, young people were given the chance for public self-expression in the idiom which they themselves have chosen – the folk song'.[15]

Protest organisations used this concert to spread the message, which included speeches by Anglican Reverend David Pope and Jim Cairns that were 'followed with close attention and drew appreciative applause from the audience'. The Vietnam Day Committee was very pleased with the event:

> We can be satisfied with the number of prominent people willing to be associated with this concert (including athletic trainer Percy Cerutty), with the singers willing to give their services free and with the great number of people willing to spend an afternoon listening to songs and messages of peace and in some measure, committing themselves to the free expression of protest.[16]

These sentiments were important in this early period of Australian involvement in the war. Anti-war marches or rallies would not have enjoyed such high attendance, but folk music attracted audiences who might otherwise have felt uncertain about engaging in acts of traditional protest. It is worth noting that, although the three-hour concert was attended by up to 10 000 people, it was not covered by commercial media outlets, which remained largely pro-war.[17]

Folk music became closely integrated into fundraising and educational activities. In January 1967, Glen Tomasetti travelled to the Anti-Vietnam Anti-Conscription Activists' Conference in Sydney to perform 'The Ballad of William White' and other songs.[18] In 1969, the Third World Folk Club – 'Sydney's only revolutionary Folk Club' – began in the Third World bookshop on Goulburn Street, with the support of Resistance.[19] The Bradfield Anti-Vietnam War Committee held a Folk

Night in the basement of St Anne's Hospital, Killara, on 12 September 1970 to raise funds to 'help make the September Moratorium a success'. It included anti-war performances by David White and Don Hopkins and a lecture by Macquarie University student Randy Nielson about the 'student's view of the Vietnam War and social action'.[20]

PLAYS, THEATRE AND DANCE

'Theatre' has a broad definition, particularly in the activist context.[21] Novel public protest tactics favoured by the New Left, such as sit-ins, teach-ins, picketing or paint throwing, created spectacle and were 'theatrical' in their very nature.[22] Although such theatre was used effectively during the Vietnam War, here I will focus solely on traditional theatrical performance, which built on a long history of using the stage to communicate political messages and comment on a range of social justice issues that continue to this day.[23]

In Australia, theatrical performance as activism increased in scale from the 1930s, largely through communist channels. The New Theatre was first instituted in 1932 as the Sydney Workers' Art Club, and aimed to 'secure the widest possible co-operation with all associations aiming at social justice', reflecting the CPA mission to unite all leftists in society to strengthen the movement.[24] From 1954 to 1968 it worked within the Waterside Workers' Federation (WWF) Cultural Committee and while it was based at the WWF federal offices in Phillip Street, Sydney, it frequently performed in the Teachers Federation Auditorium on Sussex Street.[25] At the time of writing, it is based in Newtown and remains Australia's longest-running theatre group.

During the Vietnam War, the New Theatre was associated with many 'systematically organised' events to boost support for the cause, both within or external to the New Theatre and involving a range of well-known artists. The Vietnam Action Campaign was particularly eager to integrate theatre into wider protest activities, and as early as 25 February 1966 organised a Theatre Party that featured the New Theatre revue *You Never Had it So Good*, which satirised Australian and US policies

Sit-in at the United States Consulate, Sydney, August 1967

Noel Hazard/*Tribune* collection/MLSLNSW/courtesy SEARCH Foundation

on Vietnam.[26] New Theatre Melbourne's 1967 play *On Stage – Vietnam* was performed across the country to sold-out audiences, and in Sydney was presented by the Bradfield Anti-Vietnam War Committee to an audience of over 250 people, raising $280.75 (over $4000 in 2026).[27] The Bradfield group also staged 'A Satirical Revue by the Humanist Players' at St John's Hall in Gordon on 24 May 1968 as a 'relatively painless way ... to raise funds'. They urged supporters to 'bring a party of friends to the revue', trying to encourage attendance by asking them to 'remember how you enjoyed yourselves at our sponsorship of "On Stage Vietnam"!'[28] In the same year, Thomas Kenneally's play *Childermas* was commissioned by the Australian Committee of Responsibility for Children in Vietnam and performed for the first time at the Old Tote Theatre at UNSW.[29] Such events helped protest organisations connect with the general public and expand the movement. The Sydney University Labor Club declared in December 1969 that the way forward was not sit-ins, or law-breaking, but to 'attempt to relate our protests to the power structures of Australian society', and made specific mention of 'guerrilla theatre' as one way to ensure 'more support … from the working class'.[30]

The stage was also used for another subversive art form – dance. The corporeality of dance has long been used to 'critique our current condition' and 'mirror bodily responses to social and political issues' through 'its capacity to resist, insist, invent'.[31] In 1967, Sydney's War and Peace Study Group promoted a fundraising performance by The Spectacular Mazowsze Dance Company, a renowned folk troupe instituted by the Polish state in 1948 to advance 'socialist realism'.[32] One week before the second Moratorium, the Margaret Barr Dance-Drama Group performed five dances in the Teachers Federation Auditorium, accompanied by a range of musical and spoken-word performances – the VMC sold tickets to this 'Contribution to the Moratorium' for $1 from its office at 232 Castlereagh Street.[33] Barr, a performance movement director, had worked on the New Theatre's *On Stage Vietnam* in 1967, illustrating the interconnected nature of artistic performance and political protest.[34] Dancers also performed alongside musicians, as was the case with the Newtown Moratorium Group's International Folk Concert at Redfern Town Hall where 'short talks on conscription and Vietnam' were interspersed with folk dancing led by the aforementioned Lambrakis Youth Choir.[35] The ability of dance to communicate political messages or attract non-activists to the cause was well-recognised within the NSW anti-war movement.

'PLAY AND PROTEST'

The twenty-first century understanding of games and gaming has vastly changed from the Vietnam era, but a contemporary interpretation of video games as 'communicative artifacts' that allow us to 'submerge ourselves in alternative agencies designed by another' can still be applied to the way that anti-war groups used traditional games to aid the cause.[36] Games were integrated into fundraising events. In November 1966,

Peaceful Pawns Chess Club, 1968

Noel Hazard/*Tribune* collection/MLSLNSW/courtesy SEARCH Foundation

Mr and Mrs Andrews, who lived on Veterans Parade at Narrabeen, hosted the Manly–Warringah Union of Australian Women (UAW) for an evening of games, guessing competitions and quizzes to communicate knowledge about the war in a relaxed setting and 'help finance publicity against the Holt Government's policy of war in Vietnam'.[37]

A more sustained use of gaming to spread the message emerged through the formation of the Peaceful Pawns Chess Club by Sydney chess champion Alfred Flatow of Belmore in 1968. He invited 'all opponents of the Government's Vietnam policy (Australian participation in Vietnam) who are also interested in chess' to join. The club was formally affiliated with AICD and met every Monday at their Sydney rooms.[38] This was another example of hierarchical fundraising: club membership was set at $5, including affiliation with the NSW Chess Association, but prospective members were encouraged to spend an additional $3 to become AICD members, while non-AICD members were charged 20 cents for each competition night.[39] In August 1968, Flatow, along with Victorian chess champion Trevor Hay and former Sydney champion Max Fuller, charged $1 entry to a fundraising event at the Teachers Federation Auditorium to aid their participation in the upcoming Chess Olympiad while raising funds for AICD – the proceeds were divided equally.[40]

Hay told *Tribune* the group formed because 'a number of us with similar views, who are members of the AICD, noticed the large number of chess players who turned up at peace demonstrations and decided to form a club, so as to kind of play and protest; this is the result'.[41] Modern-day gamers use similar tactics – early in 2025, some 120 000 users of the popular online game Roblox, mostly children, staged an online rally in which their avatars marched through fictional streets carrying Palestinian flags, to call for a ceasefire in Gaza.[42]

WRITERS AS ACTIVISTS

In 1966, as conscripts were sent to Vietnam, 58 Australian writers issued a statement collectively labelling the policy morally questionable because the war was not 'decisively supported by the Australian community'.[43] Many Australian writers in the period struggled against the prevalence of anti-communist and colonialist rhetoric, finding that 'life and literature were confounded'.[44] The CPA had long been committed to nurturing literature, founding the Realist Writers' Association (RWA) in Melbourne, and then Sydney, to foster the production of literature 'written about the working class, by the working class, for the working class'.[45] The RWA became the Australasian Book Society in the 1950s. The CPA's Arts Committee leader Ray Clarke said this was 'a deliberate Communist Party decision ... because there were so many people who couldn't get published' due to widespread anti-communism in society.[46] Such focused support means that the 'print culture connected to Australian communism is surprisingly rich', according to Anthony Ashbolt and Rowan Cahill.[47]

Not all writers and poets who committed themselves to protest were aligned with communist networks and organisations. During Arts Vietnam Week in 1968, the poet Roland Robinson said that he became involved from a sense of responsibility to civic values:

> Arts Vietnam could bring home to the public at large that there were 'responsible and articulate people – leading people' who denounced the war ... creative artists have got a special responsibility to speak out on issues like this. Remember what Shelley said about poets? That they're trumpets who sing into battle, the unacknowledged legislators of the world. Or Plato? That if the world had poets and philosophers for rulers it'd be a far better place.[48]

The Northern Districts Vietnam Moratorium Group encouraged newer writers to express their own activism with a peace-themed poetry competition in April 1970. Its popularity encouraged the VMC to hold a Sydney-wide competition for both adults and school children, judged by University of Sydney English academics Professor Leonie Kramer, Dr Jim Tulip and Philip Roberts.[49] It was an effective strategy for recruiting non-activists to the campaign. One entrant, 19-year-old clerk David Ailwood of Normanhurst, attached a note to his piece that said, 'I am not yet a member of the Moratorium campaign, however, I shall endeavour to correct this grevious [sic] error in the very near future', and asked to be sent Moratorium badges.[50]

The literary community was a critical voice throughout the war. At the 'People's Parliament' in November 1970, Sydney poets recited their works to a large group of 'pensioners, doctors, teachers, conservationists, politicians, [A]borigines, women and others' at an 'extensive street production' at Parliament House that was organised by ANU students and academics to support the Moratorium.[51]

Literature continues to provide a bridge between activists and the wider community. As Lebanese-Palestinian poet Hasib Hourani wrote in his 2024 collection *rock flight*:

> It's difficult to articulate what we can do from the global north but essentially, it's to choke back: boycott, stop traffic, turn a ship around, flood the train station. cut off the air supply of imperialism. this is why I fixate on suffocation. this is why I turned it into a book.[52]

Today, technology extends the reach of writers. On 29 November 2023, more than 30 independent presses, poets, writers and translators worldwide, including Pamenar Press, Kyklada Press, Stenen Press and Tamaas, hosted a Global Reading for Freedom of Expression and Solidarity with Palestine and Lebanon, during which readings and performances were livestreamed for 24 hours on YouTube and called for 'global solidarity through poetry, language and collective resistance'.[53]

FILMS AS PROTEST

Protest groups used film screenings to spread the anti-war message and raise funds. Film had been part of the leftist toolkit in Sydney since at least the 1950s, when the WWF Film Unit was formed by New Theatre members Jock Levy, Keith Gow and Norma Disher. It emulated Melbourne's Realist Film Unit, established in 1945 by RAAF veteran Ken Coldicutt.[54] The 1967 Anti-Vietnam War Anti-Conscription Activists' Conference identified film screenings as a specific tactic to gain support for the anti-war effort, particularly from rural areas.[55] Groups screened an array of war and non-war related films. Resistance screened movies like Jean-Luc Godard's *A Bout de Souffle* and the Czech director Pavel Jurácek's *Every Young Man* during their regular film nights.[56]

Freda Brown, a communist best known for her UAW and Women's International Democratic Federation (WIDF) leadership, was also involved with the New Theatre and helped facilitate film screenings to raise funds for Vietnamese medical care. After the International Committee of Solidarity with Vietnam agreed to fund a 100-bed

Hanoi Obstetrics and Gynaecology Hospital in North Vietnam in 1969, the UAW campaigned for six years to raise funds for the hospital, selling tens of thousands of Vietnam badges and screening films about Vietnam, which Freda brought back to Australia.[57] One such screening was the Australian premiere of *Life in North and South Vietnam*, held at the Building Workers' Industrial Union building at 535 George St, Sydney, on 4 September 1970, with light refreshments.[58]

Other groups campaigning around the Moratoriums screened films to educate and attract people to the cause. In the months preceding the first Moratorium rally, the VMC published a list of anti-war films distributed through AICD and the Committee of Responsibility for the Children of Vietnam to aid local groups in fundraising, such as *Far From Vietnam*, *Arts Vietnam* and *Hearts and Minds*.[59] This central assistance fostered events like the 'marathon anti-war film night' of 25 June 1970, held at the Presbyterian Church Hall on Evaline Street in Campsie, which was organised by a range of youth groups. *Inside North Vietnam* and *Threatening Skies* were shown alongside a short lecture by AICD's Bruce Gordon, with refreshments provided.[60]

Political authorities understood the propaganda value of anti-war films. ASIO paid close attention when *Tribune* announced in March 1965 that Moscow had agreed to support the Australian anti-Vietnam War movement by supplying anti-war books and films.[61] In August 1968, a screening of *Inside North Vietnam* at the Dispensary Hall in Chatswood organised by the Bradfield Anti-Vietnam War Committee was banned, even though the same film had been earlier screened in Gordon. The Bradfield committee insisted that political action and 'use of powers' were 'both arbitrary and politically discriminatory in nature'.[62]

WEARING PROTEST

The body is a versatile tool of political protest and, to 'construct compelling images that attract media attention', activists wear badges, clothing with political slogans and engage in bolder acts, including 'unclothing'.[63] Australians opposed to the war in Vietnam and to conscription wore anti-war materials, such as badges, stickers, jewellery, armbands or political clothing. The Ex-Services Human Rights Association of Australia (ESHRAA) drew attention to its veteran identity to enact 'respectable' protest by displaying RSL badges, service ribbons and medals while protesting.[64] As its newsletter *Conscience* recommended in 1966:

> Members should consider wearing a piece of black ribbon, or a cut-out black V (for Vietnam), in place of a badge – to signify sorrow at Australia's involvement in the Vietnam War and sympathy for all who are suffering because of the war. Members are invited to display this discreet sign of protest as they go about their daily activities. (It can even be worn behind an existing badge – RSL, Scout, Rotary etc).[65]

In this instance, 'wearing protest' did not just communicate anti-war messages but a certain cultural authority.

In the Moratorium period, activist bodies were used as texts more intentionally to broadcast the anti-war message to a mass audience. In February 1970, the VMC suggested that sponsors wear black armbands to mourn victims of war and demonstrate their opposition to Australian involvement in Vietnam. The Teachers' Vietnam Moratorium Group encouraged teachers to wear black armbands and badges during Moratorium Week of 3–10 May, and especially on 5 May, 'Teachers' Day'.[66] The NDVMG also asked its members to wear black 'mourning' chrysanthemums during the first Moratorium rally.[67]

Ahead of the first Moratorium rally, the VMC distributed lists of items activists might wear, indicating the extent to which such ideas had been accepted. It produced 15 000 self-adhesive stickers displaying the Moratorium symbol and date, 2000 badges and 20 000 armbands with the symbol and the words 'Vietnam Moratorium – Withdraw All Troops from Vietnam Now', as well as 15 000 car stickers with the symbol and 'Get out of Vietnam Now', which were sold by a range of organisations including AICD and UAW.[68] By the second Moratorium, the Castlereagh Street VMC office was also selling Moratorium dress pins and brooches.[69] Badge-wearing was so ingrained during the period that after the ALP failed in an attempt to delay Friday sitting dates to enable attendance at the 8 May Moratorium, politicians turned up to Federal Parliament wearing Moratorium badges.[70]

Amanda Tattersall, formerly of the National Union of Students and Unions NSW, has argued that badge-wearing is 'a mechanism for broader understanding about a campaign' and allows people who are uneasy about protest to show their political stance in a low-risk way.[71] Badge-wearing was a non-confrontational way to communicate the anti-war message and attract publicity.[72]

Some, however, treated badges as subversive. In April 1970, Principal Smith at Ibrox Park Boys High – which was from 1976 Leichhardt High, and since 2000 Sydney Secondary College – removed 40 books the school librarian Mrs Vaughan-Taylor had purchased about South-East Asia and Vietnam, claiming that they had a 'leftist bias'. Smith also objected to the wearing of Moratorium badges on school grounds, and soon afterwards suspended a school prefect for wearing a Moratorium badge 'as a protest against library censorship'. Smith took the view that the badge would divide the school, asserting that students wore Moratorium badges because they were being manipulated by protest organisations.

This dramatic response, and other cases at Sydney schools, attracted the attention of the Teacher's Moratorium Group, VMC, the Teachers Federation, the NSW Department of Education and the media. On 16 April, the *Australian,* which by 1970 was presenting a less hawkish view of the Vietnam War, reported that 'teachers at several Sydney high schools have been barred from distributing pamphlets or wearing political button badges, distributed by the Vietnam moratorium organisers'.[73] This included Manly Boys High School, where three students were suspended for wearing a Moratorium badge. Of these was 16-year-old Michael Cooke, who claimed he was being discriminated against because teachers and other students continued to wear the same badge. Ray Gardiner, a teacher, was asked to remove the badge, which he refused because, in his words, 'to me it was a personal, non-political thing, and besides there are at least half a dozen other teachers at the school wearing them openly'. On the same day, the *SMH* revealed that the issue over badges had spread to Fort Street Boys' High School and Castle Hill High School. One Castle Hill student told reporters: 'There are a group of students who feel something should be done about the Vietnam War. I cleaned my bag because scholarships are at stake here, but I will continue distributing leaflets outside the school'.[74] On 18 April, it was reported that Mr Bardwell, a teacher at St Patrick's College and ALP nominee for the seat of Goulburn, resigned after being asked to remove his Moratorium badge while teaching.[75]

The NSW Education Minister Charles Cutler responded to these events by declaring that 'party politics' should not be discussed in schools, and the *SMH* reported on 16 April that he was likely to 'take a strong stand against teacher participation in moratorium activities in schools'. In a press statement, the Teachers Moratorium Group objected to the intimidation of students and staff wearing protest badges, insisting that badges were not introducing politics into schools, as 'party politics are already there' through the 'dangerous' practice by the School Cadet Corps of presenting militarism 'to school boys as a "life adventure"'. They wrote:

> Today's senior school students are not little children to be protected from public controversies. They are nearing the age when they can be conscripted, and will soon have to vote. They are required to read widely, exercise judgement and think clearly about current matters.[76]

The VMC felt these events warranted official comment and wrote to all high school principals on 16 April 1970 to say they were:

> very disturbed by press reports during the last few days concerning intimidatory action by some Secondary School Principals against students and teachers wearing Moratorium badges ... The Moratorium Secretariat believes that any such

> intimidatory action represents a serious threat to the civil liberties of secondary teachers and the students they teach.[77]

The VMC lamented 'official' thinking in schools, and stated that 'every Secondary School principal has a responsibility to facilitate and promote the free and open discussion of all matters of public contention within the school environment' and that if they 'impede such discussion' they could be 'inviting legal action by the parents of the students involved'.[78]

The suspension of Robert Colley and three other boys at Ibrox Park after Anzac Day of 25 April amplified the controversy. Principal Smith objected to the badges on the grounds that they were sourced from an outside organisation, but Colley told Tharunka in an article titled 'The Rise & Fall of the Ibrox Reich' that he viewed them merely as 'a symbol of an event and … a statement of his personal conviction and conscience'.[79] Colley agreed to remove the badge as long as the rule about badges was reconsidered, however Smith decided the ban would remain.

As school vice-captain and winner of a special school award, Colley was a high achiever and evidently popular among students. The day after his suspension, 40 students bought and wore Moratorium badges to school. On 6 May *Tribune* reported that the NSW Department of Education was yet to respond to the range of suspensions occurring across the state, but 'many other principals and teachers believe the suspensions are "foolish" and unjustified'. They also reported that 'many students say they are entitled to express their concern about a war for which, in a very few years, they may be conscripted'.[80]

Two weeks later, *Tribune* again addressed the badge issue, pointing to the 'contradictory positions' taken by the Department over badge-wearing.[81] At Fort Street Boys High School five students had been suspended for refusing to remove badges, and one of them was David Colley, Robert's younger brother. Three days before the 8 May Moratorium, after 'several parents had made protests in person', Minister Cutler directed all five Fort Street suspensions be lifted, but the boys continued to wear their badges at school. The Department did

Ibrox Park students protest in June 1970

Noel Hazard/*Tribune* collection/MLSLNSW/courtesy SEARCH Foundation

not comment on the Robert Colley issue at Ibrox Park, but the decision appeared to be supported by Education Minister Cutler.

On 25 May 1970, Teachers Federation executive members interviewed Principal Smith, reminding him that the Federation had carried a resolution in April that students in schools should not be prevented from wearing the Moratorium badge and that 'no student or teacher should be subject to embarrassment or discrimination for doing so'.[82] This did nothing to ease the situation at Ibrox Park. On 5 June, teacher Mr Caffrey accosted Teachers' Moratorium Group members who were demonstrating outside the school and ripped up leaflets they were distributing about the Colley issue and on the removal of the library books. He chased one woman across a road while shouting 'Right boys, let's rumble the commie trash'. He also attacked Mrs Vaughan-Taylor, who was 'continually subjected to a barrage of insults'. According to *Tharunka*, Caffrey described himself 'as the spokesman for the silent majority of the staff'.[83]

The following Monday, 8 June, Smith told teachers they were not allowed to make phone calls during working hours – he was afraid that teachers would leak information to the press. On the Tuesday, Smith informed students that a televised protest demonstration was to take place outside the school that same afternoon, which prompted four boys to hold placards in front of cameras reading 'No Fascism in Schools'. Two of the boys were suspended and one was warned.[84] By Wednesday 10 June, students, teachers and parents were demonstrating outside Department of Education offices.

Two weeks later, Colley's mother Barbara authored a *Tribune* article that objected to the accusations she was being 'divisive':

> May I point out that Ibrox Park Boys' High School is now more divided than it would ever have been if Robert had been left alone to wear his badge as the quiet act of conscience that it was. It is not the badge that is divisive but the high-handed and undemocratic manner in which it has been treated.[85]

The Teachers' Moratorium Group agreed: 'the reality is that these same students who may not express their moral convictions by wearing a moratorium badge will probably be able to vote next year' – a reference to incoming changes lowering the voting age from 21 to 18, which was eventually passed through an amendment to the *Electoral Act* in 1973. They also wrote:

> The whole question of objection to the badge as 'political' and objection to politics in schools can be reduced to the simple point that though the wearing of the badge and opposition to the war is in many cases on moral grounds, it has been dubbed as 'political', simply because the Liberal Government supports our involvement in the war.[86]

The politicisation of school-aged teenagers concerned those in conservative circles. In September 1970, Peter Coleman, *Quadrant* editor, former *Bulletin* editor and a future leader of the NSW Liberal

Opposition, self-published the booklet *School Power in Australia: Is Your Child Being Manipulated by Political Operators?* An amusing write-up in *Tharunka* entitled 'Coleman power – are your parents being manipulated by parliament?' critiqued his 'lack of analysis' and concluded that Coleman was merely fearful of the 'growing level of consciousness among high school students' who 'now form, then try to express, their own ideas'.[87]

The issue received more attention in early 1971, when the NSW Department of Education used their powers to influence the future employment opportunities of some of the students involved. It refused Robert Colley a Teacher's Training Scholarship on the basis he would not be 'cooperative', even though he had earned a Commonwealth scholarship that was based on excellent examination results. The Teachers Federation 'strongly condemned the refusal of a teacher training scholarship to Robert Colley and called on the Minister for Education to rescind the decision', calling it 'clearly discriminatory, politically motivated and contrary to the long-held belief of the Federation that persons engaged in teaching within the public education system must have full civil rights without fear of discrimination or persecution'. They stated that 'there could only be one reason for his rejection – his involvement in Moratorium activities'. Colley added, 'I am sure the staff and students of my school would not have elected me class captain, prefect and school vice-captain if any of these charges were true nor would I have been given the school prize for service and co-operation'.[88]

A student from a Sydney girls high school had also been refused a Teacher's Training Scholarship the previous year. As the letter refusing her application made no mention of her academic record, the *Canberra Times* concluded the refusal was connected to her involvement with the Moratorium.[89] Despite widespread protests in support of the democratic rights of students and teachers, this recrimination shows badge-wearing, as a symbolic action to oppose war was powerful.

Similar disputes between students, teachers, the Teachers Federation and the NSW Department of Education have broken out over the wearing of the *keffiyeh*, a headdress traditionally worn by Bedouin men that has been associated with Palestinian nationhood since the first half of the twentieth century. Wasim El-Haj, a Palestinian-Australian teacher at Sydney Girls High School, had worn a *keffiyeh* to work for many years and had been asked to wear it at a school multicultural day, but was told in May 2024 he was no longer able to wear it to school because 'all symbols of Palestine are considered symbols of conflict'. El-Haj appealed to the NSW Department of Education, which upheld the views of Sydney Girls High School. The NSW Teachers Federation State Council, as well as a series of smaller associated groups, passed a motion that asserted the rights of teachers to wear the *keffiyeh* to work, and resolved not only to contact El-Haj with support but to write to Department of Education Secretary Murat Dizdar and Education Minister Prue Car.[90] This event, as well as the barring of a student from his Year 12 formal unless he apologised to the school for wearing the *keffiyeh* to graduation, prompted a series of rallies at the NSW Department of Education in Parramatta by Teachers and School Staff for Palestine, among others.[91]

SILENCE AND ABSENCE

Although the activist presence is crucial to the success of social movements, the intentional silence or absence of bodies can 'convey political ideas, demand changes, and exert pressure'.[92] Activists strategically placed their bodies in silent vigils and court rooms or other law enforcement settings to achieve various aims of the anti-war movement. In some cases, the absence or removal of bodies, through actions such as strikes or walk-offs by workers, were used to draw attention to the cause.

Silent vigils have a relationship to 'loud' protest, as some of their public-facing intentions overlap with the traditional rally, but the inclusion of the silent body creates impact by presenting a counterpoint to popular perceptions of activists as unruly or disreputable. Silent vigils were used by religious groups from the early years of Australian involvement in Vietnam. Methodist Reverend Alan Walker's

Committee for Canberra Vigil, which included 19 ministers from a range of religions, held its first event at Parliament House on 20 May 1965, to bring the government's actions 'before the bar of public conscience'.[93] The Committee, based at 138 Castlereagh Street, Sydney, invited 'as Christian citizens ... men and women from every part of Australia who share our convictions to join with us in an act of silent witness before the Federal Houses of Parliament'.[94]

Catholic Bishop of Wagga Wagga Francis Carroll also became involved in silent vigils throughout the war, marching with the Young Christian Students Group for Peace in 1970, a daring move in the face of the influence within Australian Catholicism of the decidedly pro-war National Civic Council, headed by BA Santamaria.[95] The silent vigil was also effectively used by Save Our Sons (SOS), who gathered outside army depots while conscripts were being inducted.[96]

Silence, combined with the presence of the predominantly middle-class 'respectable' woman, within a movement publicly characterised by unruliness and violence, was an intentional tactic that had a significant impact.

Two overlapping organisations established during the war to hold silent vigils were the Vietnam Candlelight Vigil and the Vigil Organising Committee (initially called the Vigil Committee). The latter group held an All-night Protest Vigil on 20 April 1966, the night before the state's first conscripts for Vietnam were to march in Sydney. The Vigil Committee evidently wished to prevent negative media attention that positioned protesters against soldiers and their families, telling supporters:

> This protest is not directed against members of the armed services or relatives and friends who may be shortly assembling to wish them a safe and speedy return. Our protest is directed against the Federal Government's Vietnam policies, especially its military commitment of 20 year old conscripts.[97]

The Vigil Organising Committee later instituted a silent vigil in Wynyard Park, every Wednesday at lunchtime, which was supported

Save Our Sons Weekly Vigil for Peace, April 1967

Noel Hazard/*Tribune* collection/MLSLNSW/courtesy SEARCH Foundation

by a range of organisations, including ESHRAA.[98] Such vigils continued throughout the war and were particularly popular during the Moratorium period, as was the case with a silent vigil at Hornsby Shopping Centre on 12 September 1970 promoted by Catholic David Mallick and Congregationalist John Munson.[99]

Activists also placed their silent bodies within the legal system as a deliberate tactic. This was used by the Committee in Defiance of the National Service Act, which intentionally breached the *Crimes Act*, and by groups such as SOS and the Vietnam Objectors' Group, which regularly attended court cases involving conscripted young men.[100] Their physical presence within courts was intended as a statement of opposition to conscription, and will be further discussed in the voluntarist context in Chapter Six.

Anti-war messages were also communicated via the strategic removal of activist bodies, through traditional strikes or work stoppages usually by key unions connected with the CPA and broader peace movement. When the government first announced that combat troops would be sent to Vietnam in early 1965, the Building Workers' Industrial Union called for their withdrawal, and the WWF staged a 24-hour strike in Sydney Harbour, holding up 37 ships. At this time, only a relatively small number of unions had majority memberships opposed to the war and this limited participation in protest.[101]

After Seamen's Union of Australia (SUA) members refused to load and man the ships *Boonaroo* and *Jeparit*, which contained *materiel* and weapons bound for Vietnam, the resulting stand-off within the union movement prompted the federal government to intervene. On 12 May 1966 the SUA Federal Executive voted to refuse any government request to man the *Boonaroo* or any other ships carrying goods to Vietnam, on the basis that such a request equated to recruiting civilian workers into the war effort. Six other maritime unions operating from Sydney opposed this action. The WWF offered to provide workers to load the ship, despite its strong ties with the CPA and peace movement. Importantly, few SUA members were opposed to manning the ship but all were reluctant to break with union policy. The ACTU, eager to avoid alienating influential pro-war unions like the Australian Workers Union, called a meeting of seven maritime unions in Sydney. It quickly became apparent that the SUA's only supporters were a small group of members of the Victorian branch of the Shipwrights and Constructors' Association who were acting in opposition to its federal executive.

The SUA eventually conceded defeat and manned the ship but in February 1967 members again walked off the *Boonaroo*, this time in Melbourne, after learning that it carried munitions bound for Vietnam. The ACTU ordered the SUA to return to work, arguing that the presence of bombs did not constitute a valid point of opposition. After this was refused, the federal government decided for the first time to install a navy crew onto the *Boonaroo*. When in March the SUA again refused to man the *Jeparit* in Sydney, against ACTU orders, and without support from any other maritime union, the Minister for Labour and National Service Leslie Bury labelled the action the 'disloyal and unAustralian machinations of the communist leaders of the Seamen's Union', and again ordered the ship be manned with a mixed navy and civilian crew.

Unionists continued to remove their bodies from sites that linked them to the war, including a 2600-strong walk-off by waterside workers in Sydney over the suspension of a worker for refusing to load bombs onto the *Jeparit* in September 1967.[102] Although these actions had varying levels of success, the level of political opposition to them suggests that the absence of worker bodies constituted a forceful part of the broader anti-war movement.

The stories in this chapter show how bodies were used by activists in a range of ways beyond the traditional rally or march, and even beyond more industrious forms of quiet protest. Beyond the intentional use of bodies as a 'text' through artistic practice, silent and absent bodies were able to disrupt public understandings of the anti-war protester as well as the tangible system of 'war-making'. Echoes of such actions in contemporary society confirm their effectiveness. In Melbourne, the Sit-Intifada has recently placed certain types of bodies in key spaces to protest on behalf of Palestine. Ihab Abu Ibrahim, a descendant of Palestinians who survived the 1948 Nakba, started the Sit-Intifada on the Victorian Parliament House steps from 9am to 9pm each day, asking supporters 'sit with us to stand for Palestine'.[103] Illustrating the multi-faceted way that activists can use their bodies to spread a message, in January 2024 the Sit-Intifada, along with community group Bukjeh, called for artists, designers, sewers, knitters and crafters to form a collective visual presence that would draw attention to the cause.[104] In Sydney, too, vigils and sit-ins have been held to protest for the same cause, including a candlelight vigil on Pitt Street Mall on 16 November 2023, a general sit-in for Palestine at Sydney Central Station on 1 December and a High School for Palestine sit-in in Sydney on 8 December.[105] Protests in Port Melbourne and Botany Bay, by maritime workers and other activists, have halted ships associated with warring states from docking.[106]

Such events show that relatively minor bodily acts can have a significant impact on social movements. In a time when larger-scale protest acts are increasingly criminalised, this is a reminder that minimalism in protest can achieve results.

CHAPTER SIX

VOLUNTARISM TO END THE WAR

In early 1968, Ian Bruce, a 17-year-old from Yagoona in southern Sydney, wrote to businessman and activist Ken Thomas to propose a Peace Ride from Sydney to the National Capital in Canberra, to lobby politicians and publicise the anti-war cause to young people in regional towns. Bruce was a member of Secondary Students for International Tolerance and Equality (SSITE), established in 1966 by high school students from suburbs across Sydney, including Fairfield, Belmore, Edgecliff, Punchbowl and Bronte.[1] Ken Thomas was so impressed with the idea that he agreed to pay $2 towards the expenses of every student who participated. The students still needed to raise $3 for bus fares, 90 cents for accommodation, and $4 for meals but were emboldened by Thomas's support to appeal for more help. SSITE attracted the attention of Methodist ministers Alan Walker and Ted Noffs, who offered to arrange accommodation for the group in a Goulburn church, while trade unionists offered funds, Anglican anti-war figure Francis James spoke at SSITE meetings, and Ex-Services Human Rights Association of Australia (ESHRAA) and AICD offered assistance with administration and publicity.[2]

SSITE declared, 'We are protesting about the war in Vietnam by presenting a petition to Parliament urging peace in Vietnam', which was soon signed by 1000 high school students.[3] SSITE's peace ride was triggered by news of the 1967 Three Point Plan to end the war in Vietnam proposed by United Nations Secretary General U Thant, which was: 'cessation of bombing in North Vietnam'; 'scaling down of all military activities by all sides in South Vietnam'; and 'willingness to enter into discussion with those who are actually fighting'.[4] The petition was a statement of support for this plan:

> THAT we the undersigned secondary students are shocked and ashamed at the unnecessary slaughter in Vietnam.
>
> THAT we are conscience bound to express our complete opposition to your Vietnam policy. Your policy is only continuing the war through mistaken self interest.
>
> THAT we believe the best means of bringing about an immediate solution to this conflict is embodied within U Thant's three-point plan.
>
> The killing must stop.
>
> And your petitions, as in duty bound, will ever pray.[5]

SSITE mobilised the time, energy and finances of fellow students and other supporters to ensure the success of the Peace Ride. The labour of volunteers was crucial. Historian Melanie Oppenheimer notes that there is no global definition of volunteering, because it varies according to culture, location and context. The nomenclature of volunteering shifts depending on who is volunteering – from pro bono work to 'lobbying', 'agitating', 'helping' or 'donating'.[6] As I will discuss, the Peace Ride for Canberra incorporated all of these elements and tells us much about gendered assumptions within protest movements.[7] Publicity surrounding the student's Peace Ride presented it as a predominantly male story. This means that women or girls who devised and organised many of its bold actions were sidelined by the media, and consequently within public memory. The enduring story of the Peace Ride does not align with the prominence of women and girls within its administrative archive. This chapter seeks to alter our understanding of activist roles, and argue that all roles, whether public or private, loud or quiet, were essential to the cause.

Communications regularly set out to students before the Peace Ride were authored by activists of all genders. In early April, organisers told students: 'make sure a copy of the petition is circulated in your school, come to the general meeting on 19th April and bring your friends, help in the actual organisation of the ride, or try to raise money on the ride'. At this initial meeting, held at the Fellowship of Australian Writers Hall at 189 Clarence Street, Sydney, organisers distributed a checklist reminding participants of the required payment and asking them to circulate the petition, hand out leaflets and SSITE newsletters, paste up posters, help with a planned folk concert or 'nag anyone who has still not decided to come into coming'. They also requested assistance at the locations they would visit on the two-day trip and funds to 'help to publish a pamphlet containing our views on Vietnam' which 'is very important and will be handed out in towns'. SSITE emphasised the importance of public outreach, reminding those joining the Peace Ride that 'the important point of the ride will be your contact with individuals', and encouraged those who had cameras or musical instruments to bring them along. Attendees, from 20 different state and private schools, were told to 'dress neatly. Be polite at all times. Know your facts about the war. Try quietly to convince people on your facts – let facts tell their own story'.

The students understood the need for promotion, urging their members to 'put publicity pressure wherever possible. If you're in any other groups, stir them. We need publicity in their leaflets etc. Can they contribute a small sum?'[8] In April, Helen Frizell of the *Sydney Morning Herald* reported in detail about this 'spontaneous idea of the secondary students', publishing a photograph of Bruce and his fellow organisers John Hughes, aged 17, and Tim Robins, aged 15, all of whom faced the draft if the war continued. The boys used this article to head off the possibility they might be accused of communist infiltration. Robins was quoted as saying the Peace Ride had emerged from a 'student movement – not a political movement'. The three boys said, 'Our movement could be used ... We're aware of this. But we don't think there could be any big infiltration among the secondary high school students', and mentioned their parents had no political connections. This was a clever move on the group's part, as two of the Peace Ride organisers were in fact 'red-diaper babies': Lee Brown was the daughter of Union of Australian Women President and prominent Communist Party member Freda Brown, while Mark Aarons was a son of the CPA National Secretary Laurie Aarons.[9]

Frizell emphasised the 'non-violent' intentions of their 'small protest' and ended on a supportive and encouraging note: 'The boys, intelligent and idealistic, have worked hard for their peace ride crusade. We can only hope that its fate is better than that of the Children's Crusade of the year 1212', referencing the unsuccessful historical journey taken by thousands of youths to remove Jerusalem from Muslim control.[10] It took a few weeks for the conservative press to catch up. A *Sunday Telegraph* reporter posed as a student and attended SSITE's 19 April planning meeting. In his report he labelled Peace Ride participants 'young dupes', writing that 'these youngsters, whether or not they thought of the idea themselves, are about to be used by every crackpot outfit round the place'.[11] On 5 May, the same newspaper published an article with the headline 'A Red Tinge to the Peace-Ride Wagon', in which a 'pupil who attends a leading girls school', presumably Lee Brown, was asked by reporters about her parents' CPA connections, which she said 'had nothing to do with her decision to go on the ride'.[12]

The departure of the Peace Ride was set for 7.15am on 13 May. The organisers told students, and their teacher chaperones Dave Bell and Lee Morrison, to meet at Sydney's Town Hall Station, and 'ask friends and parents to come and give us a big send off. Press and radio will probably be there'. Any 'worried parents' were invited to call teacher Joan Hokin for further information.

The first stop was Wollongong, at 9am, then Moss Vale at 12.30pm, Goulburn at 3pm, and Canberra at 5pm. Lee Rhiannon (née Brown), who served as the Greens Senator for NSW from 2010 until 2018, has recently shared that the reception at each of these locations varied. In Wollongong, the students were offered a breakfast prepared by

Students on the Peace Ride to Canberra, 14 May 1968

Noel Hazard/*Tribune* collection/MLSLNSW/courtesy SEARCH Foundation

supportive unionists but the police in Goulburn initially refused to let them disembark from the bus.[13]

In Canberra, the riders gathered for a folk concert organised by the Peace Ride with local students in the Wesley Hall at the National Memorial Methodist Church in Forrest, and retired to the Ainslie Hotel to spend the night. At 8.30am the next morning, 14 May, they gathered outside the US Embassy in Canberra to make a deputation to US officials, then at 11am visited the Garema Civic Centre for lunch and to sell literature about the war. At 1pm they made their way to Parliament House, where ALP Member for Lalor Dr Jim Cairns presented their petition to parliament and addressed the group. At 3.30pm they left Canberra and returned to Sydney Town Hall, arriving later that night.

We can understand the impact of the Peace Ride from the reaction of the Liberal government, which had, until then, ignored the students. On the day the students attended parliament the Attorney-General Nigel Bowen stated in the House of Representatives that the student demonstration was 'part of a planned operation'. Minister for Immigration Billy Snedden added that the student demonstration was ultimately supported by the CPA and 'the Communist inspired peace front, the Association for International Co-operation and Disarmament in Sydney'.[14] The press related the government's concerns – Melbourne's *Age* reported on 14 May that 'the Government is understood to be particularly concerned by a demonstration which will be staged in Canberra today by high school students from Sydney' and the following day Sydney's *Sun* printed the headline 'Reds dupe students' and quoted Bowen's use of the term 'sinister influences'.[15]

In the days after the Peace Ride, discussions in parliament took an even more hysterical turn. Liberal Member for Boothby John McLeay said he was 'distressed' that Jim Cairns 'told the school children never to believe people who told them they could not do anything about the war in Vietnam'. He claimed that in making these statements, Cairns was 'assisting the Communists to wage psychological warfare in this country and to achieve their form of peace, which in our language means surrender'. He referred to the CPA Eureka Youth League magazine *Target* and its urging 'that young people should campaign in the streets, destroy their draft cards and follow the shining example of William White', saying that 'in every respect this is totally unsatisfactory propaganda'.[16]

Fortunately, the Peace Ride evaded federal government interference and proved more successful than the 1212 Children's Crusade. SSITE compiled a report in the weeks after the event, which expressed appreciation for publicity and the funds it had received from trade unions and peace organisations, for meals and costs. The students recounted their brush with police in Goulburn, which they considered to be their 'first problem with the authorities and the first of the many successes of the peace ride'. The bus arrived to 'a carload of police parked just out of Goulburn, carloads along the main street, a paddy waggon driving up and down'. Police surrounded the bus and informed the students they needed to be out of Goulburn within an hour but the students defied them and headed to their planned folk concert in a nearby park:

> Spontaneously … we marched behind our banner … singing as we went we walked down one side of Goulburn's main street and back down the other giving out our material … We received the usual comments that anyone finds who demonstrates. But again people realise that such action had never been taken before, and this was all the more unique as it was being taken by secondary students. The impact went far beyond Goulburn in this area as one of the boys was interviewed on radio so people in the country districts would also [have] heard about the ride.[17]

Mark Aarons later wrote to AICD to report the Peace Ride was 'very significant in the history of the anti-Vietnam War Movement', and thanked them for all the 'moral and material support which you have given our group', and:

> All your wonderful cooperation and help in our publicity campaigns in helping to print our literature and for the literature which you supplied us for handing out on the road itself. I cannot tell you just how pleasing it was for us to receive such support and such solid moral backing for our enterprise … While I am still hot on the trail for handing out bouquets I would also wish to thank you for the use of your billing for various meetings … It was certainly very reassuring to know that we had the backing of at least some of the older generation and I once again must stress our thanks to your staff and to the very existence of your Association.[18]

AICD's Geoff Anderson replied on 6 June: 'May we commend the imaginative, competent and responsible manner in which this valuable project was executed … please be assured of our readiness to extend all possible further assistance in anticipation of the continuation of your valued initiatives'.[19]

The successful execution of a multi-day and multi-location event by high school students during the Vietnam War is a testament not only to the organisers, but also to the willingness of supporters to volunteer their time and energies to the cause. Activist organisations that lack funding can only reward participation, and the labour of volunteers, with non-financial benefits.[20] As early as the 1967 Anti-Vietnam War Anti-Conscription Activists' Conference, activists recognised the value of 'continuous activity' by volunteers, building on older traditions of volunteering as activism.[21] CPA members were certainly accustomed to supporting events such as Party Congresses by providing accommodation for interstate visitors, carrying out clerical work, cooking and serving coffee and tea.[22]

The appeal for assistance is a prominent category within the archives of quiet protest during the Vietnam years, and was a key element of strategies to build a movement. Almost every communication about upcoming events or campaigns told people exactly how they could 'help', heightening the sense that labour and time were indispensable. This 'help' was gladly provided. Voluntarism benefits not only social movements as a whole but also the individual activist, who gains social networking opportunities as well as the satisfaction of making a meaningful contribution to their community. These benefits see many in full-time paid employment gladly spending their weekends and evenings to organise for political causes.[23]

In this chapter I focus on lobbying journeys, like the Peace Ride for Canberra, and the essential supportive labours that are rarely recognised, such as clerical work, distributing leaflets, attending meetings and even babysitting. Although many forms of volunteering discussed here are comparatively mundane, and significantly quieter than other types of actions, they remain powerful, as they are not only able to provoke often dramatic responses by supporters of the war but also because, without them, louder actions would become impossible to execute.

WAYS OF 'HELPING'

The 1967 Anti-Vietnam War Anti-Conscription Activists' Conference urged suburban activists to escalate activities in their own localities, as 'a known and respected peace campaigner is a much stronger influence than an anonymous one'. The suggested method was to knock on people's doors, as this was ' the surest way of finding support' – the conference also suggested a 'door-knocking squad' could 'blitz' country districts.[24] Doorknocking was a widely used tactic throughout the entirety of the war, and is still practised by charities, activist groups and political parties.

In the months leading up to the 1966 federal election, ALP Candidate for Lowe Peter Dunn called on 'people who are opposed to CONSCRIPTION and the WAR IN VIETNAM, from all electorates ... to present the case against conservative misgovernment' to voters through doorknocking. He sought 400 volunteers, telling supporters that 'sociological studies have established that a house-to-house campaign is by far the most effective way to win votes'. Dunn hoped to attack the Liberal Party by unseating 'the minister responsible for introducing conscription', Minister for Labour and National Service William McMahon, who had represented Lowe since its establishment in 1949. Lowe proposed an 'anti-conscription drive' for 9 October 1966, and his office distributed a leaflet which included the all-important cut-off slip allowing supporters to provide names, addresses and phone numbers, and specify when and where they could assist.[25]

While many anti-war organisations had their genesis in public meetings and collective decision-making, as the war progressed activists realised doorknocking would more effectively establish contact with the masses and transform public sympathy into direct participation.[26] On 3 June 1968, a group of protest organisations including Committee of Responsibility for the Children of Vietnam (CRCV), ESHRAA, SOS, Catholics for Peace, Quaker Peace Committee, Manly–Warringah Peace Group, Australian Reform Movement (previously Liberal Reform Group), Bradfield Peace Committee and Fellowship of Reconciliation agreed 'not everyone considers protest meetings effectual' for attracting members and unanimously endorsed a 'mass doorknock' to fundraise for the CRCV. The goal was to sell 8000 copies of 'The Children of Vietnam' – an article by American lawyer William F Pepper with a preface by Dr Benjamin Spock, who was a trusted voice for parents about raising children gently and fostering their independence. The article contained devastating images of the effect of napalm burns on Vietnamese children.[27]

Effective doorknocking required a systematic approach and organiser Sheila Mason proposed a meeting at her house at 106 Rosedale Road, Pymble, on 17 June to:

> allocate volunteers from the various groups to streets in their chosen area and, over a specific weekend to take these copies round from door to door, to offer them free or for a donation, and to talk to people about the chain of events that has led to the present ghastly position. For those who feel that 'The Children of Vietnam' is too stark for them to handle, I have arranged for alternative literature from the Committee of Responsibility to be available.[28]

It is necessary to again draw attention to the disproportionate allocation of administrative and clerical protest work to women activists during the Vietnam War.[29] Although more women than ever before earned an income outside the home at this time, the Federation-era positioning of men as 'breadwinners' and women and children as dependants still held symbolic value.[30] Beverley Symons was 'very involved' in the AICD office from 1963 to 1973, and remembered 'eight years of my life just sort of went in one great huge onslaught of work – of activity, of organising these countless meetings, countless publications, committee meetings, public meetings, conferences, rallies, demonstrations'. Symons perceived the confines of her position within the movement's infrastructure when she served as AICD delegate to the 1971 Anti-War Conference in Sydney, which was:

> really my turning point if you like, in the peace movement. Now these issues of the right of women to be equally involved as men in the decision making, as well as you know making the cups of tea and filling the envelopes ... really came to the fore because it was that year when women's liberation was bursting onto the scene everywhere. I mean it just happened everywhere. And certainly it had a big impact in the peace movement. And if you read a lot of the early women's magazines, or the women's papers – those early women's liberation papers – I remember there was the big dialogue about women in the peace movement ... And the conference got under way and it was very exciting – but I hardly saw any of it. The first couple of days I was stuck in the office all the time ... So I'm churning out endless copies, and I just worked hours and hours into the night – me and others – in the back room as it were. And I can remember Mavis [Robertson] ... said to me 'Look, you've gotta take a stand. You've really gotta say to this conference "This has gotta stop – women cannot be treated like this any longer"'.[31]

Such revelatory moments propelled the formation and structure of Women's Liberation in the early 1970s that rejected the gender hierarchy that meant 'men had taken the microphone and expected women to type the minutes'.[32] Women's Liberation also emphasised consensus and cooperation, as historian and feminist activist Ann Curthoys confirms. Curthoys, who has largely shaped our understanding of the gendered roles within the Australian anti-Vietnam War movement, attended public demonstrations and was 'involved in VAC' during the war, but clarified that 'by involved, I mean I went along and folded mail-outs'.[33]

Society's view of women's work means that labour carried out by women is more likely to be categorised as 'help' over 'work', which de-emphasises its significance. When organisational activist work is viewed from a public relations (PR) standpoint, it is more commonly labelled 'dissent PR' or advocacy, rather than 'protest PR' or activism, which is more commonly associated with public and loud actions.[34] Excluding activist tactics that were largely carried out by women from definitions of 'protest' simply perpetuates gendered ideas of the nature of society at the time of the war. Oppenheimer wisely avoids this distinction by drawing varied understandings of protest together to insist that the anti-Vietnam War movement was 'propelled by volunteer activism' and so places this seemingly tedious work firmly in the broad sphere of quiet protest.[35]

Understandings of protest are decidedly gendered, but thankfully here there is a silver lining. Women were not only prominent in administering the protest archive created by the Vietnam War but also in ensuring it was preserved and archived. The gendering of protest that saw men dominate public actions and discussions and relegate women to quieter administrative roles has produced an unspoken gendering in the content of historical literature about the movement. This means that many of our lasting understandings of Vietnam-era activism have been actively and purposefully shaped by women's perspectives.

In many cases, women were undoubtedly the right people for the job. The 1967 Anti-Vietnam War Anti-Conscription Activists' Conference report identified women as the best people to run and attend 'local daytime meetings in suburban areas, directed at non-politically inclined women' and to conduct Gallup Polls on conscription in suburban shopping centres on Saturday mornings, a space where women's organisations such as SOS were active throughout the war.[36] Gendered analyses of shopping centres continue to categorise these as spaces for women over men, underlining why women activists were considered to more effectively operate there.[37]

APPEALING FOR VOLUNTEERS

The most fervent and forward requests for volunteer labour came from VAC, usually through the cut-off slip used to enlist help selling issues of its journal *Vietnam Action,* distributing leaflets or within general clerical or administrative assistance through regular 'working bees'.[38] Despite VAC's consistent focus on the public demonstration, the group constantly emphasised the value of quiet protest, writing to supporters:

'the most effective thing you can do to help "Vietnam Action" is to assist us with circulation, by taking a regular bundle to sell, by sending a gift subscription to your friends, or even just by passing this issue on to an interested friend'.[39] On 25 September 1966, in preparation for protests during the impending visit of US President Lyndon Baines Johnson, VAC held a series of working bees focused on leaflet preparation and distribution, the first in the AICD building on 17 Parker Street, Sydney. Here volunteers were asked to 'collate and staple the fifth and definitely final 5000 copies of the "American Atrocities in Vietnam" pamphlet, making a total of 25 000 in all'.[40] Two additional 'emergency working bees' were held at Bob Gould's home at 61 Holdsworth Street, Woollahra, on the weekend of 16 to 17 October, where volunteers were asked to 'prepare and post VAC newsletters to advertise activities during Johnson's visit'.[41]

VAC made it clear that it was appealing for administrative assistance to directly facilitate loud protest and increase the numbers of demonstrators on the streets. Prior to the 1966 Labor Day March, they asked for assistance conducting a 'sales drive' of the *American Atrocities in Vietnam* pamphlet, asking willing helpers to meet at Gowing's Corner on Market and George Streets on the day at 9:15am: 'This will be the best opportunity we have had so far to get to the sympathetic section of the Sydney public, so come along and help sell if at all possible'.[42] In May 1967, VAC wrote to supporters of '!!! FOUR VITAL V.A.C. WORKING BEES!!!' to be held from Sunday 14 May until Wednesday 17 May to post over 5000 leaflets advertising an upcoming demonstration. They urged: 'Please come and HELP at as many of these work parties as you can, and any willing friends you can persuade to volunteer will also be most welcome'.[43]

Of course, VAC was not alone in seeking clerical or administrative help during the war but did make notably overt statements about how indispensable volunteers were to the protest movement. Liberation organised working bees in August 1969 to set up its store at 368 Pittwater Road, North Manly: 'Come along and help! Still a lot to be done to get 368 shipshape ... working bees Wednesdays – also Thursdays and Fridays ... we need you'![44] ESHRAA's June 1966 issue of *Conscience* announced:

'Office help wanted – urgent!' in Hurstville 'to help in dealing with our ever-growing mail'. ESHRAA asked those who 'can get along there for a short spell each week' to 'phone LW [Les Waddington] and fix a time', and solicited 'an old typewriter in working order' to use in its office.[45]

Every AICD newsletter during the war requested some form of assistance. In March 1971, it asked for help in the organisation's library:

> Our Librarian, Mrs Dawn Gietzelt, who has been working for two days a week for a very nominal salary for several years past has reported that the volume of work now being handled by the library demands the employment of a full-time worker ... Mrs Gietzelt will be continuing to assist the library by contributing her services on a voluntary part time basis.[46]

In June 1972, AICD made an 'URGENT APPEAL FOR OFFICE ASSISTANCE': 'In previous newsletters we have sought the assistance of any people with time to spare to assist us in the office. However, we are now urgently making this appeal again, particularly for typists'.[47]

Volunteers were also urged to draw on their own initiative or contribute their own ideas. In the lead up to the 1969 federal election, Sonya Drabyan, from the campaign committee for 'Unconscriptable' Geoffrey Mullen in the Eastern suburbs seat of Wentworth against Minister for Labour and National Service Leslie Bury, wrote to Citizens Against the National Service Act:

> You are, of course aware of the various activities an election campaign involves: fund-raising, door-to-door interviewing, letter-boxing, poster-printing and sticking, public meetings, manning polling booths, and a great deal of typing and duplicating. Please consider carefully what you and your personal or organizational contacts could do, and let us know.[48]

In the same year, High School Students Against the War in Vietnam wrote in its tenth newsletter: 'We want to find out your school, year, what's happening in your area and whether you are willing to take part in the organisation of regional groups'.[49] The Eastern Suburbs Moratorium Group, which needed volunteers 'to hand out leaflets, letter-box etc. at any time suitable to them in shopping centres', also held a working bee at 480 Crown Street, Surry Hills, asking supporters to 'Please try to get to part of the working bee as we will need all the help we can get. Also, put on your thinking caps as we need ideas for slogans'.[50] The Draft Resistance and Counselling School asked volunteers to use their personal knowledge of the NSA to counsel potential and actual conscripts or create rosters so that help was always available.[51] The frequency and variety of these types of requests demonstrates how vital administrative facets of quiet protest were to the continuation of the movement.

As the VMC newspaper *Out Now!* announced, 'people of all walks of life will be organising and participating in a series of protests culminating in nationally coordinated action ... This is the Vietnam Moratorium Campaign'. Its three issues contained a section titled 'How to Help', which tells us much about the coordination of volunteer tasks across the campaign. These tasks included sponsorship, distributing sponsorship forms or leaflets, purchasing items to display or sell, such as badges, stickers and posters, 'contribute to, or assist with the distribution of *Out Now!*, in the city, suburbs, in offices and factories, schools, colleges, universities, sporting fixtures, cinemas and theatres', or become a 'voluntary helper' to 'assist in the Moratorium office during the day, after work till 6pm or on Saturday morning'.[52] Even babysitting was included as an essential arrangement, administered by American activist Phil Sanford.[53]

TRANSPORT AND TRAVEL

Activists used their time and energies to spread the word into rural areas or take part in the 'lobbying mission', a 'staple of anti-war and anti-conscription protest since the 1960s' which has echoes today in actions like the November 2023 bus trip to Parliament House in Canberra organised by Free Palestine Melbourne to protest in aid of

Gaza and Palestine.[54] The purpose of travelling to Canberra during the Vietnam War was manifold. The students of the Peace Ride for Canberra discussed the war with teenagers in Canberra and in rural high schools, hosted a folk concert to attract young people to the cause, distributed anti-war literature, presented their petition and met with Jim Cairns. Such diverse actions increased the number of volunteers who could participate, drawing more to the cause.[55]

Some lobbying journeys incorporated louder actions, as was the case on 11 June 1970 when anti-war protesters from a variety of groups stormed Federal Parliament.[56] They were also instigated by a variety of groups. In 1965 a collective of citizens who had no affiliations with any peace organisation presented a petition asking for peace negotiations to end the war to the US, South Vietnamese and North Vietnamese embassies in Canberra.[57] In the same year, the Committee for Canberra Vigil organised a religious vigil in the nation's capital.[58]

Activists from around the country planned large-scale Vietnam Lobby Days in Canberra. The first was jointly planned by Melbourne's Vietnam Day Committee and VAC in 1966, as a convergence of Melburnians who travelled to the capital by train or bus and Sydneysiders who conducted 'a relay march' over the almost 300 kilometres to Canberra.[59] On 15 May 1968, trade unionists from Sydney, Newcastle and Wollongong descended on the capital for a Trade Union Lobby Day for Peace, discussing the war and conscription with politicians and diplomats. It was so successful the model was adopted by unions as an area of 'continued and intensified activity', and an Interstate Liaison Committee was formed to oversee future events.[60]

AICD organised a larger Lobby Day, combining a range of quiet protest tactics, for 25 March 1969, announcing:

> A deputation from three states, having recorded its protest to the Commonwealth Government against the National Service Act and against the gaoling of 20 year old conscientious objectors for refusing to serve in the immoral Vietnam War, now calls on every Australian of goodwill to join in the urgent struggle to have these injustices removed and the men released.[61]

This required a large number of volunteers, some travelling to Canberra and others providing fundraising and logistical support from Sydney. To ensure maximum participation and avoid excluding those who did not have the capacity to travel, AICD told supporters:

> We realise that it will not be possible for you to arrange participation in all aspects of this programme but draw it to your attention as evidence of our serious intent to develop a powerful campaign in this coming election year to end the intolerable infringement of human rights imposed by this medieval legislation of the Gorton government.[62]

It also told activists how they could keep working locally: 'exercise your democratic right and responsibility; make your views known to your federal member; find out where he stands on these issues' and distributed suggested questions for politicians. Such assistance was intended to ensure activists would not exclude themselves because they felt travelling was beyond their abilities.

Administering those who could travel to Canberra was a huge task that required contributions of labour by many volunteer organisers. AICD organisers Greg Harrison, Ernie Boatswain and Ken O'Hara wrote and distributed participant forms to gather information about those travelling by car, if they could provide their own fuel, or pay $6 to travel on buses organised by AICD.[63] The buses picked up travellers at 5am on the morning of 25 March at Eddy Avenue at Central Station in Sydney, from Strathfield or Liverpool Stations, or the Crossroads Hotel, Casula. They were draped with signs declaring 'Free Zarb' advertising the plight of 21-year-old Melbourne conscientious objector John Zarb who had been imprisoned for two years under the NSA.

The AICD told volunteers to pack their own sandwiches and a thermos flask containing a warm drink for breakfast, but welcomed them to Canberra with a buffet lunch. They were advised to make 'prior appointments with their MPs wherever possible', so as to be able to engage in discussions about the war on the day, which took some of the burden of organisation from the day's administrators.[64]

TRADE UNION COMMITTEE **AICD**

587a George Street Sydney NSW Correspondence: Box 247 Post Office Haymarket NSW 2000 Telegrams: ACFICODIS Sydney Phone: 26-6201

NATIONAL LOBBY TO CANBERRA, MARCH 25TH

Rec 2617
20/3/67

PARTICIPATION FORM.

NAME MRS IRENE GALLEN

ADDRESS 35 EPSOM RD.
MOOREBANK 2170 Phone ....

ORGANISATION OR GROUP BEING REPRESENTED UNION AUSTRALIAN WOMEN

METHOD OF TRAVEL: Bus ✓ Car 602 4225.

Enclosed herewith $6.00 covering bus fare $6.00

I will be travelling by car .....
(Tick whichever applicable.)

I will be joining bus at: Eddy Ave., (Central side near George St.corner) .....
Strathfield Station (Liverpool Rd. side) .....
Liverpool Station ✓
Cross Roads Hotel .....
(Tick whichever applicable.)

This form should be completed by intending participants and lodged with fare (where travelling by bus) at A.I.C.D. rooms, 587a George St., by Friday, March 21st. Phone enquiries:

Greg Harrison : 26 3215, Ernie Boatswain : 26 6471,
Ken O'Hara : 26 6201

A sub-committee representing 30 Unions of the Association for International Cooperation and Disarmament (NSW)

Trade Union Lobby Day for Peace participation form, March 1968

People for Nuclear Disarmament/MLSLNSW

The time and energy required to organise this event – and reconcile it – becomes apparent when considering the number and range of organisations involved: Seaman's Union of Australia, Builders Labourers Federation, Building Workers Industrial Union, Waterside Workers' Federation, Federated Liquor and Allied Industries Employees' Union, Save Our Sons, AICD Women, Union of Australian Women, Water Supply Chullora and South Coast Citizens Against Conscription, which was represented by 20-year-old Mac Gudgeon, who later wrote a series of films and mini-series including, perhaps appropriately, 1989's *The Delinquents*.[65]

While the March 1969 Lobby Day was a success, Ken O'Hara spent significant time and effort afterwards writing a report that suggested points for improvement. He mentioned the need to care for volunteers properly, as bus driver Laurie Barrett only 'had 2 hours sleep in the bus in Canberra'. He also recommended attention to costs, as participants expressed dissatisfaction with being charged an additional $1.25 for lunch. O'Hara also suggested better administrative structures, such as 'earlier/better preparation in Sydney of sub-responsibilities, work teams etc'; a 'stronger coordinating team' based in the ACT and a folk concert to entertain those waiting outside parliament.

Another form of vehicular lobbying was motorcades, which usually took place in the streets surrounding major shopping centres. During the 1967 August Mobilisation to End the War in Vietnam, a 'very successful parade of placarded cars around shopping centres' was organised by the Manly–Warringah Committee for International Cooperation and Disarmament. The group wrote to members on 4 October that 'although this was done at short notice by phone, seventeen cars took part', and planned a second event for 21 October in Mona Vale.[66]

As mentioned, many types of labour necessary to the success of louder protests can be likened to PR which can include the strategic use of placards or posters. PR scholar Kevin Moloney calls this aspect of PR protest work 'weak propaganda', which is essential to making 'public debate more equal, more vigorous, more appealing, more likely to conclude with some truth'.[67] This was certainly true of the Draft Resistance Counselling Centre's use of 'cars, drivers and speakers to

Placarded car during 1970 anti-conscription protest

Noel Hazard/*Tribune* collection/MLSLNSW/courtesy SEARCH Foundation

broadcast messages publicising the Counselling Centre' in 1970, which they called 'our most effective form of contact with 20-year-olds during the last registration period'.[68]

LEGAL VOLUNTEERS

The provision of legal expertise and the funding of costs or fines, was, as discussed in Chapter Four, quiet volunteer labour, as was the physical presence of activist bodies and disruption to the court system that imprisoned draft evaders and resisters. A relatively small number of the approximately 8000 signatories to the Committee in Defiance of the National Service Act's Statement of Defiance saw the inside of a courtroom, but those who did used that time to create a permanent account of their objection to conscription, exemplifying this type of labour.

Some activists volunteered to speak on behalf of conscripted young men in courtrooms and AICD regularly sent representatives to help young conscientious objectors (COs) articulate their views more clearly.[69] Members of the Conscientious Objectors' Group were also encouraged to help in this way:

> For most conscientious objectors, inexperienced in public speaking and court procedure, it is wisest to be represented in court, even by a layman, rather than conduct it by oneself. Because it is a public statement of a personal conviction, some COs feel it would be wrong to take advantage of legal representation. But this doesn't detract from the sincerity of a case. A representative doesn't speak FOR a CO; he merely acts as a prompt to the CO's memory, so he can expound ALL his beliefs. Many young men have stepped into the witness box, their minds full of what they all say … but suddenly, in the intense drama of it all, their minds go blank. Also, unless the CO is a practised speaker, a representative would give a better address to the magistrate because he has observed the case all the way through.[70]

Friends of Rex Hewett and supporters outside the Federal Court, Sydney, 7 March 1968

Noel Hazard/*Tribune* collection/MLSLNSW/courtesy SEARCH Foundation

Others were asked to distribute literature to interested crowds and media outside courtrooms or simply to sit in courtrooms to provide quiet support. Adele Pert of SOS said that: 'if we heard of somebody that had to go to court – we'd ring up all the people we could and get them to come to court'.[71] Before CO Rex Hewett's final appearance at the Federal Court on Phillip Street, Sydney, on 7 March 1968, the Friends of Rex Hewett group appealed to supporters to 'come to the court' and 'offer assistance by contacting Rex Hewett'.[72]

The recent expansion of legal restraints on protest in the present has prompted lawyer activists to form specialty grassroots groups for this purpose, including Legal Observers NSW and Melbourne Activist Legal Support. Services provided by Legal Observers NSW include: 'organise and train teams of legal observers to monitor police action at protests', 'produce incident reports about protest policing', 'facilitate access to legal support for those facing charges in relation to a protest action, and 'engage in community legal education about protest rights', all of which echo the activities of similar Vietnam-era protesters.[73]

The quiet work of volunteers was fundamental to the anti-Vietnam War movement in NSW. Volunteers were agents of PR, whether they drove a car covered in placards or filled envelopes with communications about the war and upcoming events. Few organisations explicitly connected quieter volunteer labour and louder protest, but all realised that public disruption would not be possible without constant background work in offices, private homes and even courtrooms, as well as continual interaction with the general population. The next chapter will turn to one specific facet of this communication – spoken protest with the general public through conferences, sit-ins, public lectures and discussion groups.

CHAPTER SEVEN
SPEAKING PROTEST

In 1966, a group of 25 Catholics in Sydney established Catholics for Peace (CFP), and announced this action in a letter sent to the virulently anti-communist Archbishop of Sydney Cardinal Gilroy.[1] In August 1967, Brian Johns, the son of a waterside worker who abandoned training for the Catholic priesthood in 1966 to become a journalist – and who would eventually become managing director of SBS and the ABC – wrote an article about CFP entitled 'Catholics' Problem of Conscience' for the *SMH*. In this article, he quoted a 'left-wing intellectual' who declared:

> It's extraordinary. Catholic priests are actually attending anti-Vietnam demonstrations. Something remarkable is going on in the Catholic Church ... Good heavens, a Leftist movement has commenced in the Church.[2]

Johns wrote that the CFP described themselves as 'a coordinated group of cells for education and activity on all matters concerning peace'. While not all members were opposed to the Vietnam War or to conscription, their 'living-room studies' had begun to 'arouse a debate here that has long been going on elsewhere about the proposition that a Catholic must support a war waged by a lawfully constituted Government'.[3]

These 'living room studies' are emblematic of the religious response to the leftist shift within society that was occasioned by opposition to the Vietnam War. From January 1966, a group of Sydney lay Catholics, including activist Noreen McDonald, set to work mailing excerpts about war, peace and conscientious objection from *Pacem In Terris*

(Peace on Earth) to religious leaders. The document was an encyclical written by the late progressive Pope John XXIII, which, in the spirit of Second Vatican Council (Vatican II) reforms to the Catholic Church, addressed all humanity. In mid-1966, CFP formed and began holding group meetings on conscientious objection, while examining and seeking changes to the NSA. It also invited younger priests to 'use letter columns of the Catholic press as discussion sites', to 'organise debates, speakers at schools, youth clubs' and carried out general research on the war and conscription.[4] CFP appeared shortly before eight Melbourne Catholics formed Pax Christi and conceived a 'Catholic work for peace', in the form of an open letter supporting a call for peace by Pope Paul VI that the Archbishops of both Sydney and Melbourne had largely overlooked.[5]

On 18 June 1967, during a CFP 'Forum on Catholics, War, Vietnam' at St John's College, University of Sydney, the college Rector Dr John Burnheim controversially told the 350 attendees that 'individual Catholics ... may as a result of their own conscience consider that war is now completely unjustified'.[6] In the aftermath, CFP numbers swelled to 100 and smaller groups began to advise and provide legal aid to Catholic conscientious objectors, including Simon Townsend. They also joined anti-conscription demonstrations and distributed copies of the Pope's statement on war and Vietnam outside Catholic churches after Sunday Mass, meeting some opposition. Catholic priest and CFP member Charles Bowers, whose Australian anti-war action was so reviled by the church that he spent time in an American 'resistance commune' in the late 1960s, recalled that at one such event in Concord he saw a Saint Vincent de Paul Society member tear leaflets from the hands of a CFP activist, whose arm was 'twisted behind her back and badly bruised in the process', while 'the priest-administrator to Bishop Freeman looked on'.[7]

Catholics for Peace was just one of the many religious groups in NSW who objected to the war on the basis of Christian morality and led conversation-based events, such as teach-ins, public lectures and group discussion. These actions continued with moments of peak activity, one of which saw Sydney Methodist Reverend Alan Walker launch a

Canberra Vigil Committee in 1965. Another key event incorporating teaching and discussion was the 1970 visit of Dorothy Day, an anarchist who had co-founded the US Catholic Worker movement in the 1920s, and Eileen Egan, a member of the American PAX Association who aided Catholic conscientious objectors. They had been invited to Australia by Roger Pryke, the parish priest at Harbord, who hosted 'informal discussions' with Day during this visit on the topic of 'militant nonviolent action for social change'. Pryke told Australian activists:

> I know that our visitors have experienced a whole spectrum of nonviolent action, and also know of the experience of Cesar Chavez, Martin Luther King, Gandhi ... and have an excellent understanding of the conditions which indicate the various kinds of action. It seems to me that we are still fairly primitive in the rudimentary means we use (the vote, the strike and now the protest march), whereas other countries have seen a process of planning and of action which would make us more effective in bringing about freedom, peace, justice nonviolently.[8]

Religious groups felt that their protest would be more effective in cooperation with non-religious and left-wing activists, and their own respectability would function as 'a legitimation of anti-war dissent'.[9] Mutually beneficial cooperation of this type was common. When Youth Campaign Against Conscription (YCAC) wrote in August 1967 that it was 'heartening to see the participation of academics, clergy and Australian artists in such numbers' at a recent demonstration, this included CFP.[10] CFP meetings invited members of external organisations, such as the Women's International League of Peace and Freedom's (WILPF) Kerry Ashbolt, who attended the first group meeting on conscientious objection in May 1967.[11]

CFP members were careful to distinguish between cooperation and leftism. As Noreen McDonald told Brian Johns in 1967, 'there were very few political activists among the members', agreeing with her husband Colin, an insurance broker and member of the lay Catholic organisation Knights of the Southern Cross, that 'most would be conservative'. McDonald was undoubtedly aware of the risk of attacks from within the Church, especially BA Santamaria's anti-communist National Civic Council committee (earlier known as the Catholic Social Studies Movement or 'The Movement'). McDonald pointed out that both she and her husband had served in the Second World War and 'reacted strongly against the idea that "Catholics for Peace" is a protest movement'. Johns could not help but observe Catholics for Peace 'had its beginnings in almost classic protest style – the discovery of the Roneo machine' – a tool of quiet protest throughout the Vietnam War.[12]

McDonald's caution was warranted, for Charles Bowers was at risk of being suspended from the priesthood due to his anti-Vietnam War stance. Shortly afterwards, he voluntarily left the Church, pointing to its inability 'to take a moral stand on the Viet Nam issue' as the reason for its 'massive haemorrhage of membership' in the late 1960s.[13] The positions taken by McDonald and Bowers caused some debate in *SMH* letters to the editor. CM Burns addressed McDonald's statements by writing that 'the lady's time would have been more profitably employed' attending Church-organised activities and linked the CFP to communism:

> I distrust 'cells' established by university intellectuals. Wherever in the world such cells have been formed, even with the highest objectives, they have become the tool of unscrupulous people for subversive purposes. There is no justification for such potentially dangerous groups in Australian Catholic society.[14]

Burns said, 'Catholics for Peace has no official status in the Church', a point supported by Reverend TJ Purcell of Cronulla who wrote that any evidence of support for CFP within Sydney was 'flimsy'.[15]

There were, however, letters in support of the CFP position. Christopher Finn of Harbord – Reverend Pryke's parish – criticised Cardinal Gilroy for saying Bowers 'might need "his head punched in" for championing the peace movement'. Finn urged Gilroy 'to regard the Vietcong [soldier] not so much as a military statistic, but as primarily a human being like himself'.[16] The president of the War and Education

Research Group (WERG), teacher Eric G Earley of Kurrajong, called Johns' article 'heartening to all interested in securing world peace':

> People of all religions are deprived of life and happiness by war. War severely limits the social and educational opportunities available to the children of all participating countries … Australian Catholics who protest are to be congratulated in joining those who support [UN Secretary-General] U Thant's proposals for a peaceful settlement of the Vietnam War.[17]

Earley was active in the NSW Teachers Federation over many decades, and was a conservationist, humanist and writer who 'brought a special blend of practicality and innovation to his teaching', along with a sense of humour. Upon his death in 1996, all attending his wake were instructed in the Teachers Federation journal *Education* to 'dress colourfully and bring a joke'.[18]

Earley was among a group of teachers who met at Federation House at 166 Phillip Street, Sydney, on 8 June 1967, to form an educational protest group. Many who gathered were responding to an advertisement that had been placed in publications across the state calling on:

> Teachers, lecturers and students in all state, religious and independent educational institutions. You are invited to join the War and Education Research Group. This group is concerned by the effect of war on education and will consider what educationists can do to protect the interests of children in our own and other countries.[19]

This first WERG meeting resolved: 'A statement by educationists protesting about the effect of the war in Vietnam on children is to be inserted in as many daily papers as funds permit'. They sought educators to join their 'serious group' and contribute to their research. WERG members began researching, seeking information about war, children and education to disseminate through speaking engagements and discussion. At the end of the month they wrote to AICD: 'The War and

Education Research Group has a list of competent speakers prepared to speak on the effects of war on education and social conditions. We wish to provide speakers for public meetings, church, cultural and youth groups, trade unions and political organisations'.[20]

WERG approached the Vietnam War from a spectrum of ideological standpoints and, like CFP and other groups, feared red-smearing would cost it public support. Public communications asserted WERG was 'an independent body of educationists ... not affiliated with any political party'.[21] Members were right to be cautious.

In August 1967, WERG placed an advertisement in the *SMH* that was signed by over 500 educators and declared:

> We fear for the future of all children – children who cannot be heard. Moved by the mounting horrors of the war in Vietnam in which an estimated million children have been killed, injured or burnt, we, the undersigned educationists call upon the Australian Government to press for:
>
> 1 Unconditional cessation of the bombing of North Vietnam
> 2 Discussions between all parties to the conflict, including the National Liberation Front of South Vietnam (as proposed by U Thant).[22]

The NSW Minister for Child Welfare, Arthur Bridges, responded in parliament, saying he was 'appalled by the complete distortion of fact in the advertisement', and that the figure of one million children killed was 'misleading'. He attempted to discredit WERG by positioning them alongside Vietnamese communist forces:

> I think they were advertising for funds or for support for an anti-Vietnamese campaign, for a cessation of hostilities, or something related to that ... It was quite obvious that they were opposed to Australia's participation in South Vietnam. When it is recognized that Australia, poised as it is in the Pacific, is vulnerable to Communist encroachment from the north, it ill behoves those

> who are not appreciative of this danger to try to suggest that we should withdraw our forces. I assure honourable members, if they do not already know it, that the Australian Government, the American Government and their allies in South Vietnam would indeed be pleased to see an end to hostilities. However, it takes two people to make peace, and the forces of the Viet Cong, and the Communists who are aiding them, have deliberately abstained from attending any conference table because they want to perpetuate these hostilities.[23]

Although WERG was relatively short-lived, its efforts to educate the public about war and children through speaking and discussion were crucial to what John Murphy calls the 'reactivation of the public sphere' after the 1966 federal election. This was characterised by public meetings, lounge-room discussions, rural meetings, teach-ins at universities and preach-ins at radical churches.[24]

Speaking protest, not only to members of the public but also by communicating tactics and strategy to fellow activists, is a 'sociospatial' factor that can increase recruitment.[25] This type of 'educational awareness and community-building' is an essential precursor to direct action, to ensure that movements are working with communities that fully support them, and that the impact of actions is maximised.[26] Leafleting, public footpath discussions, doorknocking, sit-ins, strikes, public lectures, conferences and telephone calls all facilitate conversations about vital issues.[27] This chapter focuses on how activists addressed the general public, the people of Vietnam and each other through planned and spontaneous activities, in venues across the state. A constant buzz of conversation against the war entered private homes, construction sites, factories, offices, parks, churches, schools, universities, public streets and parliaments.

CONVERSATIONS AGAINST THE WAR

Anti-war organisations encouraged activists to spread the word through conversations and developed instructional materials to ensure that these were as effective as possible. One such document was 'How to Run a Discussion Group', which explained the ideal structure of formal discussion and provided possible talking points. It told activists that the aim of discussion is 'to gather all the available information on a subject, to pool it and as a result try to find the truth or at least a greater understanding'. Group members, of which there should be between six and 12 – with 'over twenty impossible' – should comfortably sit in a circle, as 'a cheerless room makes for a chilly response, and hard sitting does not evoke hard thinking'. It warned against 'crooked thinking', writing that 'there will always be a few people who are better informed than the others, and these should be encouraged to enrich the discussion but should not be allowed to talk for too long' although 'the garrulous types are easier to handle because the leader is always assisted by the offender's suffering comrades'.[28]

Protest organisations use similar tactics today. The Australian Palestinian Advocacy Network recently developed a 'A toolkit for hosting Kitchen Table Conversations for Gaza and Palestine', 'as just one of our tactics to bring in and recruit new people to our movement'. Modelled on instructions developed by the Victorian Women's Trust, the guide offers advice on selecting a space, people to invite, and topics for discussion, with the aim of 'fostering the type of environment where you can ask someone to get involved, or take action'.[29]

The work of generating discussions about the conflict and conscription began in the early years of the Vietnam War. The Cumberland Regional Peace Committee distributed a leaflet in 1965 that asked: 'Are you concerned over Vietnam?', aligning concern about the war with public responsibility by encouraging others to 'help to influence public opinion towards acceptance of the principle that negotiation must displace war as a means of settling international disputes'. People were encouraged to 'propose discussions within your organisation and initiate discussions with your local member on the futility and disastrous consequences of persisting with attempts to force military solutions of political problems'.[30] Some organisations considered discussion part of their core business – the Ex-Services Human Rights Association of Australia (ESHRAA) set a primary objective during 1965 'to provide a forum for discussion and medium of expression of the views of ex-servicemen and women devoted to the values of a free society'.[31]

Organisations who assisted potential conscripts to explore their legal options founded some of the earliest study groups. From December 1965, the Sydney Conscientious Objectors' Discussion Group, organised by a range of people including Simon Townsend, Dougald and Carol McLean, and Pat Ruffels, gathered on Wednesday evenings at 19 Devonshire Street in Surry Hills. This informal group had no listed membership but existed to 'discuss with young men who have a conscientious objection the implication of registration for national service, and to establish whether or not their beliefs are relative to their stand with respect to the National Service Act'. It also served as a conduit between young men and legal or financial advisors.[32]

Ella Outhred of Save Our Sons (SOS) and Barry Robinson of YCAC proposed an Anti-Conscription Study Group 'for all young people opposed to conscription on any grounds whatsoever':

> The aim of the group is to enable young people to clarify their ideas and exchange views on the ways they can best express their opposition. It will particularly aim to help young men who object to being conscripted into the army, including those already called up and those who are eligible for call-up in the future.[33]

The group was to meet every Monday night at 7.30pm in the YCAC rooms at 96 Phillip Street, Sydney, and supporters were encouraged to include the study group in their own conversations with others: 'Anyone interested is very welcome to attend, and we would appreciate it if you could let people know about this project'.[34] Discussion groups proliferated in the lead up to the 26 November 1966 federal election. In May 1965, the Parramatta and District Committee for International Cooperation and Disarmament told its members:

> An intense campaign to develop peace activity to its highest level in electoral areas is essential to maintain pressure upon the Federal Government. Recent events in Vietnam demonstrate that Australia's slavish adherence to American policies of support for dictatorial and corrupt regimes is arousing intense hostility from the Vietnamese people. These developments also serve to emphasise the importance and urgency of taking the maximum opportunity of Federal elections to end the morally and politically indefensible policies of the Australian Government.[35]

The Ku-ring-gai Study Group was inspired by AICD initiatives to create 'local committees in Federal Electorates, with a view to bringing this issue to the forefront as the most vital governmental question for the Australian people'. They met in the Supper Room of St John's Church Hall in Gordon in September 1966 to develop plans for 'discussion action' in surrounding suburbs.[36]

Liberal Harold Holt's landslide federal election win dashed the hopes of disheartened activists that ALP Leader Arthur Calwell would be in a position to end conscription. As described in Chapter One, Vietnam Action Campaign (VAC) issued a call out to a range of anti-war organisations across Australia and New Zealand in December 1966 that resulted in the Anti-Vietnam War Anti-Conscription Activists' Conference of 27–30 January 1967. This conference cemented the central role of discussion and speaking protest within the movement. It was one of many national conferences of anti-Vietnam War organisations as well as religious, women's and general peace groups that aimed to consolidate lessons learned and formulate plans for the future. These are examples of quiet protest, using speaking and discussion to communicate, and seeking cooperation with international attendees and speakers. They were truly democratic events, open to all. Earlier events, such as the National Anti-Conscription Conference of January 1966, had taken the movement forward, but the election defeat later that year meant that the 1967 conference set in place a strategy that was largely unchanged until the Moratorium period.

The conference emphasised democratic discussion and most sessions comprised seminar groups or meetings, rather than lectures. Sessions dissected the methods activists were already using, proposed future programs for 'organising students', and discussed 'organising at the workshop level' and the 'relevance and limit of civil disobedience'. Seminar groups considered 'concrete ideas for forward planning of anti-Vietnam War, anti-conscription activities … with a view to achieving the maximum consensus possible for a limited number of national activities'. These were some of the first discussions in a broad setting about the general aim to develop a mass movement, which was eventually achieved during the Moratorium campaign.[37]

Bob Gould wrote a conference report listing its major findings and plans shortly after the event, and distributed it, charging 10 cents per copy to cover printing. His report emphasised the need for ideological diversity within the movement – a common refrain during the Moratorium period. A large number of activists had stood behind the ALP before the 1966 election, particularly after Calwell called for 'demonstrations from one end of the country to the other', but many within the movement now questioned that stance from a range of ideological standpoints. Gould agreed, writing that 'the political comprehensiveness of the peace movement' meant that 'any formal call to join the ALP … would inevitably offend those in the movement of other political persuasions'. He acknowledged that 'members of minority political groupings like the Communist Party or the Liberal Reform Group made important contributions to the peace movement, and that even individual Liberals played a valuable role'.[38]

Gould argued that seminars, forums, talks, debates and discussions were essential to build 'maximum consensus' against the war. He suggested that women could create 'daytime meetings' to court 'non-politically inclined women' and proposed a 'special Women's Seminar' to discuss the war and conscription 'from women's point of view'. He urged activists to maintain 'continuous activity', which included 'teach-ins, meetings, discussion groups, film programs and socials', and thought high school students should initiate discussions with 'those already committed to peace in some way'. 'Diversity in peace action', through such forums as study groups, anti-war education committees, workplace debates and special meetings at unions with peace speakers would, Gould argued, allow the movement to reach a wide variety of people.

The report also laid out a plan for future communication and cooperation between activists, which Maddison and Scalmer refer to as the transmission of 'activist wisdom', a process generated by 'deliberate strategies' in which activists 'hold classes and promote discussions ... tell stories and become mentors', in both formal and informal settings.[39] Gould's call for 'increased communication between the leadership and the mass movement' reflected his awareness of the need for continual teaching through discussion.

The exhortation to 'speak protest' during the Anti-Vietnam War Anti-Conscription Activists' Conference was echoed across the movement, and conversations about the war entered offices, homes, school, unions, churches and universities. Discussions with neighbours, fellow church members, politicians and many others were a regular part of activists' lives during the entirety of the war.[40] Harold Levien pointed to the responsibility of activists to talk about the war in his 1967 booklet *Vietnam: Myth and Reality*:

> IDEAS SHOULD LEAD TO ACTION. If this booklet's analysis has convinced you our involvement in the Vietnam War is wrong and should be stopped, please don't shrug your shoulders and say 'what can I do?' Every person so convinced has a duty to his conscience to communicate to as many of his fellows as possible. A few thousand voices can soon snowball into hundreds of thousands. This is the only way government policy can be changed.[41]

In a 1968 *Tribune* article called 'Talking peace on street corners', its editor Alec Robertson described 'a recent Friday evening in Sydney', in which 80 or 90 activists who had been at a '1000-strong demonstration in Martin Place against the onerous new conscription laws' were, 'within minutes ... in action at Circular Quay, Wynyard,

Town Hall and St James tube stations, bailing up passers-by for serious discussions about Simon Townsend, Army brutality, conscription, the Vietnam War'. They wore badges stating: 'I oppose conscription. Let's talk about it'. The group collected signatures on a petition to parliament against the *National Service Act* amendments and asked for donations to cover postage for protest postcards that were to be sent to the Army Minister, but the discussions also changed attitudes. One activist shared, 'I met a woman who began by saying the Army should give Simon Townsend more of the same treatment. But after 10 minutes' talk, she took a protest card and signed it'.[42]

For some, the movement against the Vietnam War was a step towards a larger revolutionary shift. In November 1968, Liberation's Denis Freney announced the formation of a 'revolutionary socialist organisation', to be named Revolutionary Socialist Alliance (RSA), which would hold discussion groups at Gould's Third World Bookshop 'due to its convenience and the presence of many youth there after exams'. These discussions centred on the CPA, the ALP, the youth movement and the union movement, reflecting radical dissatisfaction with CPA and Labor approaches towards activism, and the belief that the figure of 'the worker' was key to the movement's success.[43] Resistance, with an adjacent ideology, formed a Socialist Study Group that discussed works like Karl Marx's *Value, Price and Profit,* and *Wage, Labour and Capital,* as well as Leon Trotsky's history of the Russian Revolution.[44] Their Radical Forums also provoked theoretical, historical and tactical discussions, held on a range of topics, including 'Non-Activist Protest', 'The CPA and Australian Society', 'Anarchism vs Marxism' and 'The Student Movement: Where Do We Go From Here?'[45]

Many public demonstrations also incorporated conversations. On 15 December 1969, a rally held in Chifley Square at 5pm, organised by the December Mobilisation Committee with members from VAC, Resistance, High School Students Against the War in Vietnam, UNSW Labor Club and Sydney University Labor Club, was followed by a 6.30pm meeting in Sydney Town Hall. The Town Hall meeting included a speaking panel and an 'all-in discussion' led by American Allen Myers, a former GI and conscript turned anti-war activist; ALP

Member for Lalor Dr Jim Cairns; Monash University physicist and ecologist Dr Alan Roberts; former American Students for a Democratic Society (SDS) member Phil Sanford; George Petersen, the progressive ALP Member for Kembla; SDS Sydney convenor Brian Glover; Bob Gould, and Wollongong wharfie Stewart West.[46]

The February 1971 National Anti-War Conference, held in Sydney between the second and third Moratorium rallies, also facilitated discussion between members of the public and activists. It included 'a series of decentralised pre-conference discussions, forums, debates, meetings etc. in jobs, local areas, schools and universities … aimed at involving both supporters of the present movement and also thousands of workers, students and others not already involved'.[47] Activists were encouraged to approach politicians, university administrators, and religious groups like the Australian Council of Churches, unions, sporting bodies, RSL sub-branches, Apex and Lions Clubs, student representative councils and local councils 'seeking their support or engaging them in dialogue about the war'. Tactics included such methods as 'mass ring-ins' to radio programs; 'town or suburb public meetings, debates, teach-ins'; canvassing door-to-door 'to get people to come to local activities, to talk about the war and conscription'; 'study groups in homes, churches, schools, etc.'; arranging high school debates and teach-ins; and holding 'lunch hour discussions … to publicise the Moratorium'.[48] A short booklet of 'factual material on the war and conscription', predominantly gleaned from newspapers and magazines, was collated with the aims of the organisation and printed by the Moratorium Secretariat 'to be used as a basis for speeches, pamphlets or whatever' by other organisations.[49]

LECTURES, FORUMS AND TEACH-INS

Although public and private conversations spread the word and expanded the movement, lectures, forums and teach-ins served as collective 'sites of agitation' and promoted 'identity formation', by bringing together large numbers of people at once.[50] Activists hosted such events to share information about the war, while politicians did so to align themselves with the movement and gain support. The Ku-ring-gai Study Group encouraged supporters to attend public forums, forgoing their October 1965 meeting to enable members to attend a Forum on Vietnam in Chatswood on 5 November and a 'Peace Workshop' by AICD held the following day. They also invited speakers to address the group about 'current international problems', such as Gordon Barton of the Liberal Reform movement and the ALP Member for the western Sydney seat of Reid, Tom Uren.[51] Uren was a war veteran and prisoner of war, and was a formidable left-wing organiser who spent a lot of time on the road in the 1960s, recalling he and Cairns 'travelled the length and breadth of Australia speaking at universities, public meetings, trade union meetings and you name it'.[52]

Phyllis Latona, then vice president of both AICD and WILPF, travelled to Jakarta, Indonesia, to engage in discussions with Vietnamese women in 1965, and on her return took part in a series of speaking engagements. In August she appeared at a Parramatta and District Committee for International Cooperation forum, 'The Human Tragedy in Vietnam', alongside Tom Uren, Methodist Reverend Errol Towner and YCAC's Barry Robinson.[53] The next month she addressed the East Hills Peace Group at the Methodist Hall in Revesby, after a screening of the film *Behind the Lines in Vietnam*.[54] In October, she joined social psychologist and academic Alex Carey at Capitol Hall on Chapel Road, Bankstown in south-western Sydney on a panel with Liberal Party member and future prime minister John Howard, who supported the war.[55] In December, she spoke to the Fairfield Peace Committee, which told members: 'Mrs Latona recently spent some time in Djakarta, where she met women from both North and South Vietnam. They had a long and interesting discussion on the present situation in Vietnam, and Mrs Latona will relate the outcome of these discussions'.[56]

Public forums featuring a range of speakers with different ideological viewpoints were used tactically to boost audiences and fill large venues. A December 1965 Sydney Town Hall 'Talk-In on Vietnam' sponsored by YCAC, SOS, AICD, Campaign for Nuclear Disarmament, WILPF and VAC, featured the editor of the *Anglican*, Francis James;

YCAC President Barry Robinson; Richard Walsh, one of the editors of the counterculture magazine *Oz*; and Richard Carleton, editor of the UNSW student paper *Tharunka*.[57] Including religious figures cast an aura of respectability – in October 1968, a Vietnam Action Society for Peace forum included Anglican Reverend John Beer, Alex Carey and conscientious objector and student Rowan Cahill.[58] Religious groups organised their own events, such as a March 1968 'Speak Out' at the Central Methodist Mission on King Street, Newcastle, that was sponsored by the Anglican/Methodist Committee of Conscience on Vietnam group. The Anglican Bishop of Newcastle James Housden chaired a discussion between Beer, Catholic priest Charles Bowers and Methodist minister Ronald Page.[59] Commemoration of old wars provided occasions to protest the current one: ESHRAA dedicated their Anzac Day commemorations in 1969 to a large public lecture by journalist Allan Ashbolt, including speeches written by Jim Cairns, Catholics for Peace, and the Australian Council of Churches. It attracted 500 people and was described as 'the only Anzac Day function worth going to' by one Sydney radio station.[60]

The 'talk-in' and 'speak-out' were variations of the 'marathon talk and discussion meetings' called 'teach-ins', inspired by US events such as the May 1965 Vietnam Day Teach-In at the University of California, Berkeley.[61] Teach-ins were more collaborative than public lectures, reflecting a shift in academic culture towards the humanities and social sciences that contributed to increasing media and government interest in scholarly research about key social issues throughout the 1960s. In 1970, political scientist Henry Albinski said teach-ins including religious ministers, parliamentarians, journalists and academics were 'among the first stages on which spirited, contentious discussion of Vietnam occurred in Australia'.[62]

The first Australian teach-in was organised by historian Robin Gollan at the Institute for Advanced Studies at the Australian National University in Canberra, on 23 July 1965. Over eight hours, 800 attendees listened to Jim Cairns, the Liberal Member for Parkes Tom Hughes, and academic historian Geoffrey Fairbairn discuss the war.[63] That same month, Channel 7 studio hosted anti-communist Catholic

BA Santamaria and Cairns – two contentious figures on opposing sides. The next day, Sydney's State Theatre became the venue for a 'preach-in'.

Sean Scalmer has written about the intentional 'staging' of teach-in events to attract press attention, maximise impact, and educate members of the public about the war.[64] Journalists at the time understood teach-ins were a phenomenon, even if, like *SMH* journalist Leicester Cotton, they questioned their value: 'It is obviously too late to protest now, but we can't see any overwhelming reason for the ugly term "teach-in" as a substitute for a debate or forum, still less for "preach-in"'. He wondered, 'did it teach or do anything more than confirm those who took part in their own previous convictions?'[65] The University of Sydney senior philosophy lecturer and staunch anti-communist William Eddy defended the teach-in:

> Such a session has its point in the context of a democracy confronted by one of the most important problems in its history. The public exposition of differing positions by competent spokesmen should give others a great deal of material upon which to reflect and put them in a position to reach informed conclusions if they have the will to do so.[66]

Teach-ins remained a feature of Vietnam War-era activism. Two days after Cotton's article was published, one was held at the University of Sydney's Wallace Theatre.[67] After the 1967 Anti-Vietnam War Anti-Conscription Activists' Conference, which included teach-ins and other types of discussions in the 'next major organised phase of action against the Vietnam War', teach-ins began to occur outside universities.[68] In 1969, ALP candidate for Mackellar Tom Reynolds, Methodist Reverend Ted Noffs, SDS Sydney's Mike Jones and student activist Russ Darnley were part of a Conscription Teach-in at the Surf Club Hall at Collaroy Beach, to which the organisers invited members of the Young Liberals and other local members of parliament.[69] During the Moratorium campaign, a teach-in and film screening at Glebe Town Hall organised by the Glebe Moratorium Committee encouraged invitees to 'make real your commitment to peace'.[70]

Public forums and teach-ins remain successful strategies today and webinar technologies allow activists to educate beyond a local audience. In October 2018, Aboriginal activist and Victoria University Professor Gary Foley spoke to a group of Australians opposed to offshore immigration detention in the Greek Centre for Contemporary Culture at 168 Lonsdale Street in Melbourne. He talked alongside Kurdish-Iranian poet and journalist Behrouz Boochani, who was imprisoned in the Australian Government's immigration detention centre on Manus Island but was able to join the meeting using Skype video conferencing on his mobile phone. The event celebrated the release of Boochani's memoir *No Friend but the Mountains,* which he had written over many months, sending WhatsApp messages and texts in Farsi to Iranian-Australian philosopher Omid Tofighian, who then translated them to English.[71]

The campaigns against the Vietnam War and conscription continuously used discussion as a tool to communicate 'activist wisdom' within the movement. NSW protesters were urged to initiate conversations about Vietnam within their communities and spread the word about events against the war. These conversations took place in private homes and group meetings, lectures and conferences, and everyday interactions between activists and the people around them. The next chapter expands the focus to the ways activists put their words on paper. The constant discussions by activists throughout the war were matched by hundreds of thousands of letters, postcards, leaflets and articles sent across the state to try to end the war.

CHAPTER EIGHT

WRITING AND PUBLISHING FOR VIETNAM

During his 30-year term as chairman of the Social Questions Committee of the General Synod of the Anglican Church, the Bishop of Armidale John Stoward Moyes had spoken out many times to support everyday Australians as they battled the state, including during the 1949 Newcastle coal strikes. He was 80 years old, retired, and living in Vaucluse when he wrote to then Liberal Prime Minister Robert Menzies on 12 March 1965 to encourage him to actively work towards peace in Vietnam.

The letter, drafted with the assistance of *Anglican* publisher Francis James and AICD and signed by 11 Anglican bishops, read:

> There are a number of us deeply concerned that our Government should be seen to be taking positive steps, with others, towards an honourable and peaceful settlement of the fighting in Vietnam ... We would hope that our nation, living as we do in the Asian world, should join with the Pope, [UN Secretary-General] U Thant and the distinguished leaders of the other Western nations ... in bringing to a close a war that is costing so many lives and reducing the economy of Vietnam to chaos.[1]

The correspondence that ensued produced the first public debate about the justness of Australian involvement in the Vietnam War.[2]

The sheer size of the protest archive in libraries and other institutions across Australia is testament to the constant flow of paper between newspapers, activists, churches, universities, unions, ex-servicemen's organisations and politicians throughout the Vietnam War years. Religious and secular activists used constant written communication to achieve their goals, through letters, articles, petitions and leaflets, as well as advertisements in newspapers. Social movement organisations are 'active subjects of political communication' that work from a grassroots perspective to create 'alternative systems of meaning and discourses'.[3] Political scientist Henry Albinski, writing in 1970, described the conscious creation of a 'pressure movement' to, as the National Campaign Against Conscription (NCAC) stated, 'not only aim to educate the general public, but also change the attitude of members of the government'.[4] Many groups, including the Cumberland Regional Peace Committee, instructed members to not only write letters to politicians in Australia, but also in the US, USSR and UK.[5]

The torrent of information became so overwhelming that in 1966 *Outlook* surveyed the journals, magazines, newspapers, newsletters, reprints and reports produced by 'a score of more of organisations' and asked, 'Is the Australian Protest Left ... suffering from a rush of printed matter to the head?'[6]

Whatever one's answer to this question, it is pleasing to see that even in the internet era, when an article, comment or meme can be posted once and seen by millions globally, the importance of written communication has not been lost. After the bold sermon made in support of immigrants and LGBTQIA+ people by Episcopal Reverend Mariann Edgar Budde on 21 January 2025 to an audience of Republican figures, including the newly inaugurated US President Donald Trump, supporters were urged on social media to send a postcard or a letter of support to the Bishop at the Episcopalian Church House in Washington DC.[7] This chapter will discuss correspondence during the Vietnam War between citizens, politicians and other influential figures, including Moyes, that was tactically used to move the nation into the desired political direction.

Moyes had sent a draft of the letter to Anglican bishops across the country before writing to Menzies, asking whether they would agree to co-sign. He expressed the hope that 'we bishops might lead public opinion in urging on the Government positive action towards a settlement of the fighting in Vietnam. This has reached a frightening stage. The Americans are getting nowhere – just as the French did earlier'.[8]

The *Age* and *SMH* printed Moyes' letter in full on 15 March, emphasising the rebelliousness of the bishops to 'have taken it on themselves to state their feelings without waiting for a meeting of the General Synod'.[9] Twelve bishops signed the letter. Bishop of Kalgoorlie Cecil Muschamp wrote, 'I love the Americans very much, but I doubt both their competence and their sincerity in international affairs – just as I sometimes doubt ours'. Bishop of Gippsland David Garnsey thanked Moyes, adding 'The whole affair is appalling'. Wangaratta's Bishop Theodore McCall wrote he was 'very much in doubt about the whole business but see nothing to object to in the letter and possibly a great deal that might be gained if it were conceivable that our Prime Minister would take the slightest notice'. Although some, like the Archbishop of Brisbane Philip Strong, told Moyes 'my views appear to differ somewhat from yours' and that he preferred not to sign, the Archbishops of Perth, Ballarat, Grafton and Carpentaria, as well as the former Archbishop of Melbourne and former Bishops of Bendigo and Tasmania, did. The Bishop of Newcastle added his name a few days later.[10]

Menzies responded, writing to the bishops, 'your letter surprises and distresses me', and accused them of 'urging some form of political action upon me and my colleagues in relation to the fighting in Vietnam'. He laid the blame for the war, and responsibility for peace, on the North Vietnamese: 'The change of heart that is needed to lay a good foundation for a fruitful negotiation and a lasting peace must occur in the Communist bodies'.[11]

The bishops refuted Menzies' claim they were shunning their responsibilities as Australian citizens by refusing to oppose communism without hesitation. They wrote on 9 April, 'The main contention of your letter is that we are indifferent to the moral and religious elements in the situation, whereas you and your Government are deeply concerned with both'. They reiterated 'the hope which was the main point of our original letter that you will use your great influence and experience to support the possibility of negotiations'.[12] The Prime Minister's final reply of 20 April was more forceful:

> My colleagues and I must decline to be cast for the roles of warmongers and supporters of illicit action on the part of the United States or South Vietnam. We are constantly aware of our duties to our country and our people. One of those duties is to do what we can to keep the peace, and to help others to keep it. Another is to be acutely aware of the need to preserve the security of Australia ... We have no desire for hostilities to spread or to grow more intense, though, if this is forced upon us, we will face the resulting situation and not seek to avoid it.[13]

This was a public battle between two bastions of respectability: religion and politics. Capturing the attention of the nation by drawing the Prime Minister into a debate about his government's decision to send troops to Vietnam was a significant feat and positioned the bishops among the allegedly unruly anti-war protesters.

Moyes was evidently unconcerned with this assumption or that a range of activists threw their support behind him. During the back-and-forth with the prime minister, AICD elected him a member on 16 March.[14] The Women's International League of Peace and Freedom (WILPF) distributed a list of answers to the questions raised within the letters, which, as public records, had been 'kindly forwarded' to them from the Prime Minister. Their examination of the correspondence showed them that: 'At no stage in the discussion did the bishops claim to be authorities on questions of foreign policy. This claim, as far as we know, was not advanced by any other body of clergy. Their plea to the Prime Minister was based entirely on humanitarian grounds'.[15] Academic Alex Carey defended the Bishops in a 30 March letter to the *SMH*, describing them as 'refreshingly courageous' and criticising the newspaper for calling them 'irresponsible' as the 'American presence in Vietnam has been associated with misery and destruction on a vast scale, and with continuing escalation which now skirts the brink of world war'.[16]

On 27 April, the Victorian branch of the Seamens' Union of Australia (SUA) held a stop work meeting where they agreed:

> This meeting commends the Anglican bishops who have issued an appeal to the Prime Minister ... calling for peace in Vietnam ... The Australian people would never tolerate interference in their independence. We have no right to deny any other people the right to freedom and independence, including the people of South Vietnam.[17]

Others wrote directly to Moyes. Most sided with his anti-war position, but some supported Menzies, such as South Australian journalist HW Chapman, who told Moyes he 'would be well advised to stick only to facts and refrain from pure mudslinging'. Mr and Mrs Paltridge of Sydney said they were 'astounded' by the first letter:

> We are amazed that a man of your learning should be so ignorant of Communist strategy to think that 'an honourable and peaceful settlement of the fighting' is possible with the Communists ... The Communist strategy is always letting good people (dupes) further their own diabolical aims and we feel that you are aiding the Communists in this way.[18]

Bishop Garnsey of Gippsland, a signatory, wrote to Moyes in mid-April to praise Moyes' 'first rate' performance in an interview on the ABC, expressing a moral distance from the pro-war position by saying that 'the constructive alternative to Communism becomes less and less within our power to promote'.[19] Minister Secombe of the Church of Christ in Ascot Park, South Australia, also wrote in solidarity:

> Congratulations on your splendid letters to the Prime Minister on the tragic situation in Vietnam. Neither the Prime Minister not President Johnson seem to be able to realise that the rebels in South Vietnam only started shooting after all other means of expressing the people's will had been brutally repressed

> and it was obvious that no free general election was going to be held.[20]

Secombe, knowing US President Lyndon Johnson belonged to the Church of Christ, wrote to the president of its federal executive to say, 'many Christians in Australia hold a different view on Vietnam to the one expressed by Sir Robert Menzies'.

Lay people also wrote to Moyes to express their support. JA Henderson, owner of Camp Maroondah in Healesville, Victoria, wrote, 'Unused as I am to mixing with bishops ... I must express my gratification with your actions on the Vietnam affair. Those humble ones of us have been greatly heartened by the stand of your colleagues'. Gertrude A Dahle, from Kew, Victoria, sent 'gratitude of a complete stranger for your courage ... 'I feel that you are helping to arouse the national conscience'. The director of the charity Community Aid Abroad, G Kennedy Tucker, wrote, 'I should like you to know how encouraged many of us were by the Statements you and other Bishops made in regard to Vietnam. It was sad that the State criticised this Christian approach to the matter'.[21]

The Anglicans who supported Moyes were not the only faith groups to join the movement. Shortly after Menzies' second reply of 24 April, the *Australian* reported that 'great concern was felt in all Protestant and Orthodox Churches about the possibility of a major war developing', and the Australian Council of Churches had also pushed the Australian Government to seek a peaceful end to the Vietnam War.[22] In July 1965, fifteen clergymen, including Moyes; Reverend Alan Walker, the founder of the Methodist Wesley Mission and Canberra vigils; and Congregational, Methodist and Presbyterian ministers, wrote a new letter saying they feared 'Australia, through its Prime Minister, is being led into a tragic escalation of the Vietnam War'.[23] On 22 October 1965, the Vietnam Day Committee in Melbourne invited Moyes to a large gathering at the Myer Music Bowl in the hope that his 'visit might stimulate more churchmen to take part in the swelling tide of concern regarding the war in Vietnam'.[24] By this time, religious involvement in this 'swelling tide' was well on its way, in many cases prompting

John Stoward Moyes speaking to a group in Sydney during the August 1967 Mobilisation to End the War in Vietnam

Noel Hazard/*Tribune* collection/MLSLNSW/courtesy SEARCH Foundation

interfaith cooperation. In April 1966, after Holt replaced Menzies as prime minister, the Australian Council of Churches, representing 11 Anglican, Nonconformist and Orthodox churches, wrote to him about their discomfort with the conscription scheme and to draw his attention to international opposition to the war. They followed up in October 1967, demanding an end to the bombing of North Vietnam and withdrawal from the war.[25]

When Moyes wrote to the bishops in March 1966 to ask if they would support another letter, many withdrew. The Bishop of Gippsland insisted that 'such an approach should be based on conference and discussion' and Bishop of Ballarat William Hardie said, 'The waters have become muddied, the facts so ignored or misrepresented or unknown that I think a further effort would undo the effect produced by our first, and to a lesser degree our second letter'. Their decisions were likely influenced by public pressure, indicated by the Bishop of Kalgoorlie's words to Moyes: 'Like you, I deplore the Vietnam

War, but I feel that now Australia is committed to it we shouldn't hinder its progress, however much we may have disagreed with it in the first place'.[26]

The brave decision by the Anglican bishops, led by Moyes, to use their influence to press the prime minister to seek peace in Vietnam led to an eruption of religious letter-writing against the war. Some saw protest as a duty after the 1968 Lambeth Conference, a global gathering of Anglican bishops held every ten years, resolved that 'war as a method of settling international disputes is incompatible with the teaching and ministry of our Lord Jesus Christ' and emphatically stated that 'it is the concern of the Church ... to uphold and extend the right of conscientious objection'. It urged 'upon Christians the duty to support international action, either through the United Nations or otherwise, to settle disputes justly without recourse to war'.[27]

The 'first group of peace dissenters' in Australia, the Quakers, have traditionally been small in number and relatively isolated, so the consistency of their objection to war since the seventeenth century is frequently overlooked. Quakers believe: 'There is a spirit within each of us that joins us all together' and it is impossible 'to deliberately harm or kill another person without damaging that spirit'. They must therefore engage in an 'active process of removing situations where violence and war may occur'.[28] Quakers regularly wrote to politicians during the Vietnam War, particularly after American Quakers set up a working committee to 'search for alternatives to military force' in Vietnam and released the booklet *Peace in Vietnam*, which provided paths to 'halt the war's expansion and help bring to an end the destruction of human life and property'.[29] Many activists groups distributed *Peace in Vietnam* – a marker of their collaboration with religious groups.

By associating with faith groups, regular activists sent a message to the nation's conservative population that protest was neither disruptive nor immoral, and aligned with religious beliefs. This cooperation was a reframing of 'civil society' ordinarily dominated by ruling classes which, according to the Marxist philosopher Antonio Gramsci, retain control via the press, church and education. Historian George Rudé argues that such control can be countered if the 'proletariat can shake off the ideological servitude by building up a counter-ideology of their own' and 'neutralise "traditional" intellectuals', such as religious leaders.[30]

The quiet protest of religious and respectable members of society had enormous power to sway public opinion. In 1968, Methodist Reverend David Pope urged Sydney activists to combat the 'vast, latent, subterranean sea of disquiet and disenchantment' within the community by speaking out against the war, acknowledging that 'in a society where a tepid mediocrity prevails, and where critical discussion is not encouraged, this is very difficult'.[31] He publicly despaired about religious support for the conflict, declaring 'The thing I want to get rid of is religion. A concept of God is meaningless', which provoked sensational responses from conservative political figures. Liberal Minister for Social Services William Wentworth referenced this controversial statement in the House of Representatives, likening Pope's words to Vladimir Lenin's belief that atheism was 'inseparable' from communism, 'a system of political lying', spread by 'apt disciples of Lenin the liar'. Wentworth said Pope was part of 'a complete system of deliberate deception', in which communists use 'people who are not ostensibly connected with the party' to discredit the war, asking 'who better for this purpose than a renegade priest?'[32]

CORRESPONDENCE AS ACTIVISM

Letter writing was a powerful tool for women's organisations such as Union of Australian Women (UAW), Women's International Democratic Federation (WIDF) and WILPF as they tirelessly fought against the war, despite the limitations placed upon them by gendered expectations of respectability. As recently emphasised by historian Kate Laing, WILPF women took care to project an image of the group as 'sensible' and 'not revolutionary'.[33] Letter-writing was a major component of the activist campaigns of such organisations, and they used it to respond to a variety of social issues, as well as their own position as women activists. WIDF, for instance, highlighted the connections between colonialism and the oppression of women, and so their stance towards

Children with balloons distributed by WILPF in Victoria Park, Sydney, 1965

Noel Hazard/*Tribune* collection/MLSLNSW/courtesy SEARCH Foundation

the Vietnam War assumed a specific character that helped to encourage women's participation in the movement.[34]

Letter writing was the primary method by which WILPF expressed opposition to the war.[35] Each meeting of its NSW branch included a dedicated report on recent correspondence. Through their Vietnam Sub-Committee, WILPF members wrote letters to local and international groups, including the Vietnam Day Committee, National Red Cross and the New Zealand Bertrand Russell Peace Foundation, as well as international newspapers like *The Times* and *Manchester Guardian*, and influential political leaders, such as US President Lyndon Johnson. They wrote regularly to conscientious objector Bill White, and wrote to the Minister for the Army, Minister for Justice and the Prime Minister to plead for White's release from prison.[36] In the mid-1960s they even formed a War Toys Sub-Committee that wrote regularly to major retailers Coles and Woolworths to suggest that they 'supply children with constructive not destructive toys'.[37]

The diligence with which the women of WILPF approached their constant communication with political authorities provides necessary nuance to the concept of 'quiet protest'. As long as politicians replied, these women continued to write – a tactic recorded in meeting minutes in July 1964: 'Members of Parliament still replying to letters sent to them by WILPF. It was decided to send them reminders and more information before Parliament re-opens'.[38] The following month, WILPF wrote to many politicians to outline its concerns about the use by American and Australian troops of the incendiary petrochemical napalm as a weapon. Liberal Attorney-General Billy Snedden's office simply wrote that the letter had been 'carefully noted', but for other politicians the letter was enormously helpful, and appreciated. Senator for South Australia James Cavanagh sent his thanks on 17 August: 'As I anticipate speaking on this question in the Senate on Tuesday, I find your information will be of great assistance and I intend to use many extracts from it'.[39] Bert James, ALP Member for the Hunter, who would later turn out to have been 'wined and dined' by Russian spies for two decades as a Soviet 'agent of influence', assured WILPF that he did not agree with the use of napalm bombs. He wrote: 'I very much appreciate your letter and your organisation's interest in these great world problems, in which we of the western world are far from faring favourably. I will do all in my power to try to have the matters raised in the National parliament when sittings resume'.[40]

WILPF members in NSW believed parliamentarians had a responsibility to communicate with the general public about key issues. The minutes of a November 1965 meeting record it was 'high time MPs were reminded that they should be available for discussions and interviews, as they are our representatives in parliament'.[41] In February 1970, WILPF expressed concern to Prime Minister John Gorton about the ethics of the Vietnamisation policy instituted in January 1969, during which the US withdrew from Vietnam and left the South Vietnamese Army of the Republic of Vietnam to fight a war the American military and its allies were not able to win. Gorton's response failed to engage with their points, merely repeating the official line that this was 'desirable in the national interest' of South Vietnam. WILPF responded: 'We appreciate the courtesy with which you deal with our correspondence, but at the same time it troubles us. We feel it shows too little understanding of the opposition to our Vietnam commitment, which is not confined to our organisation, but is widespread in Australia'.[42]

Although WILPF and other women's organisations were particularly dedicated letter writers during the Vietnam War, most other groups also used correspondence as a method of quiet protest. In 1966, the Ex-Services Human Rights Association of Australia (ESHRAA) wrote a range of letters in support of Bill White to Prime Minister Harold Holt and the Minister for the Army Malcolm Fraser. They also appealed to Prime Minister John Gorton, ex–Royal Australian Air Force, in November 1969:

> The whole dreadful business of war is a gigantic atrocity inflicted upon man by man himself ... We ask you as a fellow serviceman to take the next step in the spirit of Anzac that will lift the struggle for world peace from the ghastly field of atrocities to the more honourable heights of international dialogue and earnest seeking for workable compromise and cooperation – from the men above.[43]

Individual members of ESHRAA wrote their own letters to politicians. Self-described 'old soldier' Don Hearn wrote to Gorton in January 1970:

> After studying the 'Pros and cons' of our involvement, I am convinced history will show this to be the blackest page in Australia's short history. Consequently, if my son is conscripted to aid in the rape of Vietnam, it will be over my dead body, by means of a hunger strike. My son had to register in the last call-up.[44]

Despite the early wounds of Waddington's expulsion from the RSL, ESHRAA resolved to cooperate with the organisation in the interests of the wellbeing of soldiers and veterans. In December 1969, ESHRAA President John Collins wrote to the RSL national secretary and all state secretaries:

> The executive of ESHRAA would very gladly discuss with you any means of seeking an amnesty for imprisoned non-compliers and conscientious objectors to the existing National Service Act before Christmas. In view of the growing world opposition to the Vietnam War, we believe this move is a demanding issue for the good name of Australia.

Collins was soon able to report that the RSL 'show an interest in the subject generally' and its representatives had agreed to personal interviews with ESHRAA, showing them that 'the matter of amnesties is very much alive'.[45]

Conscription prompted many individual activists to write their own letters to political authorities. In June 1966, CFP's Noreen McDonald wrote to Fraser to object to the drafting of conscripts to service in Vietnam, and received a reply soon afterwards to assure her that most conscripted young men were 'generally positive' when surveyed on whether they wished to serve overseas.[46] Methodist John Fallding, who was exempted from active military duty during the Second World War as a religious pacifist, wrote to Minister for Labour and National Service Leslie Bury in August 1968 on behalf of Simon Townsend's conscientious objection application, to which Bury replied that he did not have any power to intervene in the judicial process.[47] Young men who were required to register for national service also wrote to government ministers to express their views towards the war and conscription. Sean Foley, who refused to register, wrote to Bury in January 1968 of his 'inability to comply in any way with … an immoral act'.[48]

Some activists used petitions or open letters to express their political views. Activists have long-engaged in petitioning as a form of political participation, and vast numbers of petitions were sent

The undersigned young Australian male citizens, being of an age making us liable for military service, declare that—

WE OPPOSE OVERSEAS CONSCRIPTION

because:

- **We believe that we may be sent to fight in Vietnam** in a war which is opposed by such world leaders as Pope Paul and thousands of the world's churchmen—the Prime Ministers of India and Canada, and most of the world's governments—General de Gaulle and Senator Fulbright, and millions of the world's citizens. **This would be a moral wrong and an unjust call upon our lives by the Government of our country.**
- We stand beside those American citizens who themselves are opposed to the war.
- We support the Australian Bishops in their call for Australia to seek a peaceful settlement in Vietnam and the thousands of Australian people in churches, in parliament, in trade unions, in community organisations and in homes and families who express opposition to this war.
- We are Australians—many of us are grandsons and sons of Anzacs and Diggers who fought as volunteers and never sought to be aggressors.

We share a fundamental belief that to safeguard the future of our nation, Australia's role in these perilous times is to seek an end to South East Asian disputes, through negotiations for peaceful settlements — not to pursue the murderous path to world conflict through prolonging the slaughter in Vietnam.

We ask: **HAS OUR GOVERNMENT DONE ALL IT CAN TO STOP THIS WAR?**

D. ROBERTS, TAS.
R. GALLAGHER, NSW
P. DUGUID, NSW
P. DAWES, NSW
R. HOWARD, ACT
R. TAPPER, QLD.
G. SYKES, NSW
R. FREEMAN, NSW
N. SIM, QLD.
I. WILLIAMS, NSW
D. MANINS, NSW
P. LOWDER, NSW
D. LEANDALE, NSW
G. KEATING, NSW
G. McLURE, NSW
N. MURDOCH, NSW
P. BROWN, NSW
G. PONTING, NSW
P. STAMP, NSW
I. HOWARD, VIC.
R. LAUGHTON, NSW
W. SHIELDS, NSW
A. DRISCOLL, NSW
D. DICKIE, QLD.

P. DAWES, NSW
G. EMANUEL, NSW
P. PRICE, NSW
I. PEERMAN, VIC.
P. DECKER, NSW
D. TIDY, NSW
M. ENGLAND, QLD.
D. POOLE, QLD.
A. DRISCOLL, NSW
T. RENNIE, NSW
T. BATTERHAM, NSW
L. WOOD, NSW
R. BYRNES, NSW
K. BRILL, NSW
R. WASHINGTON, NSW
T. DE CARLE, NSW
G. FLETCHER, NSW
M. SLAYER, NSW
M. GOLGERTH, NSW
P. CALLAGHAN, QLD
P. GARDINER, NSW
G. SMITH, QLD.
E. PHILLIPS, NSW
N. COLLEY, QLD.

R. MELROSE, NSW
M. JENKINS, NSW
P. DAWSON, NSW
P. GORDON, NSW
M. USLTER, NSW
R. WILLS, NSW
A. COLE, NSW
F. MACHRISCHEL, NSW
T. BEER, NSW
M. COLEMAN, NSW
B. CORR, NSW
R. COLLINS, NSW
R. MOORE, NSW
A. PELLEN, VIC.
D. NADEL, VIC.
I. MESSER, VIC.
M. MOULTON, NSW
A. OUTHRED, NSW
J. PERCY, NSW
P. PETERSON, NSW
E. PITT, NSW
B. ROBINSON, NSW
B. SEARLE, NSW
I. RIDDELL, QLD.

R. WALLACE, NSW
G. WATSON, NSW
J. CLARK, WA
A. MAPP, VIC.
R. WARREN, VIC.
W. KILVERT, VIC.
G. DOUBE, VIC.
D. WHITEHILL, VIC.
M. LEUNIG, VIC.
W. STEVENSON, VIC.
P. KILVERT, VIC.
M. WALKER, VIC.
R. REES, VIC.
M. HURLEY, VIC.
R. WHYTE, VIC.
P. KAINEDER, NSW
H. KING, NSW
J. MARCHANT, NSW
V. MILLS, NSW
A. MOSKVIN, NSW
W. HAYLEN, NSW
R. MANLEY, NSW
W. RUCKLEY, NSW
W. YATES, QLD.

J. OLD, NSW
H. COPLEY, NSW
T. SMITH, VIC.
J. WILLIS, VIC.
L. TESTRO, VIC.
B. ELEY, TAS.
R. LEVELLE, NSW
R. NUSSEY, WA
M. SYMONS, NSW
P. WALTER, WA
R. DE LAINE, SA
A. HARDY, NSW
D. HUNT, NSW
S. MORCOM, NSW
R. SHANKLEY, TAS.
P. ASHCROFT, NSW
J. BUCHANAN, NSW
B. AARONS, NSW
H. BELLAMY, QLD.
C. BRADFORD, NSW
P. BRENNAN, NSW
M. BURNS, NSW
K. DAVIS, NSW
E. PETTIGREW, QLD.

G. GARNSEY, NSW
J. GREGORY, NSW
J. HARWOOD, TAS.
G. HEALY, NSW
L. HEINRICH, WA
R. HEWITT, NSW
R. JONES, NSW
W. BURGESS, VIC.
I. MORGAN, VIC.
J. HASTEWELL, VIC.
R. AIKENHEAD, VIC.
R. McPHEE, VIC.
J. COX, VIC.
P. ARNOLD, VIC.
M. COUNIHAN, VIC.
M. DUBS, VIC.
A. SILVER, VIC.
M. HARVEY, VIC.
K. BARNES, VIC.
C. SMITH, VIC.
W. WOOLLARD, NSW
D. ALEXANDER, NSW
J. MOHR, NSW
S. HUSSEY, TAS.
L. MARSHALL, QLD.

Initiated by the Youth Campaign Against Conscription Committee — and supported by numerous interested community, trade union and student organisations throughout the Commonwealth of Australia.

If you believe this petition should be supported—a donation will assist it to appear again. If you are eligible or will become eligible—join this register of protest!

I support the campaign against overseas conscription.

Name ....

Address ....

State .... Age ....

Occupation ....

Donation ....

Return this form to YCAC, Room 21, 96 Phillip St., Sydney.

Youth Campaign Against Conscription petition, 1965

Noel Hazard/*Tribune* collection/MLSLNSW/courtesy SEARCH Foundation

to government ministers and published as advertisements in the commercial press during the Vietnam War. Petitioning remains important as a way for populations to express political views, although today online petitions are more common.[49]

A petition distributed by University of Sydney academic group Committee for Vietnam objecting to 'the use of torture in dealing with Vietnamese prisoners and suspects and the practice of napalm bombing' was signed by almost 240 university staff members and lodged at the prime minister's office at the Commonwealth Bank Building on Martin Place, Sydney, on 22 June 1965, then released to the press.[50] During the October 1966 visit of US President Lyndon Johnson, 140 Anglican, Methodist, Presbyterian, Congregational and Churches of Christ leaders, including John Stoward Moyes and Alan Walker, signed a statement urging the US and Australian governments to 'de-escalate the war in Vietnam' by halting the bombing of North Vietnam, taking a defensive posture and leaving Vietnam after engaging in negotiations, declaring that 'Only deeds, not words, will break the deadlock'.[51]

Open letters continue to be used to demonstrate collective opposition to political positions or decisions. On 1 February 2024, the Australian Palestine Advocacy Network (APAN) sent an open letter to ALP Prime Minister Anthony Albanese asking him to reverse the political decision to freeze funding to the United Nations Relief and Works Agency for Palestinian Refugees in the Near East and call for an immediate ceasefire, which was signed by 80 organisations and 3126 individuals across the country. Some signatories, such as Congress for International Cooperation and Disarmament, Pax Christi Australia, Quaker Peace and Legislation Committee, Catholics in Coalition for Justice and Peace, and UAW Brisbane and Newcastle branches represent groups who had been active during the Vietnam War.[52]

NEWSPAPER PROTEST

Protest organisations and individual activists understood they could circulate the anti-war message, increase the size of the movement and mobilise political participation in a streamlined way by placing their objections to the war in commercial newspapers, or on television or radio broadcasts, thereby reaching a multitude of people at once.[53] Letters to the editor sections were lively sites of dissent during the Vietnam War, but not all letters sent to newspapers were published. CPA National Secretary Laurie Aarons wrote a two-page letter to the *SMH* on 6 May 1970 that refuted a recent article questioning the purpose of protest action, citing the historian Gabriel Kolko, but this opportunity to educate the public was thwarted as the letter did not appear in the newspaper.[54]

Many letters by concerned citizens were published in newspapers. RK McNairn of Clovelly wrote in March 1966 that 'the decision to send National Servicemen to fight in Vietnam is a betrayal of the Australian concept of the "fair go"' and 'the Vietnam War is fought by the unlucky few, while the rest of the nation carries on regardless'.[55] A writer using the nom-de-plume 'Irate Mother' was similarly direct:

> The callous decision of the Government to conscript our 20-year-old sons for active service in Vietnam leaves me dumbfounded. My son is in one of the battalions to go to Vietnam. He is our only child. Many more parents of National Servicemen (I should say boys) are probably in the same position. These boys are too young to vote, too young to marry without parents' consent, too young to sign a legal document – juniors in every respect. Yet in the Government's opinion they are old enough to be forced into offering their young lives in a war, which surely they are too young to understand thoroughly.[56]

Some activists appeared to feel that correspondence with newspapers, radio or television stations was their specific contribution to the anti-war effort. Writer and journalist Hugh Mason was raised on a sheep farm in New Zealand and, like many other anti-Vietnam War activists, served in the military forces during the Second World War. After the war, he studied art and wrote for Wellington's *Southern Cross* newspaper. In 1950 he moved to Brisbane, and from 1956 worked on the wharves of Sydney, as a signwriter and in the University of Sydney's Fisher Library, while writing articles and drawing cartoons for various union and working-class newspapers. He joined the CPA soon after his migration to Australia but was expelled after the 1956 Khrushchev 'secret speech' controversy and later joined the ALP.[57] In 1958, Mason won the Dame Mary Gilmore Award for his short story 'When You Run' about the dangers of pouring molten metal in a foundry. His 1976 novel *The Last Enemy* covers the life of a man who leaves an academic position at the University of Sydney to address a past controversy in his life in New Zealand.[58]

From the mid-1960s, Mason engaged in determined correspondence with the *SMH*, often co-signed by his wife Betty, and posted from their Leichhardt home. Few were printed – they may have been too frank and pointed – but they survive in the State Library of NSW. On 8 December 1966, unhappy about the recent ALP electoral defeat, he wrote:

> From its first edition 'The Australian' set out to be a different kind of newspaper and it has been different. But I am aggrieved that it will very soon become a different paper from that which it was, that is, it will shortly become the same as the rest ... all newspapers have reduced their functions to fulfilling a PR job for the government – as long as it is well to the right of centre.[59]

He and Betty were more direct about this complaint in a letter to ALP Leader Arthur Calwell on 30 November:

> We wish to congratulate you on your leadership in a magnificent campaign. That you lost is a reflection on the sickness in our community and detracts nothing from your own principled stand. The shame, a deep shame, belongs to the electorate ... this indication of the Australian people's dangerous apathy – actual immorality – makes every word you spoke against Vietnam more vital, more urgent.[60]

Two days later, Calwell replied thanking the Masons for their support: 'We must accept the verdict of the people, but I am sure time will vindicate us and prove us right'.[61]

Activists could ensure that anti-war viewpoints were published in newspapers by purchasing advertising space to promote events or campaigns, or to publish petitions or open letters. These actions 'signalled the revival of public debate' in Australian society.[62] One of the first such community campaigns in newspapers was a Youth Campaign Against Conscription (YCAC) petition against conscription that was printed in the *Australian* on 19 June 1965.[63] The following year, AICD wrote to a range of organisations across Sydney to ask for their support in publishing a statement declaring that the government's 'policy of sending 20-year-old conscripts to fight in a dubious cause in Vietnam is causing deep concern in all sections of the community. We regard the implementation of this policy without a referendum as an intolerable infringement of the rights of young people'.[64]

One effective advertisement was published in the *Australian* on 24 June 1969 to support Sydney University Professor of Biology Charles Birch and Professor of Philosophy Charles Martin. They had both signed the Statement of Defiance and risked charges under the *Crimes Act*, and had openly protested proposed legislation to force universities and employers to supply details about draft evaders to political authorities.[65] In the published letter, more than 120 academics declared their support for the academics, and by the end of June this number had increased to 500.[66] Supporters included 'medical practitioners, clergymen, company directors, accountants, dental surgeons, architects, academics, models, actors, businessmen, waiters, school principals, tradesmen, radio broadcasters, teachers, industrial workers, lawyers, television producers, parliamentarians, trade union officials and journalists'.[67] The inclusion of this list in the original advertisement reflects not only the broad spectrum of support for Birch and Martin, but also the desire to demonstrate to the Australian public that opposition to the war and conscription was not an issue restricted to young, unruly students, but encompassed much of society.

Protest groups used this format repeatedly – as mentioned, WERG gained 500 signatories from an advertisement in the *Australian* on 26 August 1967.[68] The Citizens Committee Against the National Service Act ran a two-page ad containing hundreds of signatures on 29 June 1968 to protest recent NSA amendments.[69] On 7 May 1970, one day before the first Moratorium rally, hundreds of prominent Australians, representing a range of listed occupations including teachers, trade unionists, musicians, students, academics, architects, artists and professionals, signed a one-page advertisement in the *SMH* promoting the campaign.[70]

Newspapers were not only used by larger or more influential protest groups to publicise their views, but also by smaller groups in local papers, especially in the Moratorium period. The NDVMG regularly advertised in the *Hornsby Times*, adding cut-off slips with spaces for interested parties to add their names to be included in the group's next advertisement, with a donation.[71] Christian Action for Peace, a group led by Anglican Reverend Clive Harcourt-Norton, placed an advertisement in the *Australian* on 18 June 1970 asking: 'Can any Christian sleep in peace tonight?'[72]

Newspapers are used similarly today. In response to continuing violence in Palestine, an advertisement supported by and signed by over 500 prominent Jewish Australians, including barrister Robert Richter KC, academic Dennis Altman, lawyers Josh Bornstein and David Heilpern, and musician Ben Lee, was published in the *SMH* and the *Age* on 25 February 2025 to oppose the removal of Palestinians from Gaza. Like the open letters during Vietnam, this was a powerful and visible way to show their objection to military action in Gaza and was accompanied by other types of protests including public rallies.[73]

RADIO AND TELEVISION

Government attempts to increase secondary school attendance and university enrolment in the 1960s had created a more educated population interested in current affairs. By 1970, 90 per cent of the adult population had a television in their homes. This meant that between

1965 and 1975, the numbers watching current affairs and educational programming on the ABC during prime time increased from 74 000 to 90 000, exceeding commercial channels. The ABC would often collaborate with universities to screen teach-ins and debates, as mentioned in the previous chapter, including an April 1966 debate on Vietnam and conscription between ALP Deputy Leader Gough Whitlam and Minister for the Army Malcolm Fraser. They would also screen documentaries that related to Vietnam and the war, including a series in 1967 entitled *Getting to Know our Asian Neighbours*. Television, as a 'public socialiser', was able to draw attention to the war and attract people to activism.[74]

The federal government was aware of this power, forming an Interdepartmental Propaganda Committee in mid-1965 to investigate strikes, boycotts and any other actions that hampered the transportation of material or troops to Vietnam, including 'seditious utterances, sabotage or inciting to mutiny', with representatives from the Attorney-General's Department, Prime Minister's Department, Commonwealth Police and ASIO. The government was eager to ensure that control of the media and public opinion remained in political hands, in October ordering the Department of External Affairs to further 'exercise persuasion with broadcasting and television stations'.[75]

Activists harnessed the power of radio and television to reach audiences of different ages, lifestyles and social classes.[76] As early as 7 July 1965, the Hurstville Peace Group wrote to members of their intention to 'promote tv and radio discussions on the Geneva Agreement and Hiroshima anniversaries in the coming period'.[77] WILPF engaged in 'radio monitoring' from 1966, whereby members would listen to the radio or television continuously to pinpoint 'programmes in which it was possible for members of the public to contribute their views'. They would then create a written 'list of radio and television programs on current affairs to be prepared as a lift out supplement to the [WILPF] Bulletin so that members could keep it near their radio or TV sets'.[78]

Radio continues to be used as a tool by a range of activist organisations. Indigenous activists have broadcast continuously across

Survival, or Invasion, Day of 26 January every year since 1976 on 3CR, the station's Blak Media team spending the day discussing 'the truth about Australia's ongoing colonialism and the current campaigns to right past wrongs'.[79]

Hugh Mason also wrote regularly to the ABC to contribute his views about its Vietnam-related engagement. In a letter of March 1966, he called its coverage of Vietnam 'one-sided'; the broadcaster disagreed, providing a list of interviews or stories that opposed the Vietnam War. Mason thanked them, but replied, 'in view of your painstaking documentation of ABC coverage I cannot escape feeling ungrateful for remaining unconvinced that my criticism lacked substance'.[80]

In a happier exchange, Mason wrote to express his enjoyment of a documentary entitled *Vietnam – People and the War,* to which AT Read, the Acting Federal Director of TV Programmes, replied 'The war in Vietnam is, of course, a very important and controversial issue, and we certainly hope to televise more topical programmes on this subject'.[81] In November 1966, Mason wrote to journalist Bob Sanders, host of the ABC program *People,* to tell him how much he enjoyed the show and Sanders said, 'One letter like yours more than balances the abuse which comes from other quarters and I appreciate it very much'.[82] Perhaps emboldened, Mason wrote the following month about the imprisonment of Bill White and made 'an unsolicited suggestion' for a debate about conscientious objection for a future episode of *People* suggesting University of Sydney physicist and ecologist Professor Robert May, later Lord Robert May, as a participant. He wrote: 'needless to say my wife and I are Bob Sanders's fans and we are also fans of Bill White. The law's most tenuous moral is that you may genuinely object to all wars but you may not genuinely object to a specific war. I do not think I need labour my suggestion further'.[83]

LEAFLETS, JOURNALS AND MAGAZINES

A central resolution of the 1967 Anti-Vietnam War Anti-Conscription Activists' Conference was the publication of an anti-war journal, which

Leaflet distribution and discussion on Wynyard Street, Sydney, 12 February 1965

Noel Hazard/*Tribune* collection/MLSLNSW/courtesy SEARCH Foundation

Save Our Sons leafleting, 12 August 1965

Noel Hazard/*Tribune* collection/MLSLNSW/courtesy SEARCH Foundation

aimed to include 'the best of overseas writing on the Vietnam War, a lift-out mass distribution centre supplement, information and notices about the activities of all Australian anti-war groups and discussion of common problems by all points of view in the peace movement'.[84] This came to fruition only three months later, when the Vietnam Action Campaign (VAC) began publishing *Vietnam Action*.

Many activists believed that producing and distributing as much written material as possible was key to gaining support for the cause. Thankfully, such materials were in demand. In the first issue of *Vietnam Action*, VAC appealed for funds for a new Roneo machine to satisfy the:

> apparently insatiable demand for well-printed leaflets and pamphlets on any aspect of the Vietnam conflict. We ourselves have distributed over a quarter of a million copies, between them, of five different VAC leaflets, and with the help of the Victorian Censor, we sold nearly thirty thousand copies of *American Atrocities in Vietnam* by Eric Morden.[85]

To attract the attention of the general public, media and political authorities, communications need to be clear and effective.[86] While journals and books were popular within the movement, leaflets or pamphlets were more easily distributed and read. Excerpts of larger publications were often promoted and distributed to appeal to citizens with a variety of reading preferences. In September 1966, the Australian Quaker Peace Committee sent one chapter from *Peace in Vietnam* to protest organisations across the country, asking them to order and distribute additional copies for the price of $5 per 100 or 60 cents per dozen, with free postage.[87] WILPF decided to order 50 copies of the pamphlet to sell in its book stall 'in accordance with Branch policy of making important contributions to work for peace readily available to members for their consideration, and so that they can buy them for friends if they wish'.[88] Many other groups focused on the production and distribution of informational material, including ESHRAA through its journal *Conscience* and UAW, which researched and published articles about chemical weapon use and anti-conscription activism.[89]

The Mitchell Library holds 290 leaflets and pamphlets made by protest organisations or figures during the Vietnam War, from organisations such as Save Our Sons (SOS), AICD, Abolish Conscription Campaign (ACC), YCAC, Federal Pacifist Council of Australia, Draft Counselling Service (DCS) and smaller groups including the South Coast Citizens against Conscription and the North Shore Moratorium Youth Group. These leaflets, sold or distributed to members of the public, were often targeted at potential conscripts or groups, such as union workers and religious people. These not only promoted both loud and quiet protest actions but also provide essential 'free publicity' to other groups.[90]

Shorter-form quiet political communication continues to provoke strong responses from political authorities. In 2007, teachers were warned by the NSW Education Department to stop handing out postcards containing 'overtly political messages' that were 'critical of the Federal Government's record on public education'. The NSW Teachers Federation had produced 800 000 postcards ahead of the 2007 election that saw the ALP led by Kevin Rudd oust Liberal John Howard from power. Echoing comments about high school students wearing Moratorium badges in 1970, the Director-General of Education Michael Coutts-Trotter declared that 'schools are not political battlegrounds and we want to make sure that we serve all families with no regard to their political views'.[91] Further demonstrating the power of publishing and the written word, in 2024 the 'Withhold-Outs', who describe themselves as 'a collective of PhD candidates and staff accomplices' at the University of Melbourne and Victorian College of the Arts, organised an event responding to alleged Australian defence involvement in military operations in Gaza. This event, 'Publishing in the Academic Boycott', aimed to use 'collective power' to workshop publishing methods to ensure they would avoid collaborating with or working within the 'university-military-industrial complex'.[92]

Written protest that took place throughout the Vietnam War was able to sustain public attention between louder protest events. Correspondence was used by activists to not only spread the message, but also attempt to influence public policy through letters to politicians and other influential figures. The movement was particularly dedicated to maintaining a presence within various media, including newspapers, radio and television. The time spent researching, writing, financing, producing, distributing and then discussing activist theory and practice is incalculable, but the written evidence we have available to us through the protest archive and beyond suggests that this was incessant and effective. The writing of letters, essays, articles, chapters and other publications was a protest activity available to many who could not publicly protest, for a variety of reasons. The following chapter turns its attention to more of the quietest protesters against the Vietnam War, whose names and actions are frequently hidden in the depths of the protest archive.

CHAPTER NINE
THE QUIETEST PROTESTERS

In 1970, Jane Gray, the secretary of the Northern Districts Vietnam Moratorium Group (NDVMG), conducted a series of mail-outs to northern Sydney residents, asking whether they would like to sign up for news from the group, donate to the cause or participate in other quiet forms of protest to spread the word about the Moratorium. Interested parties were asked to return cut-off slips specifying which activities they were available to carry out, including donating, volunteering at various social events, leafleting on Saturday mornings at local shopping centres, letterboxing or distributing literature at railway stations, buying badges, stickers, posters and issues of *Out Now*, or simply adding their name to the NDVMG mailing list.[1] Gray wisely and generously kept around 150 of these slips, some of which were returned with messages from activists explaining their situation, allowing us to see the common circumstances that governed people's ability – or inability – to participate in protest. Although ample research exists about why people decide to protest, little investigation has been carried out about why others do not, meaning that these seemingly inconsequential slips of paper are valuable historical documents.[2]

In July 1970, Phyllis M Hamilton of Hornsby sent a small donation of 50 cents to convey her support for the Moratorium campaign. Hamilton had stood next to Gray during the first Moratorium rally and intended to thank her for previous correspondence but had lost her in the crowd after the event. She wrote to Gray:

> I am a pensioner & the purse empties quickly when one is interested in things that need money, hence the enclosed

> miserable 50c in stamps. I am in my 70s and have no transport for night affairs, so please excuse me from these. I am against all wars although I did wave a flag etc. in World War One I am ashamed, now, to say. Particularly am I against the Vietnam War, which seems to be more detested than previous ones.[3]

Hamilton said she was not able to participate fully in volunteering or even public demonstrations but was happy to join daytime silent vigils: 'I will stand in silence again, at any rate, when wanted'.

Three months later, LT Withers of Dural sent Gray his 'congratulations for what you have accomplished'. He wrote:

> As for myself, I feel rather guilty at being so useless ... I must admit also that both myself and my wife are not as energetic as we used to be as the years are catching up on us a bit. However I have enclosed a small donation to your local funds ... I would also be grateful if you could keep me informed of your activities.[4]

Many of these notes are from elderly activists who opposed Australian involvement in the Vietnam War, or war in general, and wished to become involved in the movement, but whose physical limitations made participation in any type of activism difficult or impossible. In February 1970, Ruth Fryer of Hornsby sent a $3 donation to the NDVMG, writing: 'Sometimes you wish you were young & strong again! But the hard work seems to be left to the young ones & middle-aged ones just try to do what they can'. On 19 March, Doris J Wilson of Asquith wrote to Gray: 'I am past the age where I can do very much more than be just a voice'. In the same month, Maynard Davies of Beecroft sent a note: 'Sorry, being rather elderly & retired folk we are unable to do more than offer future encouragement'. 78-year-old Lilliam Bertram Wood, who signed her name followed by '(spinster)', wrote on 14 April with a 50-cent donation:

> For the worthy cause for which you are working. I wish you every success as it is overdue time for putting an end to the

> world massacre of mankind. Such practice is against the commandments and God's law as commanded to us, and never should have started … Success to your efforts, dear lady. It must come at length, but Oh!! Let it be soon.

Tom Murray wrote on 21 March to express his support and apologise for his lack of activity: 'I am a man now in his 70th year and consequently not as energetic as I once may have been, not as well cashed too, so you will I am sure excuse my passive support of your ideas in general, rather than being active in extending your work'.[5]

Gray is a great-granddaughter of former NSW Premier Henry Parkes, and ran in the 1971 NSW state election, representing the short-lived Council for the Defence of Government Schools in the seat of Northcott. The seat was won with a large majority by Liberal Party candidate Jim Cameron, who would hold it until 1984, indicating the relative conservatism of the area. Gray's eagerness to avoid any public association with communism, demonstrated by her objection to the presence of communist NLF and Revolutionary Provisional Government of South Vietnam representatives at the first Moratorium, suggests that she may have attracted others who shared her more conservative opposition to the war.[6] Whether or not this is true, the eagerness expressed in the letters she received tells us that the call for activists to join the movement was heard by elderly citizens who opposed the war.

RECRUITING OLDER PROTESTERS

Discussions about the importance of involving older people in protests began as early as the 1967 Anti-Vietnam War Anti-Conscription Activists' Conference, which focused on recruiting from established peace groups and organisations of retired unionists or pensioners' rights groups operating both within and external to the CPA.[7] As such groups were frequently 'red smeared' by conservative figures, older people were encouraged to work through newer anti-Vietnam War committees to avoid alienating members of the general population from the movement.[8] The Moratorium campaigners certainly valued pensioner participation. The VMC allowed people living on the meagre pension to obtain honorary sponsor status with no charge, while charging working individuals $2 and full-time students or apprentices 50 cents.[9] Elderly activists were also directly approached for support. When AICD wrote to members asking for participants in a 20 January 1972 demonstration outside the US Consulate on Pitt Street, Sydney, it included the Original Old Age and Invalid Pensioners' Association NSW, which responded that its members had voted to support this and future AICD action.[10] Whether this 'support' included physical attendance or not, it is clear that elder persons' activism was integral to the movement.

Some elderly supporters were new to protest, whereas others were carrying over existing enthusiasm and knowledge of activism. Noreen Hewett transferred skills learned through her leadership of SOS and the UAW during the war to her involvement in the Pensioner's Association later in life.[11] Edgar Ross, a long-time CPA member, editor of Miner's Federation Journal *Common Cause*, and veteran of the 1949 NSW coalminer's strike, wrote to Gray on 21 March 1970: 'Enclosed please find 2 dollars as a small contribution. My wife and I are a "retired couple" these days. We would like to be advised of any activities of the Group and wish you all success in this most important movement'.[12]

Michael Sawtell, who described himself as a 'Dinkum Aussie', did not appear to have lost any of his fervour for opposing conscription by the Vietnam years, writing to AICD on 2 November 1970 to offer his services as a speaker against conscription:

> My Anti Friends, I was delighted to receive one of your leaflets. I could do with some more. Could you kindly leave some with my wife at this address.
>
> TELL IT IN THE STREETS MY OATH … In 1916 I was jailed for being against conscription and I would go again, if

> necessary. I am not afraid of jail … I am an old socialist and IWW member, but I am now at 87 more metaphysical.[13]

While Sawtell may not have needed to make good on this promise, First World War anti-conscription activists were certainly involved in the campaigns – a few years earlier, Melbourne's Anti-Conscription Jubilee Committee wrote to the AICD asking for names of elderly protesters who had agitated against conscription in 1916 and 1917 and who would be willing to speak at an upcoming event.[14]

Social movement scholars tell us that elderly activists should not be viewed as outliers, but instead as key participants. One of the most important factors that contribute towards individual protest participation is 'biographical availability', or the 'absence of personal constraints … such as full-time employment, marriage and family responsibilities', which is largely determined by age.[15] Sociologist Anthony Orum emphasised the importance of such availability in 1971 when he wrote: 'without people who have time on their hands, great revolutions would probably never get off the ground'. He found that 'the periodically unengaged' or those with 'unstructured work routines' such as 'the unemployed, students, the old and the young' are more able to participate fully in social movements.[16] A movement need only look beyond the 'typical' protest participant to seek additional support from older citizens.[17] Although little historical or sociological research has been carried out about non-participation in protest, the archive certainly allows us to see why many were not able to become involved in a more public way.

Participation in protest by older people is often minimised by political authorities and the media, who seek to dismiss such activities as 'rabble rousing'. Convincing members of the public that they fall outside the target audience of a social movement's mobilisation efforts can dissuade them from participating, an issue that was mentioned frequently within the Vietnam War protest archive.[18] On 20 May 1968, Teachers Federation assistant secretary WR Leslie of Woollahra wrote to the *Australian* to object to an article that labelled members of the Citizens Committee Against the National Service Act 1968

Amendments as 'middle-aged' to discount their impact by making them appear ineffectual. Leslie called it 'regrettable that the presence on the platform of such middle-aged persons as the Secretary of the New South Wales Council of Churches, a Vice-President of the New South Wales ALP, the Chairman, Mr Michael Kirby and myself (all under or around 40) were given no prominence'. He then, with tongue firmly in cheek, played to the newspaper's interpretation:

> When these elderly advocates had the fire of protesting youth about them, they sank their glistening teeth into the Anti-Communist bill of 1950, flexed their muscles on the National Service Act of 1951, and grew to maturity on the Treachery Positions of the Crimes Act, 1958. Now, in their dotage, no longer able to sit down on cold asphalt, they took to the warmth of a comfortable hall and struck out feebly against the National Service Bill of 1968. Those well known senior citizens, Gordon Barton [then 39 years of age] and Allan Ashbolt [then 47], joined forces with the venerable [then 54-year-old ALP politician] Gordon Bryant ... To be middle aged suggests having children of conscriptable age. As well, it entails experience of nearly two decades of subjection to an increasingly authoritarian government ... Surely these facts themselves are sufficient basis for citizens of any age to lend support to the ever-widening area of protest against this vicious legislation.[19]

While Leslie and company were not at retirement age, others who were may have been convinced not to participate due to ageist attitudes published in the *Australian*.

The involvement of elderly citizens in protest still has an impact today. One prominent group that has been key to climate activism in recent years is the Knitting Nannas, an 'older women's anti-coal seam gas and fossil fuel movement that has grown to encompass intergenerational ecological sustainability activism'. It was established in 2012 to respond to coal seam gas mining by Metgasco in regional NSW. The women involved had initially joined a group that offered training in non-violent direct action but felt that their activist ideas were sidelined due to preconceived ideas about older women in protest, and were 'relegated to stereotypical ageist and sexist activities of making teas, providing biscuits and taking minutes', echoing Sylvia Hale's 1971 declaration that 'women tend to type articles, not to write them'. The Knitting Nannas not only experience sexism, but also ageism, meaning that they are 'rendered invisible and inconsequential', despite their development of methods that effectively draw attention to their cause. Initially, they used knitting as a way of passing time while taking part in 'guerrilla surveillance' of mining activities, but soon the women realised the 'humour and power of strategically using their essentialist grandmotherly personas', holding knit-ins and other events that allowed them to share and develop their own ideas about activism.[20] Knitting Nanna Helen Kvelde told ABC Radio National on 25 September 2023 that she joined the group when she retired and had more spare time, saying: 'I felt like I had met my tribe, I met my family'.[21] This type of strong collective identity can motivate others who identify with the group to participate in protest. Knitting Nannas members have extended their activism into the broader movement, joining Extinction Rebellion, Rising Tide and other groups, echoing the calls for cooperation within the anti-Vietnam War movement.[22]

Kvelde's words show us that it is necessary for a social movement to meet people where they are when encouraging participation in protest. Reducing expectations and asking people to become involved, even in relatively minor ways that still have an impact on the overall movement, is crucial. This flexibility means that potential participants can themselves decide on an acceptable balance of the costs and benefits of participation and, in the long term, increases the size of social movements.[23] Protest organisations in NSW during the Vietnam War were aware that many did not have time to participate in person, understanding that people who typically join social movements have 'demographic and social characteristics that allow them to follow their interests to a greater extent than people bound to existing lines of action by such extraneous commitments as spouse, children, debts, job and occupational reputation'.[24] The Western Suburbs Moratorium Group wrote to members in 1971 when public interest in the Moratorium began to lull:

> Because a number of people who are interested in the group are unable to come along to activities, we hope to publish a newsletter like this one, regularly. If you will not be coming along and wish to receive news of what is going on locally, please contact us so that we know you wish to remain on the mailing list.[25]

This tactic would ensure the group had a better idea of how much support they had within the community and knew who they could call on for quieter protest actions moving forward.

Letters and other personal documents found in the NSW protest archive tell us that it was not just age and infirmity that limited the capacity of supporters to demonstrate publicly. EB Wilson, writing to the AICD, referred to her limited movement as a 'dependant housewife', indicating both time and familial constraints.[26]

The granular focus I have applied to the activists within this chapter is influenced by the social movement scholar Alain Touraine:

> My point of view, my effort, has always been to go down as near to the actor, as near or as close as possible, and to avoid analyses of the transformation of the world that are too general ... even in very difficult situations, it is possible to observe a social group develop a certain representation of its situation and a certain capacity to act.[27]

Focusing on fine details allows us to more effectively see who is protesting, and their reasons for limiting their participation. Such reasons include fear of police violence, limitations on employment, illness or disability, and show that activity within a protest movement, both quiet and loud, occurs in proportion to the limitations and challenges of everyday lives. Figures such as the public servants who were barred from protest by the Liberal government, and the Liberal

Reform Group's Gordon Barton, who used the electoral system to oppose the war, further demonstrate the need for a more flexible view of the activist.

ENERGY AND TIME

Illness and incapacity limited the involvement of many anti-Vietnam War activists, and they wrote to protest groups to explain their absence.[28] 'Bert' wrote to AICD's Geoff Anderson in June 1971 to explain that his wife's illness prevented him from participating.[29] CSIRO public servant FE Binet suffered from ill-health so was unable to assist with leafleting, writing to Jane Gray: 'My unsatisfactory health (after effect of a road-accident) makes it difficult for me to complete my duties in my (responsible not difficult) professional work; I CANNOT spare time for more positive activities'.[30] Binet sent a donation to the NDVMG instead. Protest organisations acknowledged such limitations: as the Eastern Suburbs Moratorium Group wrote to supporters in June 1971, 'If you cannot help physically with any of this work ... then what about financially?'[31]

From the 1970s, disability rights activism emerged from the momentum created by the anti-Vietnam War movement, and today such activists continue to support people with disabilities. On 16 August 2024, People with Disability Australia, Women with Disabilities Australia and the National Ethnic Disability Alliance released a statement also endorsed by Community Mental Health Australia, Disability Advocacy Network Australia, Down Syndrome Australia and Women with Disabilities ACT that expressed concern 'about the experiences of people with disabilities in Gaza, who are disproportionately impacted by the sustained and escalating violence, attacks and hostilities'.[32] From a more practical perspective, a zine written in the same month by British activist Max Jane references their own experiences of disability and activism to ask:

> Can't go to the demo? Me neither, but our comrades still need us ... PUTTING BODIES ON THE LINE is a vital part of our

> movements. But what if your body won't comply? YOU ARE NOT POWERLESS ... Can you PAY FOR SOMEONE'S TRAVEL to go to the demo ... Can you SPREAD THE WORD about the protest? ... Do your friends need CHILDCARE? PET SITTING? HOUSE SITTING? To enable them to go to the demo? Offer it! ... Can you GIVE OUT YOUR PHONE NUMBER to your friends going to the demo, so they can call you if they get arrested? Can you make sure your friends KNOW THEIR RIGHTS? Can you offer your friends EMOTIONAL SUPPORT to debrief ... It will take all of us![33]

In November 2023, @cripthegig wrote on Instagram: 'One of the hardest things I've found about becoming disabled is feeling like I lost my right to protest'. They shared a resource entitled *The Revolution Will Be from Bed: A Guide to Protesting for Disabled Activists* that included such actions as 'educating yourself (and others) ... donating ... contacting your political representatives ... signing petitions ... joining organisations' and emphasised that 'education is a crucial part of activism that can be done from home'.[34] Such resources reject the assumed exclusion of disabled bodies from activism and reframe their abilities as tools of effective protest.

Others lacked the time to commit to anti-Vietnam War protest. First-year Macquarie University student Ian Robertson of Eastwood shared with Jane Gray on 2 April 1970 that 'parental advice has banned political activity for me as "they say" I won't have time for my studies', telling her: 'Even though I won't be able to stand with you physically my spirit will be with you all ... I can only carry out passive support but I wish you all the best and I hope the Moratorium gets the people behind it and all that it truly does deserve'.[35] Robertson's 'passive support' was all he could manage within the limitations of his own personal circumstances, but his donation and communication of positive morale is still an act of quiet protest.

Many other activists who attempted to fit protest into typically busy lives, or who realised that participation was not possible, wrote to Gray. Con Quill of Hornsby Heights wrote on 18 July 1970 with a

$2 donation for NDVMG and another $2 for VMC: 'for various reasons I am unable to spare the time or energy to be of much assistance to you in your activities but I will always give some support to any progressive movement that is concerned with the betterment of mankind'. He confirmed his attendance at the second Moratorium's vigil parade in September and expressed a desire to meet NVDMG members. Jack Pearson of Epping wrote, evidently hastily, given his rough penmanship: 'Being heavily committed to a number of projects over the next few weeks I will not be able to give much time to helping your group but please don't hesitate to let me know what is going on and what needs doing'.

Graham Bradley donated $4 to the NDVMG on 30 August 1970 and wrote that he could not volunteer, because he was 'involved in the Moratorium organisation at Sydney and won't have time to leaflet in this area unfortunately'. J Barker asked to have their name put on the mailing list but added: 'Assistance doubtful – will help if and when possible'. Josephine Willis donated $4 but asked not to be added to the group and said, 'not sure if I would be able [to volunteer] as I may be away at the crucial time'. She wrote again on 17 April 1970 to say: 'I am greatly in sympathy with the aims of the Vietnam Moratorium Campaign but I am afraid I will not be in Sydney … I hope I'll be able to do something at the time but goodness knows what yet'. She sent a general donation of $4.50 and 50c for an upcoming advertisement in a local paper, ending the letter 'Thank you for the work you are doing for the campaign'. Kathie Herbert of Hornsby donated $1 and noted on her cut-off slip that she could help with leafleting at a shopping centre, but only after 4pm. Ruth Allen wrote on a cut-off slip that she could not help with an upcoming 'Cottage' meeting as 'I am organizing a Fete for the Cooperative for Aborigines this weekend', but sent a $4 donation.

Kevin Wallace of Waitara sent a polite letter on 28 November 1970 saying, 'With this letter I enclose a donation for the NDVMG. I would like to be "listed" and continue receiving information. Unfortunately I am unable to come to your barbecue on the 12th December'. Maxine Thomson wrote on 23 March 1970 to Jane Gray to thank her for the work and enclosed a 50 cent donation: 'At the moment, with Sue's wedding approaching faster than I would like, that is all I am prepared to do, maybe later I could be more active'.[36] These are only a handful of many Sydney residents, even merely within Jane Gray's archive, who opposed the war but could only become involved by sharing positive morale and all-important funds. Focusing solely on public protest to determine the size of protest movements will almost certainly leave any calculations short.

FEAR AND ACCEPTANCE

Some activists preferred quieter actions because public demonstrations were difficult for a variety of ideological, economic or psychological reasons. The cartoonist Bruce Petty, who was active in the movement, reflected on why some could not openly protest:

> There can be some unattractive sides to protest marches, and that began to emerge in 1968 and 1969 when some people said an impression can only be made when you confront the forces of oppression. A link was made between the US and our police as an arm of US imperialism ... It is difficult to disentangle that linkage while you're marching along and a punch-up is going on. There is not time for philosophical discourse and debating on great points of history if a police horse is laying on its side. The point being that all sides get polarised into positions that they don't quite intend. Demonstrations are tricky.[37]

The CPA recognised the existence of such 'trickiness', and constantly sought to prevent any members behaving violently during protest events, warning that if violence occurred, even if it was prompted by authorities, it would inevitably be linked to communism more broadly. The 1967 Anti-Vietnam War Anti-Conscription Activists' Conference in particular encouraged activists to control their emotional reactions during protest actions.[38]

Early demonstrations were countered with police violence that the media frequently attributed to activists. After 50 activists at a peaceful sit-in at Martin Place were apprehended and thrown into police vans,

Outlook printed a letter by 'an eyewitness and participant in the protest march' in its December 1965 issue that refuted newspaper accounts reporting that demonstrators 'spat, kicked and punched at police', and called these claims 'a hideous twisting of facts'. This letter reported that violence came from not only police, but also pro-war counter-demonstrators:

> A young girl was thrown brutally into a police van packed with men demonstrators – a man was hurled onto the road so violently by three policemen that one of his shoes was knocked off ... A group of bullies carrying Australian flags stood in a huddle and as the men in the protest march passed, they beat them upon the head and stomach, shouting obscenities. The police were informed but studiously avoided the hoodlums and moved about half a block away from them.[39]

One of the journal's regular contributors, HGP, wrote in the same issue: 'And, dusting ourselves off, we realise the sober truth, that in Menzies' Australia, power is in fact in the hands of people who believe that this is what protest is all about'.[40]

Such responses by authorities and pro-war advocates to even peaceful protest meant that the fear of public demonstrations was real. Mrs I Tell told Gordon Barton of the Liberal Reform Party on 23 November 1966 that she was planning to demonstrate against the war during the 26 November federal election although 'people tell me that I am "taking my life into my hands" by doing this ... having lived through the London bombing, and even worse experiences because of Hitler & Co., I hope I'll be able to stand up to what comes next Saturday'.[41] Mrs Tell's references to the Second World War give us some indication of her age, and suggests that the fear of protest was common among middle-aged Australians, particularly women.

Some responded to this fear by encouraging activists to cooperate with authorities to avoid reprisals by police at demonstrations. As we have seen, the Askin government developed a narrative of 'law and order', characterising the protest movement as rowdy and disorganised, and activists warned each other to 'play it cool at the Moratorium' to combat the Liberal Party's attempt to make 'demonstrations appear more violent than they are by increasing the number of arrests'.[42] During this period, Sydney's SOS, often the target of police violence during the war, was 'outraged' by the events of the second Moratorium, and its October 1970 newsletter stated 'we must stand for our beliefs or yield to pressure and become servants of a despotic state'.[43] SOS member Lilli Heyde felt that 'a bit more pragmatism would have frustrated Askin's obvious intention – which everybody now so cleverly spells out – that he did NOT want a peaceful demonstration'.[44]

Public protest or even volunteering sparked fear in many Australians who worried about the repercussions of opposing government policy. Ann McDougall of Beecroft wrote to Jane Gray two months after the second Moratorium with a $2 donation for the NDVMG, apologising for her inability to help publicise the Moratorium on upcoming weekends, citing her daughter Dierdre's party on 5 December and the need to make salads for a lapidary club barbecue on 12 December, but her letter suggests deeper reasons for staying away:

> You will note that I have hoisted my small endowment of courage & volunteered for your list, overcoming my neurotic fear of a loud knock on the door & burly ASIO officers tossing me onto a waggon. After all there would be good company at whatever unspeakable place they took me to.[45]

Gendered expectations on women to stay publicly silent, compounded with the fear of communism, prevented many from speaking out in opposition to the war. Anti-conscriptionist women regularly wrote to SOS about their fear of public protest, which according to Murphy also existed because 'in the everyday life of the middle classes decorous fear of controversy could be as repressive as the fear of communism'.[46] Even the apparently fearless leader of Melbourne's SOS Jean McLean had been hesitant, saying later that 'taking a stand against something is very scary. I used to be quite terrified'.[47] Dorothy Dalton, whose son Tony co-founded the Draft Resister's Union, said that 'going to a protest march did not come easily to me. I can remember going to one of those first Saturday morning protest marches on my own and I almost missed the tram on purpose. I was going to march but I wanted it over by the time I got there'.[48]

Some faced personal danger if they openly expressed their opposition to the war. Louise, an activist married to a police officer who was violent towards her, kept her opposition to the war secret both at home and at social events. When drawn into discussions that criticised anti-war protesters, she 'never argued or debated the point … I would say I had a different opinion. They didn't like that coming from a five-foot, two inch … blond-headed, blue-eyed woman. They didn't like it at all'. Her need for covert opposition to the war also saw her attend the Moratorium after dropping her kids off to school with her 'blonde hair under a hat', and when at the rally 'kept her head down most of the time'. She was afraid that her husband would be at the rally to subdue crowds and see her there or that she would be seen on the news, sharing that she was 'shaking very violently' on her train trip home.[49]

The dominance of the Liberal Party in NSW and federally during the Vietnam War meant that activists were operating in a 'repressive political environment' in which the cost of participation ranged from social ostracisation to unemployment and imprisonment.[50] Responses to such an environment vary as, according to Melucci, 'people have different ways of interacting with the powerful constraining conditions in which their action usually took place, both in everyday life and in political and social life'.[51] Activist groups must accept the variety of ways that people respond to specific circumstances and remain encouraging rather than critical. The 1972 August Mobilisation to End the War in Vietnam Committee was aware that some supporters of the cause would be reluctant to attend a public rally and meeting after the ramping up of police responses to protest in the state, encouraging members to join the mailing list, distribute leaflets or donate funds if it were not possible to attend: 'Don't be discouraged from attending by misinformed public opinion. Every person has a duty to his own conscience and the right of dissent is essential for a democratic community'.[52]

PUBLIC SERVANTS AND OTHER WORKERS

Nadine Jensen, a 21-year-old typist who worked at the government-run Commonwealth Hostels in Sydney and was loosely associated with VAC, decided to demonstrate her opposition to the war at a city parade on 8 June 1966 for the return of the 1st Battalion troops who served in Vietnam. She took the day off work, asked a friend to lend her some money to buy a can of red paint that was 'symbolic of the blood being shed in Vietnam', and asked another friend to mix it for her – the turpentine in the mix later 'landed her in the outpatients'. She put on a dress, worried that wearing 'her old jeans might make her a beatnik', and made her way to the city. As the troops came close to her, she poured the paint over her head and rushed forward. Initially police did not react, 'obviously thinking she was an over-enthusiastic office-girl about to throw confetti', until 'dripping wet, she threw her arms around the leader of the march, Lieut-Colonel AV Preece, Commanding Officer of the First Battalion'.[53] Jensen was charged with offensive behaviour and ordered to appear at the Central Court of Petty Sessions, where she was later fined $6 and put on a bond for 12 months.

These were not the only repercussions for Jensen. Commonwealth Hospitals dismissed her for missing a day and a half of work during the action and court appearance. She then applied for training and employment as a psychiatric nurse through the Department of Health. After her medical examination at Gladesville Psychiatric Centre, she was informed her convictions meant she could not be employed. Jensen later applied for a position at UNSW but was unsuccessful. At this point, as news of her plight began to spread across the movement, she received a stream of letters containing cheques and support 'from all sorts of people – housewives, returned men, old and young'.[54]

While Jensen's is an extremely loud example of protest, there were many who feared similar professional repercussions. Dorothy Dalton, along with her husband Les, initially advised their son Tony against contributing to medical aid for North Vietnam earlier in the war because they worried it would affect his future career prospects.[55] Even those with more established careers expressed hesitance in openly opposing the war. University of Western Australia lecturer in South Asian studies Hugh Owen wrote to Gordon Barton's Liberal Reform Group on 20 November 1966 to express his support and to complain about the *West Australian* newspaper's tendency to 'plug the Holt line on Vietnam'. He owned that 'when writing to the press I prefer not to use my University address, but my private one'.[56]

Although universities did not explicitly prevent any employee from protesting, Owen's hesitation is understandable. Public servants, as employees of the Liberal government that had initiated Australian involvement in Vietnam and the reintroduction of conscription, were not permitted to participate in anti-Vietnam War protest. The activist was frequently characterised by political authorities and the media as a young, unruly university student, but the decision to restrict public servants in this way shows that the government was aware of the broad opposition to the war in society. Despite this attempt to control government employees, public servants participated in both quiet and loud protest throughout the war.

Before the Moratorium period, visible protest acts by public servants were rarely reported or documented, likely due to the need to remain invisible. Newspaper accounts – particularly from Canberra where the proportion of public servants is significantly higher than in other cities – show us that they did occur. On 21 May 1968, the *Canberra Times* reported public servant Thomas Sharp Wilson was fined $10 for obstructing traffic in an anti-conscription protest outside the Prime Minister's Lodge the previous day.[57]

Protest groups in Canberra sought to attract public servants. On 28 July 1970, the ACT Vietnam Moratorium Committee held a meeting in Ainslie to organise the second Moratorium rally, focusing particularly on attracting the support of university students, public servants, housewives and parliamentarians.[58] Canberra activists also ensured that the third Moratorium of June 1971 was held at lunchtime, 'to accommodate people who worked, especially public servants'.[59]

Public servant activism became bolder and more organised following the first Moratorium rally, despite the persistent restrictions on protest placed upon them. This may have been due to the open support for the

Moratorium by key ALP politicians, including federal leader Gough Whitlam, as well as the encouraging numbers who participated in the 8 May 1970 rally across the country. Some began to participate openly, but others still insisted on a certain level of anonymity. CSIRO employee FE Binet mentioned earlier sent a donation to Jane Gray in the period preceding the second Moratorium of 18 September, also asking for anti-war literature to distribute. They requested that their name and address not be publicly circulated, saying: 'As I am a Commonwealth Public Servant, I must not appear in any public list of persons opposed to the government's policy (irrespective of my conviction that that power is contrary to Australia's strengthened welfare)'.[60]

Other public servants across the country felt themselves able to take a stronger stand, with protest groups forming in some capital cities. After the first Moratorium, a group of public servants in Sydney formed The Government Employees Against the War in Indo-China. One of their first actions was writing and distributing a manifesto of sorts entitled 'Public Servants Can Protest', which said many people in the Commonwealth Public Service were opposed to Australia's involvement in Vietnam and to the NSA, but also wished to organise:

> A large number of public servants were involved in the May Moratorium as individuals, and many people in the offices expressed support, although they did not march or attend the rallies. An important feature of the Moratorium was the participation of Trade Unions and industrial groups. However, the unions which represent the greatest number of Commonwealth Public Servants ... were completely silent during this nation-wide protest. In the absence of any lead from these unions, Public Servants have no choice but to form their own group to express their support for the Moratorium and its aims. The duty of a Public Servant is of course, to administer the policies of the Government. If their conscience will not allow them to do this, they may resign. However, most people who join the Commonwealth Public Service intend to make it their career and are prepared to administer laws and policies with which they

> may not agree. Nevertheless this does not prevent Public Servants from publicly commenting on issues about which they hold strong opinions, and the Public Service Act makes allowance for this.[61]

The group, led by Ken C Sunderland of Glebe but also including Ray Moran of Punchbowl, Neil Wilson of Wahroonga, Valery Murphy of Lakemba, Brian Wilson of North Parramatta, Tony Steel of Lethbridge Park and Clive Praed of Sydney, produced a leaflet to convince other public servants to join them in their stand against the war. It declared: 'Public servants have the right to protest against Australia's illegal and immoral involvement in the Indo-China conflict' and encouraged their colleagues to 'take leave and march with your fellow workers on September 18th'.[62]

Similar groups were established in Victoria and Queensland. Melbourne's ambiguously named Government Employees' Community Affairs Group was formed during the Moratorium campaign to provide 'legal and other support … when it was feared public servants might be dismissed if they took part in the march'. Around 40 members staged an all-night vigil on 9 July 1970 outside the Department of Labour and National Service at the corner of Spring and Latrobe Streets in Melbourne in support of national service objector and Premier's Department computer programmer Bob Bissett. The group remained there until 9.15am on the morning of the following day, when they moved on to Oakleigh Court where Bissett was set to appear.[63] In Brisbane, 'Public servants against the war' led a group of Commonwealth public servants marching in the second Moratorium and held a stop work meeting during the third Moratorium of 30 June 1971.[64]

Some public servants were dismissed as a result of their participation in the Moratorium. The Australian National University student newspaper *Woroni* claimed on 22 February 1971 that three public servants were disciplined for taking part in the second Moratorium rally, writing: 'One public servant, Bob Muntz was dismissed on the basis of a security dossier presumably containing details of his anti-conscription and anti-war activities which, incidentally, involve NO criminal or civil convictions'.[65]

The circumstances surrounding public servant activism against the war were addressed in 1971 by the Queensland Draft Resisters Union's journal *Resist*. In an article entitled 'The Silent Workers', they wrote:

> One quarter of Australia's workforce is silent, the public servants. They, under the Public Service Acts are not allowed to have any say on political issues. For the past few years public awareness of the position in Vietnam has forced the government to silence this workforce ... Why is this 'democratically' elected body of 'fine thinking individuals' so afraid of public servants speaking out in opposition to their policies? They seem to think that a forced silence of workers is an indication of approval ... The government must come to realise that public servants think for themselves. We should be given a fair go in this 'free and democratic' country. They buy our silence with the fact that we are fired if we show signs of opposition to their unjust laws ... It is most unjust that the government can stop free speech especially from public servants but also from people in the street ... We must waken from our sleep, take our heads out of the sand, stir the government into action.[66]

Public servants were expected to stay completely silent on the topic of Vietnam but many were prepared to take great risks to voice their opinion and showed their opposition to the war in a variety of quiet and loud ways, resisting in whatever way they personally felt comfortable.

Recently, public servants have been called on to speak publicly about events in Palestine. In May 2024, over 300 public servants signed an open letter endorsed by a range of organisations including APAN, Boycott, Divestment and Sanctions Australia, Maritime Union of Australia and PSA Unionists for Palestine to protest against the ALP government's alleged involvement in the violence in Palestine. At the time of writing, 2388 have signed the open letter, which states:

> As public servants whose work is to serve our communities, it is our obligation to voice our deep concern that you are leading

> Australia to be complicit in an additional genocide, an additional colonial project, staining this nation with more war crimes – even more than it lays claim to already – and, in negligence of the public we serve, these war crimes are again in the service of foreign powers.[67]

VOTING AS QUIET PROTEST

Opposition to Australian involvement in the Vietnam War occurred in peaks and troughs from 1962 when Australian military advisers were introduced until the withdrawal of troops in 1972, which were partly determined by the electoral calendar. The periods preceding the 1966 and 1969 federal elections, and the devastation felt within the movement by the Liberal Party victories in both cases caused alternating periods of disillusionment and determination that appear within the protest archive. Recent research about the way Australians participate in politics tell us that many people, particularly youths, feel disenchanted with the conventional political system, but still wish to influence it in positive ways, meaning they participate in 'informal, individualized and everyday' activities rather than overt activism, which includes digital political engagement.[68] Some express their disillusionment with major parties through their electoral vote, which more recently has seen Australian minor parties receive disproportionate numbers of 'protest votes'.[69] Others choose to engage in protest voting by casting their ballots for 'antiestablishment, unorthodox, ideologically extreme or other ... insurgents' from across the political spectrum.[70] During Vietnam, activists similarly encouraged others to demonstrate their opposition to the war and conscription through their democratic vote as the universal form of quiet protest in a nation with compulsory voting.

The protest archive is filled with leaflets, booklets and posters that encouraged Australians to vote against the Liberal Party's pro-war policies. Importantly, many university student activists and the young men required to register for national service at 20 years of age were unable to protest using the vote, as the voting age remained 21 until 1973. Protest organisations held public lectures with key political candidates from the ALP and other parties including the Liberal Reform Group, which will be discussed below.

In the period preceding the 1966 election, ALP candidates referred to Arthur Calwell's call for 'demonstrations from one end of the country to the other' against conscription when appealing to anti-conscriptionists for help in the campaign. One such candidate was Peter Dunn, who ran in Lowe against Deputy Leader of the Liberal Party William McMahon in 1966. One of Dunn's leaflets to constituents in Lowe read:

> You are needed to defeat William McMahon: architect of conscription, Deputy Leader of the Liberal Party and Federal Treasurer, key Liberal in New South Wales ... A swing against the deputy leader and Federal Treasurer will be a catastrophe for the conservatives and give new impetus to the anti-conscription movement. In 1961 his majority was a bare 600! Another 300 votes would have put a Labor Government in Canberra![71]

McMahon retained the seat with 21595 votes compared with Dunn's 12 687. Francis James, editor of the *Anglican*, also ran in Lowe for the Liberal Reform Group and received only 1485 votes.

Some activists with no prior experience in politics attempted to use the electoral system to reduce the strength of the ruling party by unseating a conservative political candidate. The earlier mentioned draft evader and Unconscriptable Geoff Mullen ran unsuccessfully for the seat of Wentworth against Minister for Labour and National Service Leslie Bury in the 1969 federal election. The Geoff Mullen Campaign Committee acknowledged the difficulty of unseating a Liberal in this seat but said, 'This is no mere publicity stunt. Geoff intends to fight this election tooth and nail'.[72]

Mullen's actions are reminiscent of the goals of the organisation GetUp! in the 2016 federal election, when it was key to the unseating of Liberal Member for Bass Andrew Nikolic. The ABC reported in

July 2016: 'For the past two months the left-wing activist group GetUp! has used television campaigns, billboards and volunteers and paid staff to call, doorknock, man polling booths and exit polls in a push to unseat Mr Nikolic'.[73] Ten paid GetUp! staff members and 80 volunteers working in Bass in the period preceding the election saw Nikolic lose his seat. Although GetUp! has been accused of 'hoodwinking well-meaning Australians into implementing their radical agenda' and being linked 'to a foreign network of left-wing activist groups' by conservative critics, GetUp! now boast over one million members. Although their influence has been less apparent in recent elections, they claim that their mission is to 'bring participation back into our democracy through various online and offline activities such as protests, vigils, door-knocking campaigns and donation drives' which are all reminiscent of much of the loud and quiet activism used to oppose the Vietnam War.[74]

A similar impetus drove businessman Gordon Barton to publicly split from the Liberal Party in 1966. His opposition to the Vietnam War, which he called 'the most important issue that this country has had to think about since it came into being', led him to form the Liberal Reform Group, which became the Australian Reform Movement in 1967, the Australia Party in 1969, and later merged with the New Liberal Movement to form the Australian Democrats in 1977.[75] According to Barton's *SMH* obituary, one of his 'great skills in business was finding ways around rules and regulations'. He devised a way to acquire degrees in Law, Arts and Economics from the University of Sydney while studying for just seven years. To pay for tutoring, 'he borrowed a friend's truck and began offering delivery services. This included carrying onions across the state border in the dead of night, which risked substantial fines due to harsh monopolies imposed by the government on their trade'.[76] This delivery service became the Interstate Parcel Express Company (IPEC), that is now incorporated into the Toll Group. Barton later established Tjuringa Securities in 1966 and purchased bookseller Angus & Robertson. In 1979, when IPEC expanded into Europe, Barton moved into a medieval castle in the Netherlands. After experiencing some financial problems, he relocated to Milan and eventually died in Spain in 2005.[77]

On 22 October 1966, during the Australian visit of US President Lyndon Johnson, Gordon Barton wrote 'An Open Letter to the President of the United States of America', which was published as a full-page advertisement in the *SMH*. Barton called Vietnam a 'dirty war' and wrote:

> It is unfortunate that your welcome in Australia has been clouded by the deep disagreement in this country as to our part in the Vietnamese War. I am concerned that the thought, comment and actions of our Government have reflected very little of this disagreement nor indeed much awareness of what is involved ... The fact that out of a population of eleven million we have had to depend on conscripts to make up two battalions to send to Vietnam is a sufficient indication that enthusiasm for the war is very largely confined to our politicians and their military advisers ... Whatever your military advisers say, Mr President, the burning of crops, the bombing of villages, the killing of men, women and children are no way to improve a political situation. Nor is it doing us much good. People all over the world are tired of military solutions and power politics. They are tired of anti-communism as a substitute for common sense. And above all they are tired of the killing. As one of these people, and as a person having no connection of influence with any political party or organisation whatsoever, I have written this letter as a matter of personal conscience.[78]

Less than a fortnight later, on 3 November, Barton held a meeting in his Vaucluse home to form the Liberal Reform Group, an act that Donald Horne has said 'may have been the single most important act in making the opposition to the war respectable', as it showed that even political conservatives could oppose the war.[79] Fellow transport giant and later leader of the Committee in Defiance of the National Service Act, Ken Thomas, attended this meeting, along with 40 other Liberals who shared Barton's opinion that Australian involvement in Vietnam was imprudent and inhumane.

The Liberal Reform Group's basic tenets, established at this first meeting, demonstrate Barton's continuing conservatism despite his opposition to Vietnam. These include 'loyalty to the British throne and respect for the Australian Constitution', 'support for the anti-socialist principles declared but rarely adopted by the Liberal Party' and 'the application of moral principles to Government'. However, the last two points reflect the major points at which he had separated from the Liberal Party: 'Opposition to selective (i.e. lottery-type) military conscription' and, in capitals, 'OPPOSITION TO AUSTRALIAN INVOLVEMENT IN THE VIETNAM WAR'.[80]

The following day, the *SMH* dedicated a front page article to Barton and the Liberal Reform Group announcing that a 'newly formed Independent Liberal movement in NSW will contest at least 10 Sydney seats in the Federal elections on November 25 and are expected to allocate their preferences away from the government'.[81] Barton subsequently sent a telegram to Prime Minister Harold Holt requesting he withdraw Australian troops from Vietnam, and alleging that, in keeping Australia involved in the war, Holt was acting against his own personal reservations so as to retain political power. Holt replied on 7 November that Barton's telegram had an '"Alice in Wonderland" quality about its timing and its terms which makes it difficult for me to regard it as intended for other than propaganda purposes'. He told Barton:

> By your decision to support a socialist party which would run out on our allies and which in so many other directions is fundamentally opposed to policies of the party I lead you have revealed yourselves as without entitlement to use the word 'liberal' in the description of your group. As I had noted your denial that you are in any way a labour front organisation, there can be little difference in substance if you masquerade as liberals and recommend support for Labour [sic] in preference to support of a government which has led Australia to its present strength, prosperity and international standing.[82]

Although Holt evidently felt that Barton was betraying the Liberal Party and allying with the left, the approximately 1000 letters of support Barton received following his open letter to Johnson and the *SMH* article show that it is impossible to draw clear lines between the left and right on the matter of the Vietnam War. Many saw Barton as a political candidate who shared their conservative views but disagreed with the asymmetrical nature of the conflict. One such supporter was ANU political science doctoral candidate, Oxford graduate and self-described anti-communist Greg Clark, whose opposition to the Vietnam War saw him leave the foreign service to take up his PhD. Shortly after the 1966 federal election he wrote to Barton: 'Congrats ... All the political scientists here see a quiet significance in the size of the LRG vote'.[83]

Letters from members of the public to Barton illustrate this 'quiet significance'. Peggy Wallis sent a $2 donation with a carefully written six-page letter that illustrates the difficulties faced by those who opposed the war, but felt pressured to stay silent:

> I much admire what you are doing, but I have very real domestic problems which prevent me actively participating in anything at all. This difficulty is my family, who are intensely conservative, without thinking too deeply about methods, except that it is 'respectable' to be this way. But they are adamant ... I am not happy to quietly accept what I regard as wrongs, and in my own way I have fought these when they have come across my path. I can do this by writing letters to where and who seems relevant to achieve results at the time. This is not as futile as it may sound, for I've had successes in various matters which I know you're too busy for me to describe here ... I have been working on the government by my writing, which... is all I can ever manage to do at present, but which is still better than doing nothing I feel.[84]

Wallis was aware of the power of her own quiet protest.

On 17 November, the *SMH* published a letter by Harry F Quinn of Gymea:

> It had to happen. True-blue Liberals, sickened by the Holt Government's sell-out of Liberal principles, the slaughter of innocent women and children in Vietnam and the lottery of death called conscription for our 20-year-old boys, have revolted and formed the Liberal Reform Group. The sponsors of this new Liberal group, Mr Gordon Barton and Mr Ken Thomas are both giants in the industrial world and citizens beyond reproach who deserve the thanks of all persons with a conscience.[85]

Barton also attracted the attention of ALP voters, including Patrick Burns of Greenacre who sent Barton a $10 donation on 11 November with a note: 'Your common sense and non-offensive defence policy for this country is to be commended. I have always voted Labor in past Federal elections, and shall continue to do so (certainly in the election on 26/11/66!)'.[86] Burns' words also show us why a variety of protest groups in NSW began including Barton in their communications, undoubtedly viewing him as a 'respectable' force that would be an asset to the movement.[87]

Others were not so pleased. John MH Liley of Eastwood wrote to the *SMH* that it was:

> Hard to accept that Mr Barton, who was born and brought up in Asia, can really believe that the Communists can be stopped by extending to them any hand of friendship or any gesture of peace. As far as Mr Barton's children are concerned, the issue is simple: stop the Communists in North Vietnam now, or his sons will have to fight them in North Queensland, or his daughters will be bombed by them in North Sydney![88]

Although the LRG was established only a month before the 1966 federal election, it immediately began campaigning by circulating leaflets and encouraging its supporters to engage in public anti-war demonstrations and join protest organisations. Barton's existing association with Francis James, who had served as AICD vice-president for a time, gained him much attention within the movement.[89] On

7 November, Barton told the *SMH* that he had found 10 candidates in Victoria and six in NSW, including electricians, doctors, real estate agents, lawyers and even a police detective, but would withdraw these candidates if the government changed their Vietnam position.[90] The LRG eventually contested 12 seats in NSW, and by the 1967 Senate elections gained 2.3 per cent of the NSW vote as the Australian Reform Movement.[91] After the 1966 Liberal election win, the LRG wrote to supporters: 'A majority of well-fed, semi-Christian Australians voted for frightened violence abroad and respectable inertia at home ... It is clear that most who supported the Liberal Reform Group position in Vietnam, did so as a matter of moral principle'.[92]

Many activists have considered quieter activities to be less significant than louder actions, labelling them 'advocacy' rather than 'activism'.[93] This chapter – and, in fact, this book as a whole – has aimed to challenge that view. Many quiet acts that took place in NSW during the Vietnam War caused loud, often dramatic, responses from political figures, law enforcement and members of the public. Some less disruptive acts, such as standing for election or voting, can also deeply impact society. Discounting this by removing them from the category of 'protest' also discounts many who are not able to be involved in louder forms of activism for a variety of reasons, including age, disability, fear, and the inability to make time for protest.

CONCLUSION

Palestinian journalist and filmmaker Bisan Owda began reporting the experiences of Palestinians in the face of military bombardment from her home of Gaza in October 2023, using Instagram to transmit them to the world. On 12 January 2025, a follower asked her, 'What is the most impactful thing an average person can do to help?' Owda replied, 'There's no such thing called average person because every one of us is very impactful. We have communities, we have families, we have workplaces, we have a lot of places to make real change'.[1] Owda's short response was more than a simple answer to a practical question – she captured the atmosphere across a world in which increasing numbers of citizens eagerly embraced the 'impactful' possibilities of their everyday protest actions.

In Australia, ordinary people integrate activism into their daily lives to respond to humanitarian and environmental crises, in ways that mirror the far-reaching campaign against involvement in the Vietnam War. Humanitarianism is a familiar concept to Australian citizens, who have historically responded to violence, particularly violence directed towards children, with action – during and after the Second World War, and the conflict in Vietnam.[2] Mass demonstrations, such as the 2018 School Strike 4 Climate and Sydney and Melbourne rallies for Palestine from 2023 to 2025, exceed the numbers seen at protests during the Vietnam Moratoriums and even during the Iraq War, when on 16 December 2003, half a million Australians took to the streets.

Activists today communicate aims and tactics that echo the organisation of the Vietnam era. Student climate activists have emphasised the importance of attracting both activists and 'non-activists', saying that 'strikers are increasingly attracting the involvement of people who have never been involved in climate activism before and a diversity of young people from different geographic and ethnic backgrounds'. Climate strikers have cooperated with other activist groups and supported causes such as the legal case by Wangan and Jagalingou Cultural Custodians to preserve the Doongmabulla Springs from the Adani Carmichael coal mine, encouraging donations to the associated legal fund and emails to politicians about the issue.[3]

Australian governments have recently changed laws to limit protests, earning condemnation by activists, including the NSW Council for Civil Liberties who are as responsive to social justice issues as they were during the Vietnam War.[4] These laws have seen Australia lead the charge worldwide in terms of climate protest-related arrests. In 2024, political scientists from the University of Bristol found that, since the Black Summer bushfires of 2019–2020, 20 per cent of all climate and environmental protests in Australia led to arrests, compared to an international rate of 6.3 per cent.[5] These protests also increase the number of legal encounters between activists, police and state governments. In November 2023, environmental organisation Rising Tide organised a People's Blockade of the world's largest coal port in Newcastle, NSW. Over 100 people were arrested, including a 97-year-old church minister. The following year, despite a legal challenge by police to what was intended to be a 50-hour protest, Rising Tide went ahead with a second blockade. Although 170 protesters were arrested, Rising Tide declared success because, as they wrote triumphantly on their website, they 'stopped a coal ship!'[6]

Legal responses targeting activism which physically disrupts mining and similar processes of environmental impact include the key assumption that loud and public protest are what governments, and the nations they represent, need to fear the most. Criminalising these types of acts also sets a clear political definition of protesters as disruptive lawbreakers, meaning that the average citizen, who has perhaps signed a petition or discussed key political issues with friends and family, will be less likely to define themselves as an activist, fearing that they may be identified as an undesirable type themselves. Yet, as this book has demonstrated, these and many other quieter protests can have an impact on society that is as dramatic as louder and more public forms of protest.

Defining protest as loud and public excludes the voices of those who, due to physical or mental health concerns, age, fear or the ongoing demands of patriarchal capitalist society, cannot attend public protests. As Peggy Wallis, who was limited by her family's conservatism, wrote to Gordon Barton in 1966, 'I am not happy to quietly accept what I regard as wrongs, and in my own way I have fought these when they have come across my path'. She wrote letters whenever possible, which she said was 'still better than doing nothing'.[7]

Such definitions persist today. A recent article on journalist-founded website 404 Media entitled 'You can't post your way out of fascism' reflects ideas frequently expressed by both activists and non-activists, which denounce social media–based forms of protest as ineffectual, cowardly and even lazy, claiming the individuality of online protest caters directly to 'authoritarian' forces that wish to obstruct collectively organised action.[8] Recent scholarly work analysing the intentionality and impact of 'clicktivism' counters this view, writing that it is 'legitimate political participation in that it is pursued as such'.[9] There is no doubt that collective action – whether quiet or loud – is more effective than individual action, and we need to keep encouraging people to organise together. But excluding and dismissing online activity or other quieter forms of activism that people use to communicate their dissent against repressive policies may not be the most effective approach to mobilise protest action. People cannot or do not publicly protest for a range of reasons, and many of these reasons may not have been actively chosen but are the product of individual circumstances. Criticising those who use social media in this way may mean that people for whom the internet is their only opportunity to share a collective experience may stop acting altogether, which removes a critical mass from social movements.

Could it be more productive, as many Vietnam-era organisations recognised, to provide broader possibilities for those who would like to become involved? Whitney Alese, senior editor of *The Philly Download*, a Philadelphia-based digital news source aimed at Black readers that 'encourages individuals to be civically engaged on their own terms', recently wrote:

> Resistance isn't only huge actions. Resistance can be: supporting libraries ... sending a few bucks to mutual aid, donating new/gently used items, checking in on neighbours, offering your services pro-bono, volunteering ... DO NOT CRASH OUT ... Folks are relying on you to be overstimulated, overwhelmed, & overcome so you won't resist ... Support each other ... Rest, live, & fight another day.[10]

Palestinian psychotherapist and activist Maria Fakhouri points out that approaching non-activists with 'shame and blame' is a 'deadly way to behave if we are truly invested in making progress as a movement', instead saying that 'holding these people in mind with curiosity and compassion is way more likely to succeed as a strategy' because 'a lot of folks are intimidated by activist spaces'. She goes on to say:

> If they have an inflated sense of what is being asked of them, they might discount their ability to contribute before they've given themselves a chance ... if someone in your life falls under this category, help them to realise that contributing to this movement is a group effort. Invite them to come to a protest with you! Grab a coffee beforehand, catch up. Take a genuine interest in their life. Make a day of it. Strengthen the connection you have with them, help them to feel cared for and included ... Our movement is, fundamentally, a place of love. The more we help people to experience that, the more they're likely to want to stay involved.[11]

Remaining attached to the understanding of protest as necessarily loud, or that 'direct action' can only correspond to public and possibly violent activities, means that we also misrepresent the movement in ways that continue to bind us to a patriarchal vision of society. Women were frequently assigned to administrative duties within the anti-Vietnam War movement due to the gendered nature of 'work' and men generally taking the public positions. A number of women were so dissatisfied with their treatment by the men of the movement that they shifted their efforts towards their own wider-scale liberation from the restrictions existing within Australian society. Continuing to view the less visible quiet protest work that was frequently assigned to women as 'advocacy' rather than 'activism' again limits our appreciation of many women who took an active role within the anti-Vietnam War and anti-conscription movements. Memories of the world wars have been subject to similar adjustments as historians have increasingly drawn attention to the invisible but recuperative and economically sustaining work carried out by women in caring for physically and psychologically wounded men after their return from the battlefield.[12] The Moratoriums would not have reached the heights they did without the quieter contributions of women and the administrative records they created, collected, preserved and donated to archival repositories. Today, amidst changing gender norms, we can see a leading role taken by women, girls and non-binary activists fighting for a range of reasons, including anti-colonialism, anti-militarism, Aboriginal rights and climate change, the latter dominated by young girls organising and participating in the School Strike 4 Climate rallies.

When I started this project, I never imagined that I would be able to access enough material related to the infrastructure of the movement to fill several books. While researching, collating and writing I have come across many references to similar groups in other Australian states and wondered how resolutions made at national forums such as the 1967 Anti-Vietnam War Anti-Conscription Activists' Conference or the 1971 Anti-War Conference translated elsewhere. Liberal Party leadership in NSW, combined with the relative conservatism of the NSW ALP, shaped the broader movement in this state. Other states had different political contexts: in Victoria, Liberal rule was opposed by a more progressive ALP party; and in South Australia, Labor Premier Don Dunstan, who was proactive on a range of social justice issues, led the state from 1967–1968 and then from June 1970. I was also surprised to see how many who opposed the war – both quietly and loudly – were veterans of the Second World War themselves. These questions beg further consideration but lie outside the scope of this already very full book.

Some of the most pleasurable moments I experienced while researching and writing this book were when I found myself surprised at the unexpected names and identities existing within the NSW protest archive. I only hope that I have adequately conveyed these moments of surprise, and that those reading will, like me, recognise that so many more of the faces we see and people we meet in our daily lives, irrespective of class, gender, age or ability, are activists who have engaged in protest. It is time to move beyond popular representations that continue to portray Australians who are willing to spend time and expend energy to rectify injustices in society as loud, unruly and sometimes violent. Instead, let us heed the words of writer and presenter Lance Peters, who declared on short-lived current affairs television program *Seven Days* in 1966:

> Who are the demonstrators? Let's clear up a few misconceptions. They don't all have beards. They are not all university students. Some are communists, but most are not. None of them appear to have two heads and some of them even wash.[13]

ACKNOWLEDGEMENTS

I researched and wrote this book on the unceded lands of the Pambalong clan of the Awabakal people and the Gadigal people of the Eora nation. During this time I was – and continue to be – surrounded by Awabakal and Gadigal histories of care, love and resistance. As a settler on these lands I owe a great debt to Aboriginal people. I acknowledge their sovereignty which, despite continuing processes of colonialism and dispossession, remains unchanged.

How do I sufficiently thank all who helped me take this project from glimmering threads of an idea during my postgraduate years to today? Perhaps surprisingly, these threads first came to me while I was sitting deep in military archives, occasionally finding soldiers' words in personal diaries or correspondence to loved ones that – almost silently – resisted their experiences at war. I have great respect for Australian soldiers who risked or gave their lives for ideals they believed in, as did many who fought against the Vietnam War in the 1960s and 1970s. My years studying at Flinders University are marked – in my mind, at least – by conversations with Janet Phillips (who would have loved that I have written this book) and Eric Richards, as well as by my own shift from quieter activism – which I assumed, after a strict religious upbringing, was the only avenue of resistance available to me – to actually getting out on the streets.

In Melbourne, new experiences changed me. The AHA Writing Cluster based at the University of Melbourne, chaired generously by Sean Scalmer, helped to keep my research going. Others – Joy Damousi, Sarah Pinto, Hans Pols, Jonathan Hyslop – gave me bursts of encouragement. Through Hans's always positive mentorship I met

Catharine Coleborne, who led me to the University of Newcastle, the guidance of Philip Dwyer, Elizabeth Roberts-Pedersen and Joanna Bourke, and then an incredibly supportive group of colleagues – Cathy, of course, whose generosity and kindness is constant, as well as Nancy Cushing, Kathleen McPhillips, Trisha Pender, Victoria Haskins, Justin Ellis, Laura Roche, Sacha Davis and Julie McIntyre.

This book is the product of my 2023 State Library of New South Wales David Scott Mitchell Fellowship. Thanks to everyone at the State Library who supported me throughout my fellowship – Richard Neville, and all of the librarians, but particularly Rosemarie Olk and Helen Benacek. I leave Rachel Franks till last because it's difficult to articulate how wonderful she has been in supporting me throughout my fellowship and beyond.

This book would not exist without the support of all those who fought and worked against the colonialist war in Vietnam in the 1960s and 1970s. Thanks to Lyndall Ryan, Ann Curthoys, John Docker, Rowan Cahill, Michael Matteson, and Lee Rhiannon, in particular, for sharing your stories with me, giving me treasured advice or letting me read your personal archives. Thank you to the SEARCH Foundation for access to the Communist Party of Australia and *Tribune* archives, including all the wonderful images throughout this book by Noel Hazard. Thanks to People for Nuclear Disarmament for allowing me to use the Association for International Cooperation and Disarmament archives. Thanks to the women of the movement, but particularly Jane Gray.

Many others gave me advice, helped me find archives or sat with me in conversation about this and other projects, or about activism, war, music, art or anything else really – Matthew Allen, Jarrod Cole, Danielle Leckie, Christian Thompson, Zora Simic, Jordy Silverstein, Therese Keogh, Peter Polites, Mina Polites, Dennis Grauel, Frank Bongiorno and David Lee. Thank you to all at UNSW Press for all your kindness and patience, especially the wonderful Harriet McInerney, Joumana Awad and Katherine Rajwar.

Thanks to all my family – Vicki and Chris Karageorgos, to my sister Lydia Karageorgos, Matt Pinson, Atticus Pinson, Jenny Farmacoulas, Voula Farmacoulas, Peponi, the Adelaide contingent, but especially John,

Christina and Thomas Karageorgos, and to everyone over in Greece who I always miss, especially Dina and Pavlos Foskas, Spirithoula, Spiros, Sotiris, Andreanna, and my favourites, Tasos and Pavlos. Thanks to Eleftheria Vlachos (Kotrotsios) and Vasiliki Karageorgos (Dallas) for being so strong.

I wish I knew more about what my Pappou Kosta thought about the anti-Vietnam War movement in the 1960s and 1970s, although I imagine after having migrated here as a communist after the Greek Civil War, spending some time in a migrant camp, then marrying and fathering a couple of children, his attention was probably elsewhere. I do know that, as he appeared to be a dedicated Stalinist until his death, he and I probably wouldn't have gotten on all that well during the war. He died while I was researching this book, and I thought about him many times while I was writing it.

BIBLIOGRAPHY

NEWSPAPERS, MAGAZINES, MEDIA AND ONLINE PUBLICATIONS

3CR
404media
ABC News
ABC Radio National
Australian
Australian Dictionary of Biography
Bluesky
Campsie News and Lakemba Advance
Canberra Times
Commonwealth Bureau of Census and Statistics
Conscience
Conversation
Daily Mirror
Department of Prime Minister and Cabinet: PM Transcripts
Green Left
Guardian
Honi Soit
Hornsby Times
Jewish Independent
Liverpool News
Out Now
Outlook
Overland
Peace Action in Australia
Philly Download
Ramparts
Resist
Student Underground
Sun
Sunday Telegraph
Sydney Morning Herald
Telegraph
Tharunka
Tribune
Wednesday Commentary
Woroni

HANSARD

Commonwealth, *Parliamentary Debates*, House of Representatives.
Commonwealth, *Parliamentary Debates*, Senate.
New South Wales, *Parliamentary Debates*, Legislative Assembly.

MITCHELL LIBRARY, STATE LIBRARY OF NEW SOUTH WALES

Alexander Edward Carey papers, MLMSS 5898.
Bill White Conscientious Objectors' Committee, [Leaflets, statements and news sheets relating to the Bill White Conscientious Objectors' Committee], 1967.
Communist Party of Australia records, courtesy SEARCH Foundation, MLMSS 5021; MLMSS 2389.
Daphne Gollan papers, MLMSS 8042.
Fairfax Media Limited Business Archive, MLMSS 9894.
Florence James papers, MLMSS 5877.
Francis R Harvey papers and Roger Pryke papers, 1925–2001, MLMSS 7962.
Gillian Fisher papers, MLMSS 11380.
Harold Levien papers, MLMSS 6251.
James McAuley papers, MLMSS 7920.
Jane Gray papers, MLMSS 4432.
Janet Wakefield papers, MLMSS 6969.
Janie Overton, courtesy SEARCH Foundation, MLMSS 6968.
John Fallding papers, MLMSS 7251.
John Stoward Moyes papers, MLMSS 2319.
[Leaflets from the Vietnam Action Committee], VAC, 1965–1967.
Malcolm Salmon papers, MLMSS 6105.
Nick Origlass papers, MLMSS 6614.
Noreen McDonald papers, MLMSS 3853 ADD-ON 2111.
People for Nuclear Disarmament (NSW) records, MLMSS 5522.
Ryde–Hunters Hill Flora and Fauna Preservation Society records, MLMSS 5142.
Sam Everingham papers, MLMSS 8614.
Samuel Phineas Lewis papers, MLMSS 5223.
Sydney University Labor Club records, MLMSS 10665.
Vivienne Abraham papers, MLMSS 6222.
William Phillip Orrick White papers, MLMSS 10938.
Women's International League for Peace and Freedom NSW papers, MLMSS 5395.

NATIONAL LIBRARY OF AUSTRALIA

Denis Freney papers, MS9535.

PAMPHLETS

Catholics for Peace present the three speeches given at St. John's College, University of Sydney at the Forum: Catholics, War, Vietnam, Sunday, June 18, 1967, Catholics for Peace, 1967.
Kenny, Denis, *The Evolution of the Official Catholic Attitude Towards Communism*, Catholics for Peace, 1968.

Laver, Brian and Darce Cassidy, *The Communist Party is Behind this Moratorium – Way Behind*, Brian Laver, 1970.
Levien, Harold, *Vietnam: Myth and Reality*, Harold Levien, 1967.
O'Brien, M, *Vietnam: Why are we there?*, Australian Railways Union, 1966.

PERSONAL COLLECTIONS

Personal papers of Ann Curthoys and John Docker.
Personal papers of Lee Rhiannon (née Brown).
Women in the Anti-War Movement, Interviews with Cathy Bloch, Margo Moore, Adele Pert, Claire Ray and Beverley Symons by Inara Walden and Ann Curthoys, 1993. Used with the permission of Ann Curthoys.

SECONDARY SOURCES

Aarons, Mark, *The Family File*, Black Inc, 2010.
Adi, Ana (ed.), *Protest Public Relations: Communicating Dissent and Activism*, Routledge, 2019.
Albinski, Henry S, *Politics and Foreign Policy in Australia: The Impact of Vietnam and Conscription*, Duke University Press, 1970.
Alleg, Henri, *La Question*, Éditions de Minuit, 1958.
Allimonos, Con K, 'Greek communist activity in Melbourne: A brief history', *Labour History* 86 (2004), pp. 137–155.
Almeida, Paul, *Social Movements: The Structure of Collective Mobilization*, University of California Press, 2019.
Alvarez, R Michael, D Roderick Kiewiet and Lucas Núñez, 'A Taxonomy of Protest Voting', *Annual Review of Political Science* 21, 1 (2018), pp. 135–154.
Antonopolis, Stephen and Serena Chen, 'Time and class: How socioeconomic status shapes conceptions of the future self', *Self and Identity* 20, 8 (2021), pp. 961–981.
Archer, Robin, 'Labour and liberty: The origins of the conscription referendum', in Robin Archer, Joy Damousi, Murray Foot and Sean Scalmer (eds.), *The Conscription Conflict and the Great War*, Monash University Publishing, 2016, pp. 32–59.
Ashbolt, Anthony and Rowan Cahill, 'And the lives are many: The print culture of Australian communism', *Twentieth Century Communism* 12 (2017), pp. 37–61.
Australian Society for the Study of Labour History, *Taking to the Streets Against the Vietnam War: A Timeline History of Australian Protest, 1962–1972*, viewed 2 December 2024, <https://labourhistorymelbourne.org/taking-to-the-streets-against-the-vietnam-war-a-timeline-history-of-australian-protest-1962-1972/>
Avritzer, Leonardo and Timo Lyyra, 'New cultures, social movements and the role of knowledge: An interview with Alberto Melucci', *Thesis Eleven* 48, 1 (1997), pp. 91–109.
Berglund, Oscar, Tie Franco Brotto, Christina Pantazis, Chris Rossdale and Roxana Pessoa Cavalcanti, *Criminalisation and Repression of Climate and Environmental Protests*, University of Bristol, 2024.

Blaxland, John, *The Official History of ASIO: The Protest Years: Vol. II*, Allen & Unwin, 2015.
Boochani, Behrouz, *No Friend but the Mountains*, trans. Omid Tofighian, Picador, 2018.
Bowers, Charles F, 'The Catholic Church in Sydney and the Viet Nam conflict', *Australian New Left Review* 71 (1979), pp. 33–34.
Boyte, Harry C, *The Backyard Revolution: Understanding the New Citizen Movement*, Temple University Press, 1980.
Burgmann, Verity, *Power and Protest: Movements for Change in Australian Society*, Allen & Unwin, 1993.
Cahill, Rowan, '"The two-million dollar man": Bob Gould, 1937–2011', *Labour History* 101 (2011), pp. 209–212.
Carey, Hilary M, 'The women, the war and the cardinal: Gilroy and Catholic women's organisations, 1939–1950', *Women-Church: An Australian Journal of Feminist Studies in Religion* 1 (1987), pp. 28–33.
Caswell, Michelle and Marika Cifor, 'From human rights to feminist ethics: Radical empathy in the archives', *Archivaria* 82 (2016), pp. 23–43.
Chimiak, Galia, *How Individualists Make Solidarity Work*, MPiPS, 2006.
Coleman, Peter, *School Power in Australia: Is Your Child being Manipulated by Political Operators*? Peter Coleman, 1970.
Collins, Carolyn, *Save our Sons: Women, Dissent and Conscription during the Vietnam War*, Monash University Publishing, 2021.
Cora, Dorothy, *Noreen Hewitt: Portrait of a Grassroots Activist*, Older Women's Network NSW, 2010.
Crotty, Martin, *Making the Australian Male: Middle-Class Masculinity 1870–1920*, MUP, 2001.
Curthoys, Ann, *Freedom Ride: A Freedom Rider Remembers*, Allen & Unwin, 2002.
——'Shut up you bourgeois bitch: Sexual identity and political action in the anti-Vietnam War movement', in Marilyn Lake and Joy Damousi (eds.), *Gender and War: Australians at War in the Twentieth Century*. Cambridge University Press, 1995.
Damousi, Joy, *The Humanitarians: Child War Refugees and Australian Humanitarianism in a Transnational World, 1919–1975*, Cambridge University Press, 2022.
——*Memory and Migration in the Shadow of War: Australia's Greek Immigrants after World War II and the Greek Civil War*, Cambridge University Press, 2015.
Deacon, Desley, 'Political arithmetic: The nineteenth-century Australian Census and the construction of the dependent woman', *Signs* 11, 1 (1985), pp. 27–47.
Denemark, David and Shaun Bowler, 'Minor parties and protest votes in Australia and New Zealand: locating populist politics', *Electoral Studies* 21 (2002), pp. 47–67.
Diamond, Elin, Denise Varney and Candice Amich (eds.), *Performance, Feminism and Affect in Neoliberal Times*, Palgrave Macmillan, 2017.
Ekins, Ashley, 'Overview of Australian military involvement in the Vietnam War,

1962–1975', Australian War Memorial, viewed 8 December 2024, <https://www.awm.gov.au/visit/exhibitions/impressions/impressions>

Evans, Kenneth R, Tim Christiansen and James D Gill, 'The impact of social influence and role expectations on shopping center patronage intentions', *Academy of Marketing Science* 24 (1996), pp. 208–218.

Everingham, Sam, *Gordon Barton: Australia's Maverick Entrepeneur,* Allen & Unwin, 2009.

Findlay, James, '"Give it to the Mitchell, it would be there for those that come after us': Interwar feminists' archival activism and the recasting of Australian history', *History Australia* 22, 3 (2025), pp. 448–466.

Findlay, PT, *Protest Politics and Psychological Warfare: The Communist Role in the Anti-Vietnam and Anti-Conscription Movement in Australia,* The Hawthorn Press, 1968.

Foley, Gary, 'Black power in Redfern 1968–1972', *The Koori History Website,* 2001.

——Keynote lecture at Australian Historical Association Conference, ACU, Melbourne, 6 July 2023.

Freney, Denis, *A Map of Days: Life on the Left,* William Heinemann, 1991.

Frydman, Gloria (ed.), *Protesters,* Collins/Dove, 1987.

Gibson, Ralph, 'Victorian notes on Vietnam protest action', *Communist Review* 288 (1966), p. 6.

Gilbert, Alan G, 'Religion and politics' in Ann Curthoys, Allan William Martin and Tim Rowse (eds.), *Australians from 1939,* Fairfax, Syme and Weldon Associates, 1987, pp. 197–214.

Gillan, Kevin, Jenny Pickerill and Frank Webster, *Anti-War Activism: New Media and Protest in the Information Age,* Palgrave Macmillan, 2008.

Grimshaw, Patricia, 'Keeping the records safe: Reflections on preserving sources for feminist history', *Lilith* 14 (2005), pp. 14–19.

Haerpfer, C, R Inglehart, A Moreno, C Welzel, K Kizilova, J Diez-Medrano, M Lagos, P Norris, E Ponarin and B Puranen (eds.), *World Values Survey: Round Seven – Country-Pooled,* JD Systems Institute & WVSA Secretariat, 2022.

Hagedorn, Robert and Sanford Labovitz, 'Participation in community organisations by occupation: a test of three theories', *American Sociological Review* 33, 2 (1968), pp. 272–283.

Haggard, MT, *A Chronology of Efforts to Achieve a Negotiated Settlement in Vietnam (1964–1968),* The Library of Congress Legislative Reference Service, Washington DC, 1968.

Halpin, Darren, Ariadne Vromen, Michael Vaughan and Mahin Rassi, 'Online petitioning and politics: The development of *Change.org* in Australia', *Australian Journal of Political Science* 53, 4 (2018), pp. 428–445.

Halupka, Max, 'The legitimisation of clicktivism', *Australian Journal of Political Science* 53, 1 (2016), pp. 130–141.

Hamel-Green, Michael E, 'The resisters: A history of the anti-conscription movement, 1964–1972', in Peter King (ed.), *Australia's Vietnam: Australia in the Second Indo-China War,* Allen & Unwin, 1983, pp. 100–128.

Harris, Anita, Johanna Wynn and Salem Younes, 'Beyond apathetic or activist youth: 'Ordinary' young people and contemporary forms of participation', *Nordic Journal of Youth Research* 18, 1 (2010), pp. 9–32.

Herman, Edmund S and Noam Chomsky, *Manufacturing Consent: The Political Economy of the Mass Media*, Pantheon, 1988.

Hirway, Indira, 'Understanding poverty: Insights emerging from time use of the poor', in Rania Antonopoulos and Indira Hirway (eds.), *Unpaid Work and the Economy: Gender, Time Use and Poverty in Developing Countries*, Palgrave Macmillan, 2010, pp. 22–57.

Horne, Donald, *Time of Hope: Australia 1966–1972*, Angus & Robertson, 1980.

Hourani, Hasib, *rock flight*, Giramondo, 2024.

Irving, Nick, *Global Thought, Local Action: Australian Activism During the Vietnam War 1961–1972*, PhD thesis, University of Sydney, 2017.

Irving, Terry and Rowan Cahill, *Radical Sydney: Places, Portraits and Unruly Episodes*, UNSW Press, 2010.

Irving, Terry and Sean Scalmer, 'Labour intellectuals in Australia: Modes, traditions, generations, transformations', *International Review of Social History* 50, 1 (2005), pp. 1–26.

Jordens, Ann-Mari, 'An administrative nightmare: Aboriginal conscription 1965–1972', *Aboriginal History* 13 (1989), pp. 124–134.

Klandermans, Bert, 'Promoting or preventing change through political participation: About political actors, movements and networks', in Van Zomeren, M & Dovidio, JF (eds.), *The Oxford Handbook of the Human Essence*, Oxford University Press, 2017, pp. 207–218.

——*The Social Psychology of Protest*, Oxford, 1997.

Klandermans, Bert and Dirk Oegema, 'Potentials, networks, motivations and barriers: Steps towards participation in social movements', *American Sociological Review* 52 (1987), pp. 519–531.

Knight, Nick, 'The theory and tactics of the Communist Party of Australia (M–L)', *Journal of Contemporary Asia* 28, 2 (1998), pp. 233–251.

Kuhn, Rick, 'Australia and the Vietnam War: Analyses, actions and attitudes', *Agora* 44, 2, (2009), pp. 28–34.

Laing, Kate, *Sisters in Peace: The Women's International League for Peace and Freedom in Australia, 1915–2015*, ANU Press, 2023.

Lake, Marilyn, *Getting Equal: The History of Australian Feminism*, Allen & Unwin, 1999.

Langley, Greg, *A Decade of Dissent: Vietnam and the Conflict on the Australian Home Front*, Allen & Unwin, 1992.

Larri, Larraine J, 'The craft of wisdom: Climate activist learning in the hands of Australia's Knitting Nannas', *Australian Journal of Adult Learning* 62, 3 (2022), pp. 352–375.

Larsson, Marina, *Shattered Anzacs: Living with the Scars of War*, UNSW Press, 2009.

Lavelle, Ashley, 'Labor and Vietnam: A reappraisal', *Labour History* 90 (2006), pp. 119–136.

——*Opposition Vanishing: The Australian Labor Party and the Crisis in Elite Politics*, Springer, 2018.

Lepecki, Andre, *Singularities: Dance in the Age of Performance*, Routledge, 2016.
McGregor, Katharine, 'Opposing colonialism: The Women's International Democratic Federation and decolonisation struggles in Vietnam and Algeria 1945–1965', *Women's History Review* 25, 6 (2016), pp. 925–944.
Macintyre, Stuart, *Reds: The Communist Party of Australia from Origins to Illegality*, Allen & Unwin, 1998.
McLaren, John, *Writing in Hope and Fear: Literature as Politics in Postwar Australia*, Cambridge University Press, 1996.
Maclean, Pam, 'An almost universal scheme of National Service in Australia in the 1950s', *Australian Journal of Politics and History*, 52, 3 (2006), pp. 378–397.
McPhail, Clark, 'Civil disorder participation: A critical examination of recent research', *American Sociological Review* 36, 6 (1971), pp. 1058–1073.
Maddison, Sarah and Sean Scalmer, *Activist Wisdom: Practical Knowledge and Creative Tension in Social Movements*, UNSW Press, 2006.
Marks, Russell, '"1968" in Australia: The student movement and the New Left', in Jon Piccini, Evan Smith and Matthew Worley (eds.), *The Far Left in Australia since 1945*, Routledge, 2018, pp. 134–150.
Marsh, David and Sadiya Akram, 'Political participation and citizen engagement: Beyond the mainstream', *Policy Studies* 36, 6 (2015), pp. 523–531.
Mattoni, Alice, *Media Practices and Protest Politics: How Precarious Workers Mobilise*, Routledge, 2016.
Melucci, Alberto, *Nomads of the Present: Social Movements and Individual Needs in Contemporary Society*, Hutchinson Radius, 1989.
Micheletti, Michele, *Political Virtue and Shopping: Individuals, Consumerism and Collective Action*, Palgrave Macmillan, 2003.
Milner, Lisa, 'The cultural front: Left cultural activism in the post-war era', in Piccini, Smith and Worley (eds), *The Far Left in Australia since 1945*, Routledge, 2018a, pp. 267–283.
——'The unbreakable solidarity of women throughout the world with heroic Vietnam: Freda Brown, women's organisations and the anti-Vietnam War movement', *History Australia* 15, 2 (2018b), pp. 255–270.
Moloney, Kevin, *Rethinking Public Relations: PR Propaganda and Democracy*, 2nd edn., Routledge, 2006.
Moloney, Kevin and David McKie, 'Changes to be encouraged: Radical turns in PR theorisation and small-step evolutions in PR practice', in Jacquie L'Etang, David McKie, Nancy Snow and Jordi Xifra, *The Routledge Handbook of Critical Public Relations*, Routledge, 2016, pp. 151–161.
Murphy, John, *Harvest of Fear: A history of Australia's Vietnam War*, Allen & Unwin, 1993.
Naser, Amal, *Explainer: What are your rights to protest in Australia?*, UNSW Australian Human Rights Institute, <https://www.humanrights.unsw.edu.au/research/commentary/explainer-what-are-your-rights-to-protest-australia>
Nguyen, C Thi, *Games: Agency as Art*, Oxford University Press, 2020.
Noone, Val, *Disturbing the War: Melbourne Catholics and Vietnam*, Spectrum, 1993.

Oliver, Bobbie, *Hell No! We Won't Go! Resistance to Conscription in Post-War Australia*, Interventions Inc, 2022.

Oppenheimer, Melanie, *All Work No Pay: Australian Civilian Volunteers in War*, Ohio Productions, 2002.

——*Volunteering: Why We Can't Survive Without It*, New South, 2008.

Orum, Anthony M, 'On Participation in Political Protest Movements', *The Journal of Applied Behavioural Science* 10, 2 (1974), pp. 181–207.

Percy, John, 'The campaign against the Vietnam War', 6 June 1995, <https://www.angelfire.com/pr/red/vietnam_war/campaign_against_the_vietnam_war.htm>

Piccini, Jon, 'The Ex-Services Human Rights Association of Australia, the Vietnam War, and the remaking of the Anzac tradition', *AJPH* 68, 1 (2022), 54–71.

Polaska, Dominika Vergara and Galia Chimiak, 'Organizing Without Organizations: On informal social activism in Poland', *International Journal of Sociology and Social Movements* 36, 9/10 (2016), pp. 662–679.

Probert, Belinda, 'Award restructuring and clerical work: Skills, training and careers in a feminized occupation', *Journal of Industrial Relations* 34, 3 (1992), pp. 436–454.

Quakers Australia, 'Know Thy Friend: Robin McLean', Interview by Pamela Leach, 5 December 2015, <https://australianfriend.org/know-thy-friend-robin-mclean>

Raajpoot, Nasser A, Arun Sharma and Jean-Charles Chebat, 'The Role of Gender and Work Status in Shopping Centre Patronage', *Journal of Business Research* 61 (2008), pp. 825–833.

Raeburn, Norman S, 'Incite, Urge and Encourage: Section 7A and the National Service Act', *University of Tasmania Law Review* 3, 4 (1970), pp. 285–311.

Ranalli, Ralph, 'Civil upheaval in Iran: Why widespread discontent with the country's religious regime may have reached a tipping point', Interview with Peyman Asadzade, Harvard Kennedy School, 19 December 2022, <https://www.hks.harvard.edu/faculty-research/policy-topics/international-relations-security/civil-upheaval-iran-why-widespread>

Rice, Stephen KJ and Jennifer L Bartlett, 'Legitimating organisational decisions: A study of media framing of the Australian Government's legitimacy strategy and public opinion on the war in Iraq', *Journal of Communication Management* 10, 3 (2006), pp. 274–286.

Riseman, Noah, 'The curious case of Mervyn Eades: National service, discrimination and Aboriginal people', *Australian Journal of Politics and History* 59, 1 (2013), pp. 63–79.

Ross, Edgar, *A History of the Miners Federation of Australia*, The Australian Coal and Shale Employees' Federation, 1970.

Rudé, George, *Ideology and Popular Protest*, Lawrence & Wishart, 1980.

——'Ideology and popular protest', *Historical Reflections/Réflexions Historiques* 3, 2 (1976), pp. 69–77.

Sandy, Geoffrey A, 'Australian Christian conscientious objectors during the Vietnam War Years', *Religions* 12, 1 (2021), pp. 373–392.

——'Conscientious non-compliers: The Vietnam War years', *Victorian Historical Journal* 92, 2 (2021), pp. 331–357.

Saunders, Malcolm, 'The ALP's response to the anti-Vietnam War movement: 1965–1973', *Labour History* 44 (1983), pp. 75–91.

——'The trade unions in Australia and opposition to Vietnam and conscription: 1965–1973', *Labour History* 43 (1982), pp. 64–82.

Saunders, Malcolm and Ralph Summy, *The Australian Peace Movement: A Short History*, ANU Peace Research Centre, 1986.

——'Salient themes of the Australian peace movement: An historical perspective', *Social Alternatives* 3, 1 (1982), pp. 23–32.

Sawer, Marian and Merrindahl Andrew, 'Collectivism, consensus and concepts of shared leadership in movements for social change', in Joy Damousi, Kim Rubenstein and Mary Tomsic, *Diversity in Leadership: Australian Women, Past and Present*, ANU Press, 2014, pp. 283–300.

Scalmer, Sean, *Dissent Events: Protest, the Media and the Political Gimmick in Australia*, UNSW Press, 2002.

Scates, Bob, *Draftmen Go Free: A History of the Anti-conscription Movement in Australia*, NLA, 1988.

Seal, A, 'Protest Poetry', in Roland Greene, Stephen Cushman, Clare Cavanagh, Jahan Ramazani and Paul Rouzer (eds.), *The Princeton Encyclopedia of Poetry and Poetics*, 4th edn, Princeton University Press, 2012, pp. 1121–1122.

Shandro, Alan, 'Lenin and hegemony: The Soviets, the working class and the party in the revolution of 1905', in Sebastian Budgen, Stathis Kouvelakis and Slavoj Zizek (eds.), *Lenin Reloaded: Towards a Politics of Truth*, Duke University Press, 2008, pp. 308–331.

Silverstein, Jordana, *Cruel Care: A History of Children at Our Borders*, Monash University Publishing, 2023.

Snow, David A, Louis A Zurcher and Sheldon Ekland-Olson, 'Social networks and social movements: A microstructural approach to differential recruitment', *American Sociological Review* 45 (1980), 787–801.

Summy, Ralph V, 'Militancy and the Australian peace movement, 1960–1967', *Politics* 5, 2 (1970), pp. 148–162.

Sutton, Barbara, *Bodies in Crisis: Culture, Violence and Women's Resistance in Neoliberal Argentina*, Rutgers University Press, 2010.

Symons, Beverley and Rowan Cahill, *A Turbulent Decade: Social Protest Movements and the Labour Movement, 1965–1975*, Australian Society for the Study of Labour History, 2005.

Terracini, Paul, 'Moyes, Menzies and the Vietnam War: New insights into the public correspondence between the Prime Minister and the Bishops', *Journal of Religious History* 36, 1 (2012), pp. 70–88.

Toch, Hans, *The Social Psychology of Social Movements*, The Bobs-Merrill Company, 1965.

Touraine, Alain, 'The importance of social movements', *Social Movement Studies* 1, 1 (2002), pp. 89–95.

Tsounis, Mick, 'Greek left in Australia', *Australian Left Review* 29 (1971), pp. 53–60.

Vaughan, Michael, Ariadne Vromen, Pablo Porten-Chee and Darren Halpin, 'The role of novel citizenship norms in signing and sharing online petitions', *Political Studies* 72, 1 (2022), pp. 26–47.

Verhulst, Joris and Stefaan Walgrave, 'The first time is the hardest? A cross-national and cross-issue comparison of first-time protest participants', *Political Behaviour* 31 (2009), pp. 455–484.

Vromen, Ariadne, 'GetUp! in Election 2016' in Anika Gauja, Peter Chen, Jennifer Curtin and Juliet Pietsch, *Double Disillusion: The 2016 Australian Federal Election*, ANU Press, 2018, pp. 397–420.

——'Political engagement in the Australian digital context', *Papers on Parliament* 69 (2018), pp. 93–115.

Warren, Tracey, 'Class- and gender-based working time? Time poverty and the division of domestic labour', *Sociology* 37, 4 (2004), pp. 733–752.

White, Richard J and Patricia Burke Wood, 'Editorial: Activism with(out) organisation', *International Journal of Sociology and Social Policy* 36, 9/10 (2016), pp. 570–577.

NOTES

INTRODUCTION

1 Fairfax Media Limited Business Archive [Fairfax], Mitchell Library, State Library of New South Wales [MLSLNSW], MLMSS 9894/535, Committee in Defiance of the National Service Act [CDNSA], 3 July 1969.

2 Samuel Phineas Lewis Papers, MLMSS 5223/23, CDNSA, 3 September 1969.

3 *Crimes Act 1960* (Cth.). See also Norman S Raeburn, 'Incite, Urge and Encourage: Section 7A and the National Service Act', *University of Tasmania Law Review* 3, 4 (1970), pp. 285–311.

4 Lewis papers, MLMSS 5223/23, CDNSA, 1 September 1969.

5 John Blaxland, *The Official History of ASIO: The Protest Years,* Vol. II, Allen & Unwin, 2015, pp. 182, 185.

6 Lewis papers, MLMSS 5223/23, CDNSA, 22 September 1969.

7 Beverley Symons and Rowan Cahill, *A Turbulent Decade: Social Protest Movements and the Labour Movement, 1965–1975,* Australian Society for the Study of Labour History, p. ix.

8 UN Independent International Commission of Inquiry on the Occupied Palestinian Territory, including East Jerusalem, and Israel, *Legal analysis of the conduct of Israel in Gaza pursuant to the Convention on the Prevention and Punishment of the Crime of Genocide,* UN Human Rights Council Resolution A/HRC/60/CRP.3, 16 September 2025, <https://www.ohchr.org/sites/default/files/documents/hrbodies/hrcouncil/sessions-regular/session60/advance-version/a-hrc-60-crp-3.pdf>

9 NSW *Roads and Crimes Legislation Amendment Act 2022,* No. 7.

10 Amal Naser, 'Explainer: What are your rights to protest in Australia?', UNSW Australian Human Rights Institute, <https://www.humanrights.unsw.edu.au/research/commentary/explainer-what-are-your-rights-to-protest-australia>

11 NSW Police, 'Two charged following unauthorised protest – Singleton', 22 June 2023, <https://www.police.nsw.gov.au/news/news?sq_content_src=%2BdXJsPWh0dHBzJTNBJTJGJTJGZWJpenByZC5wb2xpY2UubnN3Lmdvdi5hdSUyRm1lZGlhJTJGMTA3MTc3Lmh0bWwmYWxsPTE%3D>; Romy Stephens and Madeline Lewis, 'Anti-coal protests block Port of Newcastle rail lines in ongoing disruptions', *ABC Newcastle,* 21 June 2023, <https://www.abc.net.au/news/2023-06-21/coal-protests-block-rail-lines-to-newcastle-port/102504056>

12 Knitting Nannas, 2024, viewed 25 March 2025, <https://knitting-nannas.com/>

13 Isobel Roe, 'Pro-Palestinian protesters take to waters at Port Botany in blockade campaign against Israeli ships', *ABC News,* 11 November 2023, <https://www.abc.net.au/news/2023-11-11/pro-palestinian-rally-port-botany-blockade-israeli-ship/103093816>
14 Capers Thornbury, @Capers.thornbury, Instagram, 14 November 2023; Palestine Children's Relief Fund, viewed 15 October 2023, <www.pcrf.net>
15 Lewis papers, MLMSS 5223/23, CDNSA, 26 August 1969.
16 Lewis papers, MLMSS 5223/23, CDNSA, 5 December 1969.
17 Lewis papers, MLMSS 5223/23, Nigel Bowen, undated.
18 Lewis papers, MLMSS 5223/23, 22 September 1969.
19 Jane Gray papers, 1968–1980, MLSLNSW, MLMSS 4432/1, AICD, December 1969.
20 Gray papers, MLMSS 4432/1, AICD, December 1969.
21 Raeburn 1970, pp. 293–294.
22 Lewis papers, MLMSS 5223/23, CDNSA, 22 September 1969.
23 Lewis papers, MLMSS 5223/23, Mabel Wilson, November 1969.
24 Richard J White and Patricia Burke Wood, 'Editorial: Activism with(out) organisation', *International Journal of Sociology and Social Policy* 36, 9/10 (2016), p. 571.
25 Women's International League for Peace and Freedom NSW Branch Records, 1960–1990 [WILPF], MLSLNSW, MLMSS 5395/1, 19 March 1966.
26 Symons and Cahill 2005, p. vii.
27 See Ann Curthoys, *Freedom Ride: A Freedom Rider Remembers,* Allen & Unwin, 2002.
28 Gary Foley, 'Black power in Redfern 1968–1972', *The Koori History Website,* 2001, p. 1.
29 Foley 2001, p. 13.
30 See WAR, Warriors of the Aboriginal Resistance Vic Chapter, @war_collectivevic <https://www.instagram.com/war_collectivevic/>; Rafqa Touma, 'Invasion Day 2025: a guide to protest marches and events across Australia on 26 January, *The Guardian,* 25 January 2025, <https://www.theguardian.com/australia-news/2025/jan/25/invasion-day-2025-a-guide-to-protest-marches-and-events-across-australia-on-26-january>
31 George Rudé, 'Ideology and popular protest', *Historical Reflections/Réflexions Historiques* 3, 2 (1976), p. 69.
32 Alberto Melucci, *Nomads of the Present: Social Movements and Individual Needs in Contemporary Society,* Hutchinson Radius, 1989, pp. 70–71.
33 Sarah Maddison and Sean Scalmer, *Activist Wisdom: Practical Knowledge and Creative Tension in Social Movements,* UNSW Press, 2006, p. 81.
34 Robert Hagedorn and Sanford Labovitz, 'Participation in community organisations by occupation: a test of three theories', *American Sociological Review* 33, 2 (1968), p. 273.
35 Paul Almeida, *Social Movements: The Structure of Collective Mobilization,* University of California Press, 2019, p. 101.
36 Almeida 2019, p. 108.

37 Anthony M Orum, 'On participation in political protest movements', *The Journal of Applied Behavioural Science* 10, 2 (1974), pp. 196–197. See also Joris Verhulst and Stefaan Walgrave, 'The first time is the hardest? A cross-national and cross-issue comparison of first-time protest participants', *Political Behaviour* 31 (2009), p. 460.
38 Clark McPhail and David Miller 1971, cited in Clark McPhail, 'Civil disorder participation: A critical examination of recent research', *American Sociological Review* 36, 6 (1971), p. 1071.
39 McPhail 1971, p. 1071.
40 See Michele Micheletti, *Political Virtue and Shopping: Individuals, Consumerism and Collective Action*, Palgrave Macmillan, 2003; David Marsh and Sadiya Akram, 'Political participation and citizen engagement: beyond the mainstream', *Policy Studies*, 36, 6 (2015), 523–531; Max Halupka, 'The legitimisation of clicktivism', *Australian Journal of Political Science* 53, 1 (2016), pp. 130–141.
41 People for Nuclear Disarmament (NSW) records, 1912–1985, MLSLNSW, MLMSS 5522/40, Sylvia Hale, 17–21 February 1971.
42 See Ann Curthoys, 'Shut up you bourgeois bitch: Sexual identity and political action in the anti-Vietnam War movement', in Marilyn Lake and Joy Damousi (eds). *Gender and War: Australians at War in the Twentieth Century*, Cambridge University Press, 1995; Verity Burgmann, *Power and Protest: Movements for Change in Australian Society*, Allen & Unwin, 1993; Carolyn Collins, *Save our Sons: Women, Dissent and Conscription during the Vietnam War*, Monash University Publishing, 2021.
43 Patricia Grimshaw, 'Keeping the records safe: Reflections on preserving sources for feminist history', *Lilith* 14 (2005), p. 15.
44 James Findlay, '"Give it to the Mitchell, it would be there for those that come after us": interwar feminists' archival activism and the recasting of Australian history', *History Australia* 22, 3 (2025), pp. 448–466.
45 Michelle Caswell and Marika Cifor, 'From human rights to feminist ethics: Radical empathy in the archives', *Archivaria* 82 (2016), p. 24.
46 Ralph Ranalli, 'Civil upheaval in Iran: Why widespread discontent with the country's religious regime may have reached a tipping point', Interview with Peyman Asadzade, Harvard Kennedy School, 19 December 2022, <https://www.hks.harvard.edu/faculty-research/policy-topics/international-relations-security/civil-upheaval-iran-why-widespread>

CHAPTER ONE

1 Collins 2021, p. 50.
2 People for Nuclear Disarmament (NSW) records, 1912–1985, MLSLNSW, MLMSS 5522/51, Ella Outhred, 19 July 1968.
3 PND records, MLMSS 5522/50, 30 July 1968.
4 PND records, MLMSS 5522/51, Caravan Against Conscription, 25 July 1968.
5 PND records, MLMSS 5522/50, ACC, 30 July 1968.
6 PND records, MLMSS 5522/50, Caravan Against Conscription, 25 July 1968.

7 PND records, MLMSS 5522/51, Caravan Against Conscription, undated.
8 PND records, MLMSS 5522/51, Rex Hewett Committee, undated.
9 PND records, MLMSS 5522/52, Les Bromfield, 9 August 1968.
10 Harry C Boyte, *The Backyard Revolution: Understanding the New Citizen Movement*, Temple University Press, 1980, p. 2.
11 George Rudé, *Ideology and Popular Protest*, Lawrence & Wishart, 1980, p. 36.
12 Malcolm Saunders and Ralph Summy, 'Salient themes of the Australian peace movement: An historical perspective', *Social Alternatives* 3, 1 (1982), p. 23.
13 Nick Origlass papers, 1907–1992, MLSNSW, MLMSS 6614/14, APC, February 1950.
14 Malcolm Saunders and Ralph Summy, *The Australian Peace Movement: A Short History*, ANU Peace Research Centre, 1986, p. 33; Saunders and Summy, 'Salient themes', p. 25.
15 Burgmann 1993, p. 4.
16 See Maddison and Scalmer 2006.
17 PT Findlay, *Protest politics and Psychological Warfare: The Communist Role in the Anti-Vietnam and Anti-Conscription Movement in Australia*, The Hawthorn Press, 1968, p. 24.
18 Findlay 1968, pp. 5–6, 15; Bert Klandermans, 'Promoting or preventing change through political participation: About political actors, movements and networks', in M Van Zomeren and JF Dovidio (eds.), *The Oxford Handbook of the Human Essence*, Oxford University Press, 2017, p. 214.
19 Ralph Gibson, 'Victorian notes on Vietnam protest action, *Communist Review* 288 (1966), p. 6.
20 *Tribune*, 18 November 1964, p. 11.
21 Findlay 1968, pp. 6, 8.
22 Findlay 1968, pp. 23, 28; Maddison and Scalmer 2006, pp. 115, 126.
23 Blaxland 2015, p. 169.
24 Alan Shandro, 'Lenin and hegemony: The Soviets, the working class and the party in the revolution of 1905', in Sebastian Budgen, Stathis Kouvelakis and Slavoj Zizek (eds.) *Lenin Reloaded: Towards a Politics of Truth*, Duke University Press, 2008, p. 325.
25 Audrey Blake, cited Stuart Macintyre, *Reds: The Communist Party of Australia from Origins to Illegality*, Allen & Unwin, 1998, p. 289.
26 Communist Party of Australia [CPA] papers, 1920–1987, MLSLNSW, MLMSS 5021/75, CPA, 16 March 1965.
27 CPA papers, MLMSS 5021/1, CPA, June 1967.
28 CPA papers, MLMSS 5021/2, CPA, March 1970.
29 CPA papers, MLMSS 5021/2, Alec Robertson & John Grimshaw, 1970.
30 Nick Knight, 'The theory and tactics of the Communist Party of Australia (M-L)', *Journal of Contemporary Asia* 28, 2 (1998), pp. 233–251; Rick Kuhn, 'Australia and the Vietnam War: Analyses, actions and attitudes', *Agora* 44, 2, (2009), p. 32.
31 Henry S Albinski, *Politics and Foreign Policy in Australia: The Impact of Vietnam and Conscription*, Duke University Press, 1970, p. 113.

32 John Murphy, *Harvest of Fear: A history of Australia's Vietnam War*, Allen & Unwin, 1993, pp. 255–256.
33 Origlass papers, MLMSS 6614/14, RSA, 26 November 1968.
34 Denis Freney, *A Map of Days: Life on the Left*, William Heinemann, 1991, pp. 236, 264.
35 Ashley Lavelle, *Opposition Vanishing: The Australian Labor Party and the Crisis in Elite Politics*, Springer, 2018, p. 53.
36 Malcolm Saunders, 'The ALP's response to the anti-Vietnam War movement: 1965–1973', *Labour History* 44 (1983), p. 76.
37 Saunders and Summy 1982, p. 27.
38 Murphy 1993, p. 209.
39 Ralph V Summy, 'Militancy and the Australian peace movement, 1960–1967', *Politics* 5, 2 (1970), pp. 155–156.
40 Commonwealth, *Parliamentary Debates*, House of Representatives, 14 April 1970, p. 1052 (Gough Whitlam).
41 Commonwealth, *Parliamentary Debates*, House of Representatives, 14 April 1970, p. 1052 (Tom Hughes, Attorney-General).
42 Gray papers, MLMSS 4423/1, Jane Gray, 28 April 1970.
43 CPA papers, MLMSS 5021/1, CPA, June 1967; Freney 1991, p. 224.
44 PND records, MLMSS 5522/52, Anti-Conscription Jubilee Committee, 27 July 1966.
45 CPA papers, MLMSS 5021/67, AICD, July 1970.
46 Murphy 1993, p. 159.
47 William Phillip Orrick White papers, 1965–2008, MLSLNSW, MLMSS 10938/1, PVC, 1967; Fairfax, MLMSS 9894/1563, Bob Gould, 1974.
48 Sydney University Labor Club records, MLMSS 10665/2 [SULC], *Wednesday Commentary*, 4, 13 (1968), 1.
49 Origlass papers, MLMSS 6614/13, PVC, 1967.
50 Findlay 1968, pp. 35–36.
51 White papers, MLMSS 10938/1, PVC, 1967.
52 James McAuley correspondence and subject files, 1932–1997, MLMSS 7920/19, Bob Gould, 1967.
53 McAuley papers MLMSS 7920/19, PVC, 1967.
54 Findlay 1968, pp. 35–36.
55 McAuley papers 7920/19, ASIO, undated.
56 Malcolm J Saunders, 'The trade unions in Australia and opposition to Vietnam and conscription: 1965–1973', *Labour History* 43 (1982), p. 80; Murphy 1993, p. 258.
57 Donald Horne, *Time of Hope: Australia 1966–1972*, Angus & Robertson, 1980, pp. 92, 98.
58 Almeida 2019, p. 101.
59 McPhail 1971, p. 1071; Orum 1974, pp. 196–197.
60 Indira Hirway, 'Understanding poverty: Insights emerging from time use of the poor', in Rania Antonopoulos and Indira Hirway (eds.), *Unpaid Work and the Economy: Gender, Time Use and Poverty in Developing Countries*, Palgrave

Macmillan, 2010, 26; Tracey Warren, 'Class- and gender-based working time? Time poverty and the division of domestic labour', *Sociology* 37, 4 (2004), pp. 747–748.

61 Stephen Antonopolis and Serena Chen, 'Time and class: How socioeconomic status shapes conceptions of the future self', *Self and Identity* 20, 8 (2021), p. 976; Almeida 2019, pp. 113, 115.

62 Haerpfer, C et al., World Values Survey: Round Seven – Country-Pooled, JD Systems Institute & WVSA Secretariat, 2022.

63 Joy Damousi, *Memory and Migration in the Shadow of War: Australia's Greek Immigrants after World War II and the Greek Civil War,* Cambridge University Press, 2015; Mick Tsounis, 'Greek Left in Australia', *Australian Left Review* 29 (1971), p. 55.

64 CPA papers, MLMSS 5021/2, CPA Aristotle Branch, 1970.

65 Tsounis 1971, pp. 55, 59.

66 Con K Allimonos, 'Greek communist activity in Melbourne: A brief history', *Labour History* 86 (2004), p. 149.

67 Terry Irving and Rowan Cahill, *Radical Sydney: Places, Portraits and Unruly Episodes,* UNSW Press, 2010, pp. 293–294.

68 Origlass papers, MLMSS 6614/13, VAC, October 1965.

69 Findlay 1968, pp. 23.

70 PND records, MLMSS 5522/35, AICD, 1966.

71 Bulletin 7: Characteristics of the Population and Dwellings: Local Government Areas. NSW Census of Population and Housing, Commonwealth Bureau of Census and Statistics, 30 June 1971, p. 106.

72 PND records, MLMSS 5522/52, Newtown Moratorium Group, 1970.

73 Malcolm Salmon papers, 1927–1986, MLMSS 6105/4, CPA 1970.

CHAPTER TWO

1 *How Not to Join the Army: Advice for 20 Year Olds,* Resistance, 1968, pp. 2, 3, 5.

2 John Percy, 'The campaign against the Vietnam War', 6 June 1995, <https://www.angelfire.com/pr/red/vietnam_war/campaign_against_the_vietnam_war.htm>

3 *Canberra Times,* 27 June 1968, p. 3.

4 *Tribune,* 3 July 1968, p. 1.

5 Percy 1995.

6 *Canberra Times,* 25 June 1968, p. 3.

7 *Canberra Times,* 27 June 1968, p. 3; *Canberra Times,* 28 June 1968, p. 3.

8 *Woroni,* 11 July 1968, p. 4.

9 *Tribune,* 30 October 1968, p. 4.

10 *Canberra Times,* 2 July 1968, p. 2.

11 *Canberra Times,* 5 July 1968, p. 2.

12 *Canberra Times,* 10 July 1968, p. 21.

13 *Canberra Times,* 16 July 1968, p. 7.

14 Commonwealth, *Parliamentary Debates,* House of Representatives, 28 September 1968, p. 1525; 4 March 1969, p. 365 (Malcolm Mackay).

15 Sean Scalmer, *Dissent Events: Protest, the Media and the Political Gimmick in Australia,* UNSW Press, 2002, pp. 7, 52.
16 Commonwealth, *Parliamentary Debates,* House of Representatives, 31 July 1901, p. 3315 (James Hume Cook).
17 Martin Crotty, *Making the Australian Male: Middle-Class Masculinity 1870–1920,* Melbourne University Press, 2001, p. 25.
18 Robin Archer, 'Labour and liberty: The origins of the conscription referendum', in Robin Archer et al. (eds.), *The Conscription Conflict and the Great War,* Monash University Publishing, 2016, p. 32.
19 Pam Maclean, 'An almost universal scheme of national service in Australia in the 1950s', *Australian Journal of Politics and History* 52, 3 (2006), pp. 378–397.
20 Murphy 1993, pp. 217–218.
21 Val Noone, *Disturbing the War: Melbourne Catholics and Vietnam,* Spectrum, 1993, p. 104.
22 Greg Langley, *A Decade of Dissent: Vietnam and the Conflict on the Australian Home Front,* Allen & Unwin, 1992, p. 82.
23 Rowan Cahill, *Past and Presents,* 1 May 2025, <https://rowancahill.net/blog/f/pasts-presents>
24 Geoffrey A Sandy, 'Australian Christian conscientious objectors during the Vietnam War years', *Religions* 12, 1 (2021[a]), p. 3.
25 Geoffrey A Sandy, 'Conscientious non-compliers: The Vietnam War years', *Victorian Historical Journal* 92, 2 (2021[b]), pp. 331–357.
26 Florence James papers, 1890–1993, MLMSS 5877/46, Martin Tuck, undated.
27 Langley 1992, p. 37.
28 Noah Riseman, 'The curious case of Mervyn Eades: National service, discrimination and Aboriginal people', *Australian Journal of Politics and History* 59, 1 (2013), pp. 63–79.
29 Ann-Mari Jordens, 'An administrative nightmare: Aboriginal conscription 1965–1972', *Aboriginal History* 13 (1989), pp. 125–126.
30 Hamel-Green 1983, p. 126.
31 *Australian,* 29 June 1968, p. 8.
32 Bobbie Oliver, *Hell No! We Won't Go! Resistance to Conscription in Post-War Australia,* Interventions Inc, 2022; Collins 2021.
33 Sandy 2021a, p. 337.
34 Murphy 1993, p. 121.
35 Saunders 1993, p. 25.
36 Commonwealth, *Parliamentary Debates,* Senate, 6 October 1971, p. 1180 (Jim Cavanagh).
37 Cited in Albinski 1970, p. 40; Kuhn 2009, p. 29.
38 Albinski 1970, p. 202.
39 Bob Scates, *Draftmen Go Free: A History of the Anti-conscription Movement in Australia,* NLA, 1988, p. 7.
40 Gray papers, MLMSS 4432/1, Lambeth Conference (of the Anglican Communion), 1968.
41 Gray papers, MLMSS 4432/1, Jane Gray, 1970.

42 M O'Brien, *Vietnam: Why are we there?*, Australian Railways Union, 1966, pp. 2–3.
43 Saunders 1993, p. 69; ACTU, cited in Scates, 1988, p. 33.
44 White, cited in Sandy 2021, p. 345.
45 Bill White Conscientious Objectors' Committee, Leaflets, statements and news sheets relating to the Bill White Conscientious Objectors' Committee, 1967, MLSLNSW, William White, 1966.
46 Langley 1992, p. 64.
47 Lewis papers, MLMSS 5223/23, Peter Meehan, 4 October 1966.
48 White papers, MLMSS 10938/1, WWF, 1969.
49 White papers, MLMSS 10938/1, AICD, December 1966.
50 White papers, MLMSS 10938/1, Glen Tomasetti, undated.
51 White papers, MLMSS 10938/1, 23 December 1966.
52 White papers, MLMSS 10938/1, Bill Muir, 24 December 1966.
53 White papers, MLMSS 10938/1, D.M. Hunt, 8 February 1972.
54 Bill White Conscientious Objectors Committee, April 1967.
55 White papers, MLMSS 10938/1, Various letters and notes, 1966.
56 Lewis papers, MLMSS 5223/23, NSWTF, 1965.
57 *Telegraph*, 20 July 1966, p. 2.
58 PND records, MLMSS 5223/23, NSWTF, 11 February 1967.
59 PND records, MLMSS 5223/23, Teachers' Vietnam Moratorium Group, March 1970.
60 John Fallding – papers, 1930–1998, MLMSS 7251/1, ACC, 19 May 1968; Oliver, p. 99.
61 Lewis papers, MLMSS 5223/23, Australian Quaker Peace Committee, undated.
62 Quakers Australia, 'Know Thy Friend: Robin McLean', Interview by Pamela Leach, 5 December 2015, <https://australianfriend.org/know-thy-friend-robin-mclean>
63 Sydney University Labor Club records, MLSLNSW (SULC) MLMSS 10665/2 *Wednesday Commentary* 4, 17 (1968), 2.
64 PND records, MLMSS 5522/35, NCAC, 20 January 1969.
65 Fallding papers, MLMSS 7251/1, NCAC, 9 February 1969.
66 Bill White Conscientious Objectors Defence Committee, April 1967.
67 White papers, MLMSS 10938/1, ESHRAA, 1966.
68 Allan Ashbolt and Michael Charlton, 'Returned Servicemen's League', ABC, 31 August 1963, <https://www.abc.net.au/news/2011-08-08/rsl---1963/2833754>
69 See Jon Piccini, 'The Ex-Services Human Rights Association of Australia, the Vietnam War, and the remaking of the Anzac tradition', *Australian Journal of Politics and History* 68, 1 (2022), pp. 54–71.
70 Langley 1992, p. 29.
71 White papers, MLMSS 10938/1, ESAA, 25 November 1966.
72 White papers, MLMSS 10938/1, ESHRAA 20 June 1967.
73 White papers, MLMSS 10938/1, Les Waddington, January 1971.

74 Russell Marks, '"1968" in Australia: The student movement and the New Left', in Jon Piccini et al. (eds.), *The Far Left in Australia since 1945*, Routledge, 2018, p. 142.
75 PND records, MLMSS 5522/51, Carol McLean, undated.
76 Australian Academy of Science, Interview with Lord Robert May, 2011, <https://www.science.org.au/learning/general-audience/history/interviews-australian-scientists/lord-robert-may-physicist-and-1>
77 PND Records, MLMSS 5522/51, Stephen Bock, Ken McLeod and Murray Sime, 19 September 1969.
78 Vivienne Abraham – papers, 1917, 1934–1993, MLMSS 6222/15, DCS, *The Ins and Outs of Conscription*, 1970.
79 Gray papers, MLMSS 4432/1, DRCC, 21 July 1970.
80 Abraham papers, MLMSS 6222/15, DCS, *The Ins and Outs of Conscription*, 1970.
81 PND records, MLMSS 5522/54, SDS, 1970.
82 PND records, MLMSS 5522/54, SDS, 1970.
83 PND records, MLMSS 5522/54, SDS, 13 January 1971.
84 Hamel-Green 1983, p. 109.
85 SULC records, MLSLNSW MLMSS 10665/2, SULC, *Wednesday Commentary* 2, 2 (1966), p. 2.
86 Marks, 142; Cited in Hamel-Green 1983, p. 113.
87 Nick Irving, *Global Thought, Local Action: Australian Activism During the Vietnam War 1961–1972*, PhD thesis, University of Sydney, 2017, 160; Scates 1988, p. 30.
88 PND records, MLMSS 5522/35, The Unconscriptables, 21 September 1968.
89 PND records, MLMSS 5522/35, Sonia Drabyan, Geoff Mullen Campaign Committee, 3 March 1969.
90 PND records, MLMSS 5522/51, DRU, 1971/2.
91 Hamel-Green, cited in Langley 1992, p. 152.
92 Hamel-Green 1983, p. 122.
93 Oliver 2022, 165; Horne 1980, p. 56.
94 PND records, MLMSS 5522/51, DRU, 1 June 1972.
95 PND records, MLMSS 5522/51, DRU, 26 November 1972.
96 PND records, MLMSS 5522/51, DRU, 1972.
97 Langley 1992, p. 153.
98 Scalmer 2002, 7.

CHAPTER THREE

1 Murphy 1993, p. 242.
2 Gray papers, MLMSS 4432/1, AICD, 2 December 1969.
3 Murphy 1993, pp. 245, 251.
4 CPA papers, MLMSS 5021/67, Leo Martin, MLC, 1970.
5 Langley 1992, pp.135, 144.
6 Murphy 1993, pp. 244.
7 Gray papers, MLMSS 4432/1, VMC, 1970.

8 Brian Laver and Darce Cassidy, *The Communist Party is Behind this Moratorium – Way Behind*, Brian Laver, 1970.
9 CPA papers, MLMSS 5021/67, John Sendy, Bernie Taft and Laurie Carmichael, 1970.
10 CPA papers, MLMSS 5021/67, AICD, 1970.
11 CPA papers, MLMSS 5021/67, AICD, 1970.
12 CPA papers, MLMSS 5021/67, VMC, 30 September 1970. See also National Library of Australia, Papers of Denis Freney, MS9535; Freney 1991.
13 Murphy 1993, p. 257.
14 National Museum of Australia, *Vietnam Moratoriums,* viewed 14 November 2024, <https://www.nma.gov.au/defining-moments/resources/vietnam-moratoriums>
15 Saunders 1982, p. 71.
16 Saunders 1983, p. 86.
17 Maddison and Scalmer 2006, p. 104.
18 Bert Klandermans and Dirk Oegema, 'Potentials, Networks, Motivations and Barriers: Steps Towards Participation in Social Movements', *American Sociological Review* 52 (1987), p. 521.
19 Klandermans 2017, 'Promoting or Preventing', pp. 215–216.
20 Chris Dite, 'Public Housing Can Only Be Won Through Struggle', *Overland,* 9 October 2024, <https://overland.org.au/2024/10/public-housing-can-only-be-won-through-struggle/?fbclid=PAZXh0bgNhZW0CMTEAAa bvfhQrR1EeeDvIpyntEmyV8jpL4Fu6jEoKsru6O6f2Tex7DpI1nUS8y sE_aem_7P5gnzy2gm9geezclt43MQ>
21 Gray papers, MLMSS 4432/1, VMC, 16 July 1970.
22 Gray papers, MLMSS 4432/1, VMC, 8 August 1970.
23 Freney 1991, p. 263.
24 Saul Alinsky, 'Organising Protest', *Out Now,* 2 (1970), p. 5.
25 Gray papers, MLMSS 4432/1, VMC, 4 April 1970.
26 Maddison and Scalmer 2006, p. 115.
27 CPA papers, MLMSS 5021/50, VMC, 27 April 1970. See also Janie Overton – papers, 1925–1991, Courtesy SEARCH Foundation, MLNSW, MLMSS 6968/1, AICD, March 1970.
28 Gray papers, MLMSS 4432/1, David Mallick and John Munson, 14 August 1970.
29 PND records, MLMSS 5522/52, Railway Moratorium Committee, *Railway Moratorium Bulletin,* May 1971, p. 7.
30 Origlass papers, MLMSS 6614/13, VMC, March 1970; 1 September 1970.
31 Gray papers, MLMSS 4432/1, NDVMG, 24 February 1970.
32 *Liverpool News,* 14 March 1940, p. 2; National Archives of Australia (NAA), Tenno Koolberg RAAF records, A9301/443313; NAA, Tenno Koolberg Naturalisation papers, A714/54/18228.
33 UNSW Wests Water Polo Club, 'Our History', viewed 19 November 2024, <https://www.unswwests.com/our-history>; G Stutsel, 'AUSSI – The Formation and Early History', viewed 19 November 2024, <https://assets.

sportstg.com/assets/console/document/documents/20150615053231Early_History_by_GStutsel_edited.pdf>
34 Gray papers, MLMSS 4432/1, NDVMG, March 1970.
35 *Hornsby Times*, 15 April 1970, p. 20.
36 Gray papers, MLMSS 4432/1, 11 May 1970.
37 Gray papers, MLMSS 4432/1, Jane Gray, 22 March 1970.
38 Gray papers, MLMSS 4432/1, Jane Gray, March 1970.
39 Gray papers, MLMSS 4432/1, NDVMG, March 1970.
40 Origlass papers, MLMSS 6614/13, VMC, March 1970.
41 *SMH*, 7 May 1970, p. 7.
42 *SMH*, 9 May 1970, p. 2; *Tribune*, 13 May 1970, p. 3.
43 Gray papers, MLMSS 4432/1, VMC, 8 June 1970.
44 Gray papers, MLMSS 4432/1, VMC, 7 September 1970.
45 Origlass papers, MLMSS 6614/13, Ken O'Hara, 2 October 1970.
46 Gray papers, MLMSS 4432/1, VMC, 1970.
47 Saunders 1983, pp. 86–87.
48 John Gorton, 'Dr Cairns Calls for Demonstrations', Media Release no. 42/973, 26 March 1970, Department of the Prime Minister and Cabinet: PM Transcripts, <https://pmtranscripts.pmc.gov.au/release/transcript-2203>
49 Saunders 1983, p. 87.
50 Gray papers, MLMSS 4432/1, Jane Gray, 28 April 1970.
51 Gray papers, MLMSS 4432/1, Jane Gray, 4 April 1970.
52 *Tribune*, 23 September 1970, p. 1.
53 *Tharunka*, 16 September 1970, p. 2. See also *Tribune*, 21 November 1972, p. 2.
54 CPA papers, MLMSS 5021/67, VMC, 22 September 1970.
55 Gray papers, MLMSS 4432/1, Jane Gray, 22 September 1970.
56 NSW, *Parliamentary Debates*, Legislative Assembly, 29 September 1970, pp. 6114–6115 (Sydney Einfeld).
57 CPA papers, MLMSS 5021/67, VMC, 30 September 1970.
58 CPA papers, MLMSS 5021/67, VMC, October 1970.
59 Gray papers, MLMSS 4432/1, VMC, 8 June 1970.
60 Daphne Gollan papers, ca. 1918–2002, MLSLNSW, MLMSS 8042/18, VMC, 1971.
61 *The Guardian*, 5 February 2025, <https://www.theguardian.com/australia-news/2025/feb/05/queensland-university-apologises-for-hurt-after-jewish-group-heads-slide-showed-stereotype-at-anti-racism-event-ntwnfb>; Elizabeth Strakosch et al., 'The QUT Symposium: Holding the Line Against Rising Racism', *Overland*, 31 January 2025, <https://overland.org.au/2025/01/the-qut-symposium-holding-the-line-against-rising-racism/>
62 Ryde–Hunters Hill Flora and Fauna Preservation Society records, 1960–1988, MLSLNSW [R-HH FPPS], MLMSS 5142/4, VMC, 1971.
63 R-HH FFPS papers, MLMSS Ted Marr, 18 February 1971.
64 R-HH FFPS papers, MLMSS Denis Freney, 18 February 1971.
65 Origlass papers, MLMSS 6614/13, VMC, February 1971.

66 PND records, MLMSS 5522/34, Newcastle Trades Hall Council Workers' Club, 19 March 1971.
67 PND records, MLMSS 5522/34, Fred Olsson, 25 March 1971; CPA papers, MLMSS 5021/67, VMC, September 1970; October 1970.
68 Origlass papers, MLMSS 6614/13, VMC, 24 January 1971.
69 *Tribune,* 14 July 1971, p. 8; *Canberra Times,* 1 July 1971, p. 9.
70 Gray papers, MLMSS 4432/1, VMC, 8 June 1970.
71 *Tribune,* 7 July 1971, p. 10.
72 Scates, cited in Langley 1992, p. 147.

CHAPTER FOUR

1 Marks 2018, p. 141.
2 *Tharunka,* 14 September 1965, p. 14.
3 SULC records, 10665/2, *Wednesday Commentary* 2, 1 (1966), p. 1.
4 *Wednesday Commentary* 2, 2 (1966), pp. 1–3.
5 *Wednesday Commentary* 2, 6 (1966), p. 1.
6 *Wednesday Commentary* 2, 7 (1966), p. 1.
7 *Wednesday Commentary* 2, 12 (1966), p. 1; *Tribune,* 29 June 1966, p. 11.
8 Findlay 1968, pp. 48–49.
9 Albinski 1970, pp. 73, 74, 152.
10 Australian Society for the Study of Labour History, *Taking to the Streets Against the Vietnam War: A Timeline History of Australian Protest, 1962–1972,* viewed 2 December 2024, <https://labourhistorymelbourne.org/taking-to-the-streets-against-the-vietnam-war-a-timeline-history-of-australian-protest-1962-1972/>
11 Langley 1992, p. 117.
12 *Defence Forces Protection Act 1967.*
13 Commonwealth, *Parliamentary Debates,* Senate, 7 September 1967, p. 622 (Justin O'Byrne).
14 *Tribune,* 11 October 1967, p. 12.
15 *Tharunka,* 5 September 1967, p. 6.
16 Origlass papers, MLMSS 6614/13, SULC, July 1967.
17 Henri Alleg, *La Question,* Éditions de Minuit, 1958.
18 People's Inquiry into Campus Free Speech on Palestine, viewed 27 February 2025, <https://www.palestineinquiry.com/home>; Ella McGrath, 'Greens launch "Palestine Inquiry" into free speech on campus', *Honi Soit,* 21 February 2025, <https://honisoit.com/2025/02/greens-launch-palestine-inquiry-into-free-speech-on-campus/>
19 *Tribune,* 18 October 1967, p. 11.
20 Origlass papers, MLMSS 6614/13, Denis Freney, 27 February 1968.
21 Findlay 1968, p. 54.
22 Michael Hyde, 'Getting out of the boat', *Overland,* 199, 2010, <https://overland.org.au/previous-issues/issue-199/feature-michael-hyde>
23 Scalmer 2002, p. 52.
24 Origlass papers, MLMSS 6614/13, AICD, October 1967; Findlay 1968, p. 54.

25 PND records, MLMSS 5522/52, AICD, June 1972.
26 Gollan papers, MLMSS 8042/18, Medical Aid to Indochina, July 1972.
27 Gollan papers, MLMSS 8042/18, National Vietnam Aid Appeal, 1975.
28 Lisa Milner, 'The unbreakable solidarity of women throughout the world with heroic Vietnam: Freda Brown, women's organisations and the anti-Vietnam War movement', *History Australia* 15, 2 (2018), pp. 264, 266.
29 Melanie Oppenheimer, *Volunteering: Why We Can't Survive Without It*, NewSouth, 2008, p. 87; See also Marilyn Lake, *Getting Equal: The History of Australian Feminism*, Allen & Unwin, 1999, p. 173.
30 Orum 1974, p. 193.
31 PND records, MLMSS 5522/34, AICD, 1969.
32 Lewis papers, MLMSS 5223/23, August Mobilisation to End the War in Vietnam, 1972.
33 CPA papers, MLMSS 5021/50, AICD, March 1971.
34 Klandermans and Oegema 1987, p. 530.
35 Klandermans 2017, p. 212.
36 White papers, MLMSS 10938/1, ESHRAA, April 1967. See also Piccini 2022, p. 61.
37 Marina Larsson, *Shattered Anzacs: Living with the Scars of War*, UNSW Press, 2009.
38 PND records, MLMSS 5522/34, AICD.
39 Harold Levien, *Vietnam: Myth and Reality*, Harold Levien, 1967.
40 Harold Levien – papers, 1952–1967, MLSLNSW MLMSS 6251.
41 Oppenheimer 2008, p. 89.
42 White papers, MLMSS 10938/1.
43 PND records, MLMSS 5522/54, Geoff Anderson, 8 March 1966.
44 Milner 2018b, pp. 258, 260.
45 Origlass papers, MLMSS 6614/13, SOS, 1966.
46 Janet Wakefield – papers, 1938–1992, MLSNSW MLMSS 6969/1, SOS, April–May 1972.
47 PND records, MLMSS 5522/50, Annandale–Petersham Moratorium Group, 1970.
48 PND records, MLMSS 5522/50, M Christian, Bradfield Anti-Vietnam War Committee, 25 November 1968.
49 PND records, MLMSS 5522/50, Bradfield Anti-Vietnam War Committee, April 1970.
50 Francis R Harvey papers, ca. 1970–2005, and Roger Pryke papers, 1925–2001, MLSNSW MLMSS 7962/5, ICCV Australian branch, 1 August 1967.
51 White papers, MLMSS 10938/1, ESHRAA, *Conscience*, 9, 20 June 1966.
52 Communist Party of Australia [CPA] records, 1922–23, 1945–1967, courtesy SEARCH Foundation, MLSNSW MLMSS 2389/2, VAC Newsletter, 5, December 1965.
53 Origlass papers, MLMSS 6614/13, VAC, 1966.
54 Levien papers, MLMSS 6251/3, VAC, 1968.
55 Origlass papers, MLMSS 6614/13, VAC, 1969.

56 Fairfax Archive, MLMSS 8984/1563, Bob Gould, 1974.
57 Almeida 2019, pp. 110–113.
58 Dominika Vergara Polaska and Galia Chimiak, 'Organizing without organizations: On informal social activism in Poland', *International Journal of Sociology and Social Movements* 36, 9/10 (2016), 662, 665.
59 Summy 1970, p. 150.
60 PND records, MLMSS 5522/54, Canterbury District Peace and Disarmament Committee, 1965.
61 PND records, MLMSS 5522/50, Alec Fisher, Bradfield Anti-Vietnam War Committee, December 1967.
62 PND records, MLMSS 5522/51, Caravan against Conscription, 1968; Fairfield Peace Committee, 1968; Origlass papers, MLMSS 6614/13, Resistance, 1968.
63 Origlass papers, MLMSS 6614/13, Resistance newsletter 18, April–May 1969.
64 PND records, MLMSS 5522/54, WILPF, 1965.
65 Origlass papers, MLMSS 6614/13, VAC, 1965.
66 Origlass papers, MLMSS 6614/13, High School Students Against the War in Vietnam, Newsletter no. 10, 1969.
67 PND records, MLMSS 5522/54, Western Suburbs Moratorium Group, 1970; 1971.
68 Claire Ray, Interviewed by Inara Walden, 15 July 1993. Used with permission of Ann Curthoys.
69 PND records, MLMSS 5522/34, AICD ticket book, 1967.
70 Origlass papers, MLMSS 6614/13, VMC, December 1970.
71 Findlay 1968, pp. 36, 43.
72 Origlass papers, MLMSS 6614/13, AICD, undated.
73 Rowan Cahill, '"The two-million dollar man": Bob Gould, 1937–2011', *Labour History* 101 (2011), 211.
74 Origlass papers, MLMSS 6614/13, Third World Bookshop, 1967.
75 Origlass papers, MLMSS 6614/13, VAC, 1969.
76 Gary Foley, Keynote lecture at Australian Historical Association Conference, Australian Catholic University, Melbourne, 6 July 2023.
77 Margo Moore, interviewed by Inara Walden & Ann Curthoys, 21 June 1993. Used with permission of Ann Curthoys.
78 Gray papers, MLMSS 4432/1, Community Action for Peace, 6 May 1971.
79 Ashley Ekins, 'Overview of Australian military involvement in the Vietnam War, 1962–1975', Australian War Memorial, viewed 8 December 2024, <https://www.awm.gov.au/visit/exhibitions/impressions/impressions>
80 CPA papers, MLMSS 5021/75, CPA, 1970.
81 Noone 1993, p. 228.
82 McAuley papers, MLMSS 7920/19, PVC, 1967.
83 PND records, MLMSS 5522/34, MJ Holmes, 24 March 1968.
84 Noone 1993, p. 195.
85 CPA papers, MLMSS 5021/67, Ken McLeod, 11 October 1970.
86 Orum 1974 193; Klandermans 2017, p. 208.

87 White papers, MLMSS 10938/1, ESHRAA, undated.
88 Vivienne Abraham papers, MLSLNSW MLMSS 6222/15, Inter-Church Committee on Peace, July 1968.
89 Abraham papers, MLMSS 6222/15; DCS, *The Ins and Outs of Conscription*, 1970; 4432/1, DRCC, 21 July 1970.
90 PND records, MLMSS 5522/34, Berenice Buckley, 6 August 1971.
91 NSWCCL, *Right to Protest*, viewed 23 February 2025, <https://www.nswccl.org.au/right_to_protest>
92 Murphy 1993, pp. 145–146.
93 *Tribune*, 27 October 1965, p. 1.
94 Leaflets from the Vietnam Action Committee, Vietnam Demonstration Defence Fund, 1965.
95 CPA records, MLMSS 2389/2, VAC Newsletter no. 5, December 1965.
96 PND records, MLMSS 5522/54, John Child, 7 March 1967.
97 Origlass papers, MLMSS 6614/13, Demonstration Defence Fund Committee, 1967.
98 PND records, MLMSS 5522/54, John Child, 3 July 1967.
99 PND records, MLMSS 5522/54, John Child and Alec Fisher, 1 November 1967.
100 *Tribune*, 14 October 1970, p. 3.
101 PND records, MLMSS 5522/52, Phyllis Latona and Denis Freney, 1970.
102 *Tribune*, 18 November 1970, p. 3.
103 CPA papers, MLMSS 5021/67, Leo Martin, 1970.

CHAPTER FIVE

1 Roger Milliss, *Tribune*, 2 October 1968, p. 7.
2 Milliss 1968.
3 Commonwealth, *Parliamentary Debates*, House of Representatives, 9 October 1968, p. 1724 (Lance Barnard; John Gorton, Prime Minister).
4 Lisa Milner, 'The Cultural Front: Left Cultural Activism in the Post-War Era', in J Piccini et al. (eds.), *The Far Left in Australia since 1945*, Routledge, 2018 (2018a), pp. 267–269.
5 Noreen McDonald – further papers, 1939, 1962–1987, mainly concerning Catholics for Peace (Australia), MLMSS 3853 ADD-ON 2111, YCAC Newsletter, August 1967.
6 Gollan papers, MLMSS 8042/18, Vietnam Moratorium Campaign Newsletter, 6 July 1970.
7 CPA papers, MLMSS 5021/67, VMC, 1970.
8 Barbara Sutton, *Bodies in Crisis: Culture, Violence and Women's Resistance in Neoliberal Argentina*, Rutgers University Press, 2010, p. 172.
9 Anna Kelsey-Sugg and Bhakthi Puvanenthiran, 'Spate of Resignations Follow Creative Australia's Decision to Drop Artist Khaled Sabsabi from Venice Biennale', *ABC News*, 17 February 2025, <https://www.abc.net.au/news/2025-02-16/industry-reacts-to-creative-australia-sabsabi-

venice-biennale/104941402>; Khaled Sabsabi and Michael Dagostino, @Peacefender, 14 February 2025; Nour Haydar and Sarah Collard, 'National Gallery of Australia says it covered Palestinian flags on tapestry after security assessment', *The Guardian*, 21 February 2025, <https://www.theguardian.com/australia-news/2025/feb/21/national-gallery-of-australia-says-it-covered-palestinian-flags-on-tapestry-after-security-assessment-ntwnfb>; Palestine Action Group Canberra, @Palestinianactiongroupcbr, 23 February 2025.

10 Dee Jefferson, 'Creative Australia awards Khaled Sabsabi $100 000 grant months after dumping from Venice Biennale', *The Guardian*, 14 October 2025, <https://www.theguardian.com/culture/2025/oct/14/khaled-sabsabi-creative-australia-grant-venice-biennale-dumping>

11 Sutton 2010, p. 174.

12 Klandermans 2017, p. 212; Maddison and Scalmer 2006, pp. 202–203.

13 Milner 2018a, pp. 278–280.

14 Cathy Bloch, Interview with Inara Walden, 29 June 1993. Used with permission of Ann Curthoys.

15 CPA records, MLMSS 2389/2, Vietnam Day Committee Bulletin no. 3, 1965.

16 CPA records, MLMSS 2389/2, Vietnam Day Committee Bulletin no. 3, 1965.

17 Murphy 1993, pp. 141–142.

18 Noone 1993, p. 108.

19 Gollan papers, MLMSS 8042/18, Resistance Newsletter no. 22, Dec 1969–January 1970, p. 2.

20 PND records, MLMSS 5522/52, Bradfield Anti-Vietnam War Committee, September 1970.

21 Kevin Gillan et al., *Anti-War Activism: New Media and Protest in the Information Age,* Palgrave Macmillan, 2008, pp. 76–77; Alice Mattoni, *Media Practices and Protest Politics: How Precarious Workers Mobilise,* Routledge, 2016.

22 Scalmer 2002, p. 7. See also Maddison and Scalmer 2006, p. 205.

23 Elin Diamond et al. (eds.), *Performance, Feminism and Affect in Neoliberal Times,* Palgrave Macmillan, 2017.

24 New Theatre, 1936, cited in Milner 2018a, p. 271.

25 Milner 2018a, p. 272.

26 Origlass papers, MLMSS 6614/13, Bob Gould, VAC, February 1966.

27 PND records, MLMSS 5522/52, Keith Atkins, Bradfield Anti-Vietnam War Committee, 1967.

28 PND records, MLMSS 5522/52, M Christian, Bradfield Anti-Vietnam War Committee, May 1968.

29 Albinski 1970, p. 148.

30 McAuley papers, MLMSS 7920/19, SULC, December 1969.

31 Kevin Gillan, Jenny Pickerill and Frank Webster, *Anti-War Activism: New Media and Protest in the Information Age,* Palgrave Macmillan, 2008, p. 76; Andre Lepecki, *Singularities: Dance in the Age of Performance,* Routledge, 2016, pp. 14–15.

32 PND records, MLMSS 5522/52, War and Peace Study Group, November 1967.
33 Gray papers, MLMSS 4432/1, VMC, September 1970.
34 PND records, MLMSS 5522/52, Margaret Barr Dance-Drama Group, September 1970.
35 PND records, MLMSS 5522/52, Newtown Moratorium Group, 1970.
36 C Thi Nguyen, *Games: Agency as Art*, Oxford University Press, 2020, p. 1.
37 PND records, MLMSS 5522/52, Manly–Warringah UAW and Congress for International Cooperation and Disarmament, November 1966.
38 PND records, MLMSS 5522/52, PWCC letter, 1968.
39 PND records, MLMSS 5522/52, PWCC Membership Form, 1968.
40 PND records, MLMSS 5522/52, PWCC letter, August 1968.
41 *Tribune*, 28 August 1968, p. 8.
42 Nomadic Voyager, @Nomadic.voyager2, 22 January 2025.
43 Horne 1980, p. 52.
44 McLaren 1996, p. 179. See also A Seal, 'Protest Poetry', in Roland Greene, Stephen Cushman, Clare Cavanagh, Jahan Ramazani and Paul Rouzer (eds.), *The Princeton Encyclopedia of Poetry and Poetics*, 4th edn, Princeton University Press, 2012, pp. 1121–1122.
45 Frank Hardy, cited in Milner 2018a, p. 274.
46 Ray Clarke, cited in Milner 2018a, p. 274; John McLaren, *Writing in Hope and Fear: Literature as Politics in Postwar Australia*, Cambridge University Press, 1996, pp. 112, 115–116.
47 Anthony Ashbolt and Rowan Cahill, 'And the lives are many: the print culture of Australian communism', *Twentieth Century Communism* 12 (2017), pp. 37–61. See also Terry Irving and Sean Scalmer, 'Labour intellectuals in Australia: Modes, traditions, generations, transformations', *International Review of Social History* 50, 1 (2005), pp. 1–26.
48 Roland Robinson, cited in Milliss 1968. See also Horne 1980, p. 58; SULC papers, MLMSS 10665/1, *Wednesday Commentary*, 4, 17 (1968).
49 Gray papers, MLMSS 4432/1 Jane Gray 2 April 1970.
50 Gray papers, MLMSS 4432/1 David Ailwood, 28 April 1970.
51 Gollan papers, MLMSS 8042/18, VMC Newsletter, September 1970.
52 Hasib Hourani, *rock flight*, Giramondo, 2024, p. 81.
53 Stenen Press, Global Reading for Freedom of Expression and Solidarity with Palestine and Lebanon – Trailer, YouTube, <https://www.youtube.com/watch?v=wAUsWlcsnmM>
54 McLaren 1996, pp. 61–62; Jock Levy, cited in Milner 2018a, pp. 277–278.
55 Findlay 1968, pp. 35, 38.
56 Gollan papers, MLMSS 8042/18, Resistance Newsletter no. 22 Dec 1969–Jan 1970, p. 2.
57 Milner 2018b, p. 267.
58 Gillian Fisher further papers, MLSLNSW MLMSS 11380/1, 'Film Night', *Out Now*, 2, 24 August 1970.
59 Origlass papers, MLMSS 6614/13, VMC, 1970.

60 PND records, MLMSS 5522/50, Balmain Group of the Vietnam Moratorium Campaign, 1970.
61 Blaxland 2015, p. 161.
62 PND records, MLMSS 5522/52, Bradfield Anti-Vietnam War Committee, 10 August 1968.
63 Sutton 2010, p. 173.
64 Piccini 2022, pp. 61, 66.
65 White papers, MLMSS 10938/1, ESHRAA, *Conscience*, no. 9, 20 June 1966, p. 2.
66 Lewis papers, MLMSS 5223/23, Teachers Vietnam Moratorium Group, 1970.
67 Gray papers, MLMSS 4432/1, VMC, February 1970; NDVMG, 17 February 1970.
68 Origlass papers, MLMSS 6614/13, VMC, 1970; Third World Bookshop, 1970; Milner 2018b, p. 267.
69 CPA papers, MLMSS 5021/67, VMC, 30 July 1970.
70 Ashley Lavelle, 'Labor and Vietnam: A reappraisal', *Labour History* 90 (2006), pp. 126–127.
71 Amanda Tattersall, cited in Maddison and Scalmer 2006, p. 88.
72 Klandermans and Oegema 1987, p. 522.
73 *Australian*, 16 April 1970.
74 *SMH*, 16 April 1970.
75 *Canberra Times*, 18 April 1970, p. 3.
76 Lewis papers, MLMSS 5223/23, Teachers' Moratorium Group, 13 April 1970.
77 Lewis papers, MLMSS 5223/23, VMC, 16 April 1970.
78 Lewis papers, MLMSS 5223/23, VMC, 16 April 1970.
79 *Tharunka*, 23 June 1970, p. 2.
80 *Tribune*, 6 May 1970, p. 1.
81 *Tribune*, 20 May 1970, p. 1.
82 *Tribune*, 27 May 1970, p. 1.
83 *Tharunka*, 23 June 1970, p. 2.
84 *Tharunka*, 23 June 1970, p. 2.
85 *Tribune*, 24 June 1970, p. 11.
86 Lewis papers, MLMSS 5223/23, Mrs C Tucker, Teachers' Vietnam Moratorium Group, June 1970.
87 Peter Coleman, *School Power in Australia: Is Your Child Being Manipulated by Political Operators*? Peter Coleman, 1970; *Tharunka*, 16 September 1970, p. 6.
88 *Tribune*, 10 February 1971, p. 3; 'Robert Colley Denied Scholarship: A Clear Case of Victimisation', *Education: Journal of the NSW Public School Teachers Federation* 52, 3 (1971), p. 24.
89 *Canberra Times*, 25 November 1970, p. 3.
90 Unionists for Palestine, @Unionistsforpalestine , 24 February 2025; Wasim El-Haj, LinkedIn, <https://www.linkedin.com/in/wasim-el-haj-25a773122>
91 Sydney Students for Palestine, @Sydstudents4palestine, 12 December 2024; 'Rally: Stop anti-Palestinian racism in schools!, *Green Left*, viewed 6 April

2025, <https://www.greenleft.org.au/content/rally-stop-anti-palestinian-racism-schools>
92 Sutton 2010, p. 174.
93 Findlay 1968, p. 16.
94 PND records, MLMSS 5522/51, Committee for Canberra Vigil, 1965.
95 Noone 1993, pp. 243–244.
96 Murphy 1993, p. 202; Milner 2018b, p. 260.
97 PND records, MLMSS 5522/54, Vigil Committee, 1966.
98 PND records, MLMSS 5522/54, Vigil Organising Committee, 1968; White papers, MLMSS 10938/1, ESHRAA, *Conscience* 9, 20 June 1966, p. 2.
99 Gray papers, MLMSS 4432/1, David Mallick and John Gunson, 14 August 1970.
100 Lewis papers, MLMSS 5223/23, CDNSA, 3 September 1969; Murphy 1993, 214; Dorothy Cora, *Noreen Hewett: Portrait of a Grassroots Activist*, Older Women's Network NSW, 2010, p. 25; Albinski 1970, p. 150.
101 Saunders 1982, p. 65.
102 Saunders 1982, pp. 67–69.
103 'The Sit-Intifada', 3CR, 6 April 2024, <https://www.3cr.org.au/palestine/episode/conversation-ihab-abu-ibrahim-palestinian-activist-and-founder-%C2%A0-sit-intifada>; Zena Chamas, 'From hunger strikes to 12 hour sit-ins, protesters are going to great length to end the war in Gaza', *ABC News*, 16 November 2023, <https://www.abc.net.au/news/2023-11-17/protesting-for-gaza-to-end-war-and-sending-weapons-to-israel/103104478>
104 Bukjeh, @Bukjeh, 8 January 2024.
105 Palestine Action Group, @PalestineActiongroup, 28 November 2023; Palestine Action Group, @palestineactiongroup, 12 November 2023.
106 Australian Services Union Action for Palestine, @asu_action4palestine, 11 November 2023.

CHAPTER SIX

1 PND records, MLMSS 5522/52, SSITE, 1968.
2 Helen Frizell, 'Students plan a $3 peace ride', *SMH*, 19 August 1968, p. 1.
3 'Secondary Students Peace Ride for Canberra', 1968, Personal collection of Lee Rhiannon (née Brown).
4 MT Haggard, *A Chronology of Efforts to Achieve a Negotiated Settlement in Vietnam (1964–1968)*, Library of Congress Legislative Reference Service, 1968.
5 PND records, MLMSS 5522/52, Secondary Students Peace Ride Committee, 1968.
6 Oppenheimer 2008, p. 12.
7 Curthoys 1995.
8 PND records, MLMSS 5522/52, SSITE Newsletter 1968.
9 Mark Aarons, *The Family File*, Black Inc, 2010, p. 274.
10 Frizell 1968, p. 6.
11 'School heads should halt this march!', *Sunday Telegraph*, 21 April 1968, p. 2;

Lee Brown (Rhiannon), Secondary Students Peace Ride for Canberra report, 1968, Personal collection of Lee Rhiannon (née Brown).

12 'A red tinge to the peace-ride wagon', *Sunday Telegraph*, 5 May 1968, p. 2.

13 Lee Rhiannon (née Brown), Radical Sydney Conference, Herbert Greedy Hall, Marrickville, Saturday 15 March 2025.

14 Commonwealth, *Parliamentary Debates*, House of Representatives, 14 May 1968, p. 1386; 9 May 1968, p. 1259 (Nigel Bowen, Attorney-General; Billy Snedden).

15 *Age*, 14 May 1968, 3; *Sun*, 15 May 1968, p. 1.

16 Commonwealth, *Parliamentary Debates*, House of Representatives, 16 May 1968, p. 1544 (John McLeay).

17 Rhiannon collection, Lee Brown (Rhiannon), Secondary Students Peace Ride for Canberra report, 1968.

18 PND records, MLMSS 5522/52, Mark Aarons, 2 June 1968.

19 PND records, MLMSS 5522/52, Geoff Anderson, 6 June 1968.

20 Maddison and Scalmer 2006, p. 23; Polaska and Chimiak 2016, p. 666.

21 McAuley papers, MLMSS 7920/19, PVC, 1967.

22 See Salmon papers, MLMSS 6105/2, CPA, 1970 as an example of the type of volunteer work requested.

23 Galia Chimiak, *How Individualists Make Solidarity Work*, MPiPS, 2006, pp. 207–208; Maddison and Scalmer 2006, p. 245.

24 McAuley papers, MLMSS 7920/19, PVC, 1967.

25 Origlass papers, MLMSS 6614/13, Peter Dunn, 'You are needed to defeat William McMahon', 1966.

26 Bert Klandermans, *The Social Psychology of Protest*, Oxford, 1997, p. 23; Almeida 2019, p. 106; Hans Toch, *The Social Psychology of Social Movements*, The Bobs-Merrill Company, 1965, p. 11; CPA records, MLMSS 2389/2, VDDF, 1965.

27 See William F Pepper, 'The Children of Vietnam', *Ramparts* 5, 7 (1967), pp. 45–68.

28 Sam Everingham papers, MLMSS 8614/2, Sheila Mason, 3 June 1968.

29 See Belinda Probert, 'Award Restructuring and Clerical Work: Skills, Training and Careers in a Feminized Occupation', *Journal of Industrial Relations* 34, 3 (1992), pp. 436–454.

30 Melanie Oppenheimer, *All Work No Pay: Australian Civilian Volunteers in War*, Ohio Productions, 2002, p. 11; Desley Deacon, 'Political Arithmetic: The Nineteenth-Century Australian Census and the Construction of the Dependent Woman', *Signs* 11, 1 (1985), pp. 29–30.

31 Beverley Symons, interviewed by Inara Walden, 9 September 1993. Used with permission of Ann Curthoys.

32 Marian Sawer and Merrindahl Andrew, 'Collectivism, consensus and concepts of shared leadership in movements for social change', in Joy Damousi, Kim Rubenstein and Mary Tomsic (eds.), *Diversity in Leadership: Australian Women, Past and Present*, ANU Press, 2014, p. 284.

33 Curthoys 1995; Langley 1992, p. 62.

34 Kevin Moloney and David McKie, 'Changes to be encouraged: Radical turns in PR theorisation and small-step evolutions in PR practice', in Jacquie L'Etang, et al. (eds.), *The Routledge Handbook of Critical Public Relations*, Routledge, 2016, p. 156.
35 Oppenheimer 2008, pp. 87, 89; Lake 1999, p. 173.
36 McAuley papers, MLMSS 7920/19, PVC, 1967.
37 Kenneth R Evans, Tim Christiansen and James D Gill, 'The impact of social influence and role expectations on shopping center patronage intentions', *Academy of Marketing Science* 24 (1996), pp. 216–217. See Nasser A Raajpoot, Arun Sharma, Jean-Charles Chebat, 'The role of gender and work status in shopping centre patronage', *Journal of Business Research* 61 (2008), pp. 825–833.
38 Origlass papers, MLMSS 6614/13, VAC Newsletter, 1966.
39 Leaflets from the Vietnam Action Committee, VAC Leaflet, 20 April 1967.
40 Origlass papers, MLMSS 6614/13, VAC Newsletter 4, September 1966.
41 Origlass papers, MLMSS 6614/13, VAC Newsletter 5, October 1966.
42 Origlass papers, MLMSS 6614/13, VAC Newsletter 5, October 1966.
43 Leaflets from VAC, May 1967.
44 Origlass papers, MLMSS 6614/13, Liberation Newsletter 1, August 1969.
45 White papers, MLMSS 10938/1, ESHRAA, *Conscience*, 9 (1966), p. 2.
46 CPA papers, 5021/50, AICD Newsletter, March 1971.
47 Alexander Edward Carey papers, ca. 1915–1987, MLSLNSW MLMSS 5898/24, AICD Newsletter 2, 3, June 1972.
48 PND records, MLMSS 5522/35, Sonia Drabyan, Geoff Mullen Campaign Committee, 3 March 1969.
49 Origlass papers, MLMSS 6614/13, High School Students Against the War in Vietnam Newsletter 10, March 1969.
50 PND records, MLMSS 5522/51, Eastern Suburbs Moratorium Group, June 1971.
51 Gray papers, MLMSS 4432/1, DRCC, 21 July 1970.
52 Fisher papers, MLMSS 11380/1, *Out Now*, 24 August 1970, p. 8.
53 Gray papers, MLMSS 4432/1, NSW VMC, 4 April 1970.
54 Irving 2017, 142; Free Palestine Melbourne, @FreePalestinemelb, 8 November 2023.
55 Klandermans and Oegema 1987, pp. 521–522, 525.
56 Scalmer 2002, p. 68.
57 Irving 2017, p. 88.
58 PND records, MLMSS 5522/51, Committee for Canberra Vigil.
59 CPA records, MLMSS 2389/2, Vietnam Day Committee Bulletin 3, 1966.
60 *Tribune*, 17 April 1968, p. 10; 19 June 1968, p. 8.
61 PND records, MLMSS 5522/34, AICD, 20 March 1969.
62 PND records, MLMSS 5522/34, AICD, 10 February 1969.
63 Origlass papers, MLMSS 6614/13, National Lobby to Canberra participation form, 25 March 1969.
64 PND records, MLMSS 5522/34, AICD, 20 March 1969.

65 PND records, MLMSS 5522/34, Ken O'Hara, 1969.
66 PND records, MLMSS 5522/52, Manly–Warringah Committee for International Cooperation and Disarmament, 4 October 1967.
67 Kevin Moloney, *Rethinking Public Relations: PR Propaganda and Democracy*, 2nd edn, Routledge, 2006, p. 2; Ana Adi (ed.), *Protest Public Relations: Communicating Dissent and Activism*, Routledge, 2019.
68 Gray papers, MLMSS 4432/1, DRCC, 21 July 1970.
69 PND records, MLMSS 5522/35, Brian Aarons, undated.
70 PND records, MLMSS 5522/52, COG Circular 3, 24 August 1965.
71 Adele Pert, Interviewed by Inara Walden, 22 July 1993. With permission from Ann Curthoys.
72 Origlass papers, MLMSS 6614/13, Friends of Rex Hewett, 1968.
73 Legal Observers NSW, viewed 27 February 2025, <https://legalobserversnsw.org/>

CHAPTER SEVEN

1 Hilary M Carey, 'The Women, the War and the Cardinal: Gilroy and Catholic Women's Organisations, 1939–1950', *Women-Church: An Australian Journal of Feminist Studies in Religion* 1 (1987), 28–33; *Daily Mirror*, 31 January 1949, p. 2.
2 *SMH*, 23 August 1967, p. 2.
3 *SMH*, 23 August 1967, p. 2.
4 Harvey and Pryke papers, MLMSS 7962/5, CFP meeting report, 1967.
5 Noone 1993, pp. 158–160, 293–294.
6 *Catholics for Peace present the three speeches given at St. John's College, University of Sydney at the Forum [on] Catholics, War, Vietnam, Sunday, June 18, 1967*, CFP, 1967; See also Denis Kenny, *The Evolution of the Official Catholic Attitude Towards Communism*, CFP, 1968.
7 CF Bowers, 'The Catholic Church in Sydney and the Viet Nam conflict', *Australian New Left Review* 71 (1979), pp. 33–34.
8 Gray papers, MLMSS 4432/1, Roger Pryke, 20 July 1970.
9 Alan G Gilbert, 'Religion and Politics' in Ann Curthoys, Allan William Martin and Tim Rowse (eds.), *Australian from 1939*, Fairfax, Syme and Weldon Associates, 1987, p. 210.
10 McDonald papers, MLMSS 3853 ADD-ON 2111, YCAC Newsletter, August 1967, p. 2.
11 Harvey and Pryke papers, MLMSS 7962/5, CFP meeting report, 1967.
12 *SMH*, 23 August 1967, p. 2.
13 Gilbert 1987, p. 211.
14 *SMH*, 29 August 1967, p. 2.
15 *SMH*, 4 September 1967, p. 2.
16 *SMH*, 25 August 1967, p. 2.
17 *SMH*, 29 August 1967, p. 2.
18 'Eric Earley', *Education: The Journal of the NSW Public School Teachers Federation* 77, 11 (1996), p. 14.
19 *Tharunka*, 6 June 1967, p. 18.

20 PND records, MLMSS 5522/54, War and Education Research Group, June 1967. See also 'War and Education Research Group', *Education: Journal of the NSW Public School Teachers Federation* 48, 11 (1967), 95.
21 PND records, MLMSS 5522/54, Eric G Earley, 1967.
22 *SMH*, 26 August 1967, p. 12.
23 NSW, *Parliamentary Debates*, Legislative Council, 29 August 1967, pp. 817–818 (Arthur Bridges).
24 Murphy 1993, pp. 145–146.
25 David A Snow, Louis A Zurcher and Sheldon Ekland-Olson, 'Social networks and social movements: A microstructural approach to differential recruitment', *American Sociological Review* 45 (1980), pp. 789–790.
26 Almeida 2019, pp. 107, 110–111.
27 Orum 1974, p. 193.
28 Fisher papers, MLMSS 11380/1, How to run a discussion group, undated.
29 APAN, 'How-To: Kitchen Table Conversations' toolkit, viewed 19 September 2024, <https://apan.org.au/wp-content/uploads/Kitchen-table-conversations.pdf>
30 PND records, MLMSS 5522/51, M Charlwood, Cumberland Regional Peace Committee, 1965.
31 White papers, MLMSS 10938/1, ESHRAA Newsletter 3, 25 November 1965, p. 1.
32 PND records, MLMSS 5522/54, Sydney Conscientious Objectors' Discussion Group, undated.
33 Origlass papers, MLMSS 6614/13, Ella Outhred and Barry Robinson, 1966.
34 White papers, MLMSS 10938/1, ESHRAA, *Conscience* 9, 20 June 1966, p. 1.
35 PND records, MLMSS 5522/52, F Moss, 23 May 1966.
36 PND records, MLMSS 5522/51, John Walker, September 1966.
37 Leaflets from the Vietnam Action Committee, MLSLNSW, Bob Gould, Barry Robinson and Geoff Anderson, January 1966.
38 McAuley papers, MLMSS 7920/19, PVC, 1967.
39 Maddison and Scalmer 2006, 7, p. 58.
40 Albinski 1970, p. 109.
41 Levien 1967, p. 31.
42 Alec Robertson, 'Talking peace on street corners', *Tribune,* 19 June 1968, p. 8. See also Langley 1992, pp. 16, 20 for examples of Garrie Hutchinson and John Little being persuaded by discussion to oppose the war.
43 Origlass papers, MLMSS 6614/14, Denis Freney, 10 November 1968.
44 Gollan papers, MLMSS 8042/18, Resistance Newsletter, 22 Dec 1969–Jan 1970.
45 Origlass papers, MLMSS 6614/13, Resistance Newsletter, April–May 1969, p. 18.
46 PND records, MLMSS 5522/51, December Mobilization Committee, 4 December 1969; Gollan papers, MLMSS 8042/18, High School Students Against the War in Vietnam, *Student Underground*, 12 (1969).

47 Origlass papers, MLMSS 6614/13, VMC, February 1971.
48 Gray papers, MLMSS 4432/1, VMC, Moratorium News Sheet 1, 1970.
49 Lewis papers, MLMSS 5223/23, Ken McLeod and Phil Sanford, 1970.
50 Maddison and Scalmer 2006, pp. 204–209.
51 PND records, MLMSS 5522/51, Ku-ring-gai Study Group, October 1965; February 1966; 1967.
52 Langley 1992, p. 107.
53 PND records, MLMSS 5522/52, Parramatta and District Committee for International Cooperation, August 1965.
54 PND records, MLMSS 5522/51, East Hills Peace Group, 1965.
55 PND records, MLMSS 5522/52, Forum on Vietnam, 1965.
56 PND records, MLMSS 5522/51, Fairfield Peace Committee, 1965.
57 CPA records, MLMSS 2389/2, VAC Newsletter 5, December 1965.
58 PND records, MLMSS 5522/54, Vietnam Action Society for Peace, 1968.
59 PND records, MLMSS 5522/54, Committee of Conscience on Vietnam, 1968.
60 McDonald papers, MLMSS 3853/MLK3002, ESHRAA, *Conscience,* March 1970; Piccini 2022, pp. 68–69.
61 Findlay 1968, p. 18; Irving, pp. 104–106.
62 Albinski 1970, pp. 142–147.
63 *Canberra Times,* 13 July 1965, p. 14.
64 Scalmer 2002, pp. 44–45.
65 *SMH,* 2 August 1965, p. 11.
66 *SMH,* 6 August 1965, p. 2. See also Lorraine Barlow, 'Eddy, William Henry Charles (Harry) (1913–1973)', Australian Dictionary of Biography, National Centre of Biography, ANU, viewed 8 January 2025, <https://adb.anu.edu.au/biography/eddy-william-henry-charles-harry-10094/text17813>
67 PND records, MLMSS 5522/51, Hurstville Peace Group, 7 July 1965.
68 Findlay 1968, p. 36.
69 Origlass papers, MLMSS 6614/13, Conscription Teach-in, July 1969; PND records, MLMSS 5522/52, Manly–Warringah Committee for International Cooperation and Disarmament, 20 July 1969.
70 PND records, MLMSS 5522/51, Glebe Moratorium Committee, April 1970.
71 Omid Tofhigian, 'Translator's Tale: a window to the mountains', in Behrouz Boochani, *No Friend But the Mountains,* trans. Omid Tofighian, Picador, 2018, xi–xvii.

CHAPTER EIGHT

1 John Stoward Moyes papers, 1875–1972, MLNSW, Moyes papers, MLMSS 2319/5, John Stoward Moyes, 12 March 1965; Summy 1970, p. 154.
2 Paul Terracini, 'Moyes, Menzies and the Vietnam War: New insights into the public correspondence between the Prime Minister and the Bishops', *Journal of Religious History* 36, 1 (2012), p. 70.
3 Mattoni 2016, pp. 12, 64.
4 Albinski 1970, p. 109; PND records, MLMSS 5522/52, NCAC, 1969.

5 PND records, MLMSS 5522/51, M Charlwood, Cumberland Regional Peace Committee, undated; NCAC Newsletter, 20 January 1969.
6 'Too many Words?', *Outlook* 10, 4 (1966), p. 13.
7 Shannon Axe, Episcopalians on Facebook, Facebook, 23 January 2025, <https://www.facebook.com/groups/Episcopalians/posts/9103546393045673/>
8 Moyes papers, MLMSS 2319/5, John Stoward Moyes, 5 March 1965.
9 *Age*, 15 March 1965, p. 7.
10 *Age*, 16 March 1965, p. 6.
11 Department of the Prime Minister and Cabinet, PM Transcripts, 'Vietnam – exchange of letters between Prime Minister, the Rt. Hon. Sir Robert Menzies, KT, CH, QC, MP and the Rt. Rev J S Moyes, CMG, and certain Archbishops and Bishops', 24 March 1965, viewed 10 April 2025, <https://pmtranscripts.pmc.gov.au/sites/default/files/original/00001098.pdf>
12 Moyes papers, MLMSS 2319/5, John Stoward Moyes, 9 April 1965.
13 Department of the Prime Minister and Cabinet, PM Transcripts, 20 April 1965.
14 Findlay 1968, p. 54.
15 WILPF papers, MLMSS 5395/3, WILPF, 1965.
16 Moyes papers, MLMSS 2319/5, Alex Carey, 30 March 1965.
17 Moyes papers, MLMSS 2319/5, BM Bolan, 4 May 1965.
18 Moyes papers, MLMSS 2319/5, Mr and Mrs Paltridge, 3 April 1965.
19 Moyes papers, MLMSS 2319/5, David Garnsey, 20 April 1965.
20 Moyes papers, MLMSS 2319/5, Minister Secombe, 23 April 1965.
21 Moyes papers, MLMSS 2319/5, J.A. Henderson, 31 May 1965; Gertrude A. Dahle; G. Kennedy Tucker, 25 May 1966.
22 Terracini 2012, p. 84.
23 *Peace Action in Australia* 7, 4 (1965), p. 12.
24 Moyes papers, MLMSS 2319/5, Vietnam Day Committee, 22 October 1965.
25 Albinski 1970, p. 124; Harvey and Pryke papers, MLMSS 7962/5, Harold Perkins, 11 October 1967.
26 Moyes papers, MLMSS 2319/5, David Garnsey; William Hardie; Cecil Muschamp, 23 March 1966.
27 Gray papers, MLMSS 4432/1, Lambeth Conference (of the Anglican Communion), 1968.
28 Saunders and Summy 1982, p. 23; Quakers Australia, 'Faith and Values', viewed 21 January 2025, <https://www.quakersaustralia.org.au>
29 WILPF papers, MLMSS 5395/1, Jean Richards, Australian Quaker Peace Committee, 8 September 1966; Albinski 1970, p. 122.
30 Rudé 1980, p. 23.
31 David Pope, 27 January 1967, cited in Murphy 1993, p. 161.
32 Commonwealth, *Parliamentary Debates*, House of Representatives, 26 September 1968, p. 1616 (William Wentworth).
33 Agnes Stapledon, 1966, cited in Kate Laing, *Sisters in Peace: The Women's International League for Peace and Freedom in Australia, 1915–2015*, ANU Press, 2023, p. 230.

34 Katharine McGregor, 'Opposing colonialism: The Women's International Democratic Federation and decolonisation struggles in Vietnam and Algeria 1945–1965, *Women's History Review* 25, 6 (2016), 925. See also Milner 2018a, p. 261.
35 Laing 2023, p. 237.
36 WILPF papers, MLMSS 5395/1, WILPF NSW minutes, 9 August 1966.
37 WILPF papers, MLMSS 5395/1, WILPF NSW minutes 7 July 1965; 13 July 1965, 6 September 1965.
38 WILPF papers, MLMSS 5395/1, WILPF NSW minutes, 14 July 1964.
39 WILPF papers, MLMSS 5395/2, James Cavanagh, 17 August 1964.
40 WILPF papers, MLMSS 5395/2, Bert James, 17 August 1964; *Age*, 26 December 2014, <https://www.theage.com.au/politics/federal/asio-spy-case-file-on-labor-mp-albert-james-reveals-kgb-meetings-20141226-12dwlq.html>
41 WILPF papers, MLMSS 5395/1, WILPF NSW Minutes, 9 November 1965.
42 WILPF papers, MLMSS 5395/3, Margaret Forte, 12 May 1970.
43 McDonald papers, MLMSS 3853/MLK3002, ESHRAA, 27 November 1969.
44 McDonald papers, MLMSS 3853/MLK3002, ESHRAA, *Conscience*, January 1970, 5.
45 McDonald papers, 3853/MLK3002, John Collins, December 1969.
46 McDonald papers, 3853/MLK3002, Malcolm Fraser, 17 June 1966.
47 Fallding papers, MLMSS 7251/1, Leslie Bury, 21 August 1968.
48 PND records, MLMSS 5522/52, NCAC press release, 4 January 1969.
49 Darren Halpin, et al., 'Online petitioning and politics: the development of *Change.org* in Australia', *Australian Journal of Political Science* 53, 4 (2018), p. 440; Michael Vaughan, et al., 'The role of novel citizenship norms in signing and sharing online petitions', *Political Studies* 72, 1 (2022), pp. 42–43.
50 Findlay 1968, p. 18; Lewis papers, MLMSS 5223/23, Committee for Vietnam, 19 June 1965.
51 *SMH*, 21 October 1966, p. 1.
52 IPAN, Open Letter to Prime Minister Albanese on Gaza, <https://ipan.org.au/open-letter-to-prime-minister-albanese-on-gaza-february-2024/>
53 Klandermans 2017, p. 207.
54 CPA papers, MLMSS 5021/75, Laurie Aarons, 6 May 1970.
55 *SMH*, 17 March 1966, p. 4.
56 *SMH*, 17 March 1966, p. 4.
57 New Theatre, Person – Hugh Mason, viewed 17 January 2025, <https://newtheatrehistory.org.au/wiki/index.php/Person_-_Hugh_Mason>
58 *SMH*, 17 August 1962, p. 20; *Tribune*, 10 May 1961, 6; *SMH*, 20 May 1961, p. 15.
59 Hugh Mason papers, [ca. 1956]–2015, MLNSW MLMSS 10370/1, Hugh Mason, 8 December 1966.
60 Mason papers, MLMSS 10370/1, Hugh Mason, 30 November 1966.
61 Mason papers, MLMSS 10370/1, Arthur Calwell, 2 December 1966.
62 Murphy 1993, p. 155.
63 Origlass papers, MLMSS 6614/13, YCAC, May 1965; Murphy 1993, pp. 143, 155, 234.

64 PND records, MLMSS 5522/51, Ku-ring-gai Study Group, 13 April 1966.
65 Murphy 1993, p. 217.
66 Hamel-Green 1983, p. 115.
67 *Australian*, 24 June 1969, p. 4.
68 *SMH*, 26 August 1967.
69 PND records, MLMSS 5522/51, Citizens Committee Against the National Service Act, *Australian*, 29 June 1968.
70 *SMH*, 7 May 1970, p. 7.
71 *Hornsby Times*, 15 April 1970, p. 20.
72 *Australian*, 18 June 1970, p. 7.
73 *SMH*, 25 February 2025, p. 9; Deborah Stone, 'Jews speak out against forced transfer of Palestinians', *Jewish Independent*, 25 February 2025, <https://thejewishindependent.com.au/jews-speak-out-against-forced-transfer-of-palestinians>
74 Albinski 1970, pp. 14–16; Klandermans and Oegema 1987, pp. 519–531; Orum 1974, 181–207; Almeida 2019, pp. 104–105.
75 Blaxland 2015, pp. 164–165. See also Edmund S Herman and Noam Chomsky, *Manufacturing consent: The political economy of the mass media*, Pantheon, 1988; Stephen KJ Rice & Jennifer L Bartlett, 'Legitimating organisational decisions: A study of media framing of the Australian Government's legitimacy strategy and public opinion on the war in Iraq', *Journal of Communication Management* 10, 3 (2006), pp. 274–286.
76 Mattoni 2016, pp. 12–13, 64. See also Maddison and Scalmer 2006, in which the importance of media is repeatedly emphasised.
77 PND records, MLMSS 5522/51, Hurstville Peace Group, 7 July 1965.
78 WILPF papers, MLMSS 5395/1, WILPF NSW Minutes, 9 August 1966.
79 3CR Radical Radio, Invasion Day 2025, 26 January 2025, <https://www.3cr.org.au/invasionday2025>
80 Mason papers, MLMSS 10370/1, D Robson, 18 March 1966.
81 Mason papers, MLMSS 10370/1, Hugh Mason, 29 July 1966.
82 Mason papers, MLMSS 10370/1, Hugh Mason, November 1966.
83 Mason papers, MLMSS 10370/1, Hugh Mason, 8 December 1966.
84 Findlay 1968, pp. 37, 42, 43.
85 Findlay 1968, p. 43. See Leaflets from the Vietnam Action Committee, VAC, *Vietnam: Why must the protest go on?*, undated.
86 Gillan, Pickerill and Webster 2008, p. 41.
87 WILPF papers, MLSS 5395/1, Jean Richards, Australian Quaker Peace Committee, 8 September 1966.
88 WILPF papers, MLSS 5395/1, A Michaelis, 16 September 1966.
89 Milner 2018b, p. 258.
90 Findlay 1968, p. 24.
91 'Teachers warned over political postcards', *ABC News*, 12 September 2007, <https://www.abc.net.au/news/2007-09-12/teachers-warned-over-political-postcards/667826>
92 The Withhold-Outs, viewed 26 March 2025, <https://withhold-outs.hotglue.me/>

CHAPTER NINE

1 Gray papers, MLMSS 4432/1, NDVMG, March 1970.
2 Almeida 2019, p. 108.
3 Gray papers, MLMSS 4432/1, Phyllis M Hamilton, 21 July 1970.
4 Gray papers, MLMSS 4432/1, LT Withers, 14 September 1970.
5 Gray papers, MLMSS 4432/1, Doris J Wilson, 19 March 1970; Maynard Davies, March 1970; Lilliam Bertram Wood, 14 April 1970; Tom Murray, 21 March 1970.
6 Gray papers, MLMSS 4432/1, Jane Gray, 4 April; 28 April 1970.
7 CPA papers, MLMSS 5021/2, Bill McDougall, 1970.
8 Findlay 1968, p. 24.
9 Gray papers, MLMSS 4432/1, VMC, 1970.
10 PND records, MLMSS 5522/34, Original Old Age and Invalid Pensioners' Association NSW, 15 January 1972.
11 Cora 2010, p. 12.
12 Gray papers, MLMSS 4432/1, Edgar Ross, 21 March 1970. See also Edgar Ross, *A History of the Miners Federation of Australia,* The Australian Coal and Shale Employees' Federation, 1970.
13 PND records, MLMSS 5522/50, Michael Sawtell, 2 November 1970.
14 PND records, MLMSS 5522/50, Anti-Conscription Jubilee Committee, 1967.
15 Almeida 2019, p. 108; Verhulst and Walgrave 2009, p. 455.
16 Orum 1974, p. 196.
17 Klandermans and Oegema 1987, pp. 521–522, 525.
18 Klandermans and Oegema 1987, p. 519.
19 PND records, MLMSS 5522/51, WR Leslie, 20 May 1968.
20 Larraine J Larri, 'The craft of wisdom: climate activist learning in the hands of Australia's Knitting Nannas', *Australian Journal of Adult Learning* 62, 3 (2022), pp. 353–354, 356, 362.
21 Verhulst and Walgrave 2009, p. 461.
22 ABC Radio National, *Life Matters,* 25 September 2023, <https://www.abc.net.au/listen/programs/lifematters/not-just-a-youth-movement-older-protesters/102890706>
23 Klandermans and Oegema 1987, p. 520.
24 Snow, Zurcher and Ekland-Olson 1980, p. 794.
25 PND records, MLMSS 5522/54, Western Suburbs Moratorium Group, 1971.
26 PND records, MLMSS 5522/34, EB Wilson, 15 March 1969.
27 Alain Touraine, 'The Importance of Social Movements', *Social Movement Studies* 1, 1 (2002), p. 90.
28 Klandermans and Oegema 1987, p. 529.
29 Gray papers, MLMSS 4432/1, 5522/34, Bert, June 1971.
30 Gray papers, MLMSS 4432/1, FE Binet, 1970.
31 PND records, MLMSS 5522/51, Eastern Suburbs Moratorium Group, June 1971.
32 People with Disability Australia, 'Joint Statement: On the rights of people

with disability in Gaza', People with Disability, 16 August 2024, <https://pwd.org.au/joint-statement-on-the-rights-of-people-with-disability-in-gaza/>

33 Max Jane, @totoroandtangerine, 7 August 2024.

34 Cripthegig, (@Cripthegig), 'crips for a free palestine !!!!!', 3 November 2023, <https://www.instagram.com/p/CzJ11wzsf4W/?img_index=1>

35 Gray papers, MLMSS 4432/1, Ian Robertson, 2 April 1970.

36 Gray papers, MLMSS 4432/1, C Quill, 18 July 1970; Jack Pearson, 1970; Graham Bradley, 30 August 1970; J Barker, 1970; J Willis, 17 April 1970; Kathie Herbert, 1970; Ruth Allen, 1970; Kevin Wallace, 28 November 1970; Maxine Thomson, 23 March 1970.

37 Bruce Petty, cited in Langley 1992, p. 99.

38 Findlay 1968, pp. 27, 38.

39 'The Press', *Outlook* 9, 6 (1965), p. 7.

40 HGP, 'Sit down and speak up: View from the ground', *Outlook* 9, 6 (1965), p. 6.

41 Everingham papers, MLMSS 8614/2, I Tell, 23 November 1966.

42 *Tharunka*, 16 September 1970, 2; *Tribune*, 23 September 1970, p. 1.

43 Collins 2021, p. 232; Cora 2010, p. 26.

44 Collins 2021, p. 233.

45 Gray papers, MLMSS 4432/1, Ann McDougall, July 1970.

46 Murphy 1993, pp. 146–147.

47 Jean McLean, cited in Gloria Frydman, *Protesters*, Collins Dove, 1987, p. 25.

48 Dorothy Dalton, cited in Frydman 1987, p. 98.

49 Langley 1992, pp. 110, 138, 141.

50 Klandermans 2017, p. 211.

51 Leonardo Avritzer and Timo Lyyra, 'New cultures, social movements and the role of knowledge: An interview with Alberto Melucci', *Thesis Eleven* 48, 1 (1997), pp. 91–92.

52 Lewis papers, MLMSS 5223/23, August Mobilisation to End the War in Vietnam Committee, 1972.

53 HGP, 'The Individual Protester', *Outlook* 10, 4 (1966), p. 13; *SMH*, 9 June 1966, p. 5.

54 HGP 1966, p. 13.

55 Frydman 1987, p. 105.

56 Everingham papers, MLMSS 8614/2, Hugh Owen, 20 November 1966.

57 *Canberra Times*, 21 May 1968, p. 10.

58 *Woroni*, 21 July 1970, p. 2.

59 *Canberra Times*, 29 June 1971, p. 3.

60 Gray papers, MLMSS 4432/1, FE Binet, 1970.

61 PND records, MLMSS 5522/51, The Government Employees Against the War in Indo-China, 1970.

62 PND records, MLMSS 5522/51, The Government Employees Against the War in Indo-China, 1970.

63 *Age*, 9 July 1970, p. 8.

64 CPA papers, MLMSS 5021/67, Public Servants Against the War, 1970; *Canberra Times*, 29 June 1971, p. 3.

65 *Woroni*, 22 Feb 1971, p. 14.

66 *Resist*, June 1971, p. 5.

67 Mostafa Rachwani, 'Australian public servants call on government to cease supplying all military parts and weapons to Israel', *Guardian*, 30 May 2024, <https://www.theguardian.com/australia-news/article/2024/may/30/australia-public-servant-open-letter-israel-weapons-military-war-gaza-rafah>; 'Public servants condemn Australian Government complicity in Palestinian genocide', viewed 26 March 2025, <https://docs.google.com/forms/d/e/1FAIpQLSfgDnXEEa5xZYAHjUyh-YPHgyCuo1q2_i0ucO3DnAfqDtFE7A/viewform>

68 Anita Harris, Johanna Wynn and Salem Younes, 'Beyond apathetic or activist youth: "Ordinary" young people and contemporary forms of participation', *Nordic Journal of Youth Research* 18, 1 (2010), p. 10; Ariadne Vromen, 'Political engagement in the Australian digital context', *Papers on Parliament* 69 (2018), pp. 93–115.

69 David Denemark and Shaun Bowler, 'Minor parties and protest votes in Australia and New Zealand: locating populist politics', *Electoral Studies* 21 (2002), pp. 47–67.

70 R Michael Alvarez, D Roderick Kiewiet, and Lucas Núñez, 'A Taxonomy of Protest Voting', *Annual Review of Political Science* 21, 1 (2018), p. 136.

71 Origlass papers, MLMSS 6614/13, Peter Dunn, September 1966.

72 PND records, MLMSS 5522/35, Sonia Drabyan, Geoff Mullen Campaign Committee, 3 March 1969.

73 Alex Blucher, 'Election 2016: Finger-pointing begins over Liberal losses in Tasmania', *ABC News*, 4 July 2016, <https://www.abc.net.au/news/2016-07-04/election-2016-finger-pointing-begins-liberal-losses-tasmania/7565690>

74 Ariadne Vromen, 'GetUp! in Election 2016' in Anika Gauja, et al., *Double Disillusion: The 2016 Australian Federal Election*, ANU Press, 2018, pp. 397–420; Mark Rolfe, 'GetUp's brand of in your face activism is winning elections – and making enemies', *Conversation*, 17 May 2019, <https://theconversation.com/getups-brand-of-in-your-face-activism-is-winning-elections-and-making-enemies-116672>; GetUp!, Statement of Independence, viewed 15 February 2025, <https://www.getup.org.au/>

75 Horne 1980, p. 54.

76 *SMH*, 11 April 2005, p. 18.

77 Sam Everingham, *Gordon Barton: Australia's Maverick Entrepeneur*, Allen & Unwin, 2009.

78 *SMH*, 22 October 1966, p. 11.

79 Horne 1980, p. 54.

80 Everingham papers, MLMSS 8614/2, Liberal Reform Group, 1966.

81 *SMH*, 4 November 1966, p. 1.

82 Everingham papers, MLMSS 8614/2, Harold Holt, 7 November 1966.

83 Everingham papers, MLMSS 8614/2, Greg Clark, 29 November 1966.

84 Everingham papers, MLMSS 8614/2, Peggy Wallis, 19 November 1966.

85 *SMH*, 17 November 1966, p. 2.

86 Everingham papers, MLMSS 8614/2, Patrick Burns, 11 November 1966.
87 Everingham papers, MLMSS 8614/2, Sheila Mason, 3 June 1968.
88 *SMH,* 17 November 1966, p. 2.
89 Tony Stephens, 'James, Alfred Francis (1918–1992)', Australian Dictionary of Biography, National Centre of Biography, ANU, 2016, viewed 20 January 2026, <https://adb.anu.edu.au/biography/james-alfred-francis-16270/text28209>
90 *SMH,* 7 November 1966, p. 1.
91 Horne 1980, pp. 53–54. See also Noone 1993, p. 111; Murphy 1993, p. 150.
92 Everingham papers, MLMSS 8614/2, Liberal Reform Group, December 1966.
93 Moloney and McKie 2016, p. 156.

CONCLUSION

1 Bisan Owda, @wizard_bisan1, 12 January 2025.
2 Joy Damousi, *The Humanitarians: Child War Refugees and Australian Humanitarianism in a Transnational World, 1919–1975,* Cambridge University Press, 2022; Jordana Silverstein, *Cruel Care: A History of Children at Our Borders,* Monash University Publishing, 2023.
3 School Strike 4 Climate Australia, 2025, <https://www.schoolstrike4climate.com/>; Nagana Yarrbayn, 'Groundbreaking human rights case launched to protect sacred Doongmabulla Springs', 2025, <https://standing-our-ground.org/>
4 NSWCCL, 'Sign the Petition! Demand a public review of the NSW Anti-Protest Laws', <https://www.nswccl.org.au/take_action_now_protect_protest - :~:text=NSWCCL condemns these legislative changes,for offences committed by protesters>
5 Oscar Berglund, et al., *Criminalisation and Repression of Climate and Environmental Protests,* University of Bristol, 2024, p. 6.
6 Jordyn Beazley, 'Protesters scale back blockade of world's biggest coal port but NSW police ready for mass "disruption" at Newcastle', *Guardian,* 5 November 2024, <https://www.theguardian.com/australia-news/2024/nov/05/rising-tide-protest-newcastle-worlds-biggest-coal-port-blockade#:~:text=In%20 2023%2C%20police%20accepted%20the,%2Dyear%2Dold%20church%20 minister>; Rising Tide, *People's Blockade 2024,* <https://www.risingtide.org.au/2024-highlights>
7 Everingham papers, MLMSS 8614/2, Peggy Wallis, 19 November 1966.
8 Janus Rose, 'You can't post your way out of fascism', 404media, 5 February 2025, <https://www.404media.co/you-cant-post-your-way-out-of-fascism>
9 Halupka 2016, p. 139.
10 Whitney Alese, @thereclaimed.bsky.social, 21 February 2025, <https://bsky.app/profile/thereclaimed.bsky.social/post/3lgr7t4svdk2m>; *The Philly Download,* <https://www.thedownload.news/>
11 Maria Fakhouri, @mar._unfiltered, 5 June 2024.
12 Larsson, *Shattered Anzacs.*
13 Lance Peters, 1966, cited in Langley 1992, p. 96.

INDEX

www.ingramcontent.com/pod-product-compliance
Lightning Source LLC
LaVergne TN
LVHW100922110826
845155LV00036B/46

* 9 7 8 1 7 6 1 1 7 0 2 6 3 *